In Search of Ancient Scotland

Bruce statue, Bannockburn

In Search of Ancient Scotland

A Guide for the Independent Traveler

Gerald M. Ruzicki

Dorothy A. Ruzicki

ASPENGROVE

PUBLISHING

Aspen Grove Publishing
Post Office Box 1493, Mead, Washington 99021-1493

Maps by Rodger Hartman
Cover design by Mendocino Graphics
Printed in the United States of America

Publisher's Cataloging-in-Publication
(Provided by Quality Books, Inc.)

Ruzicki, Gerald M.
    In search of ancient Scotland : a guide for the independent
traveler / Gerald M. Ruzicki, Dorothy A. Ruzicki. -- 1st ed.
    p. cm.
    Includes bibliographical references and index.
    LCCN: 99-63546
    ISBN: 0-9664496-0-6

    1. Scotland--Guidebooks. 2. Scotland--Antiquities.
3. Historic sites--Scotland--Guidebooks. I. Ruzicki, Dodie.
II. Title.

DA870.R89 2000   914.1104'086
                                  QB199-1550

Cover photo: Cairnholy I, Cairnholy Chambered Cairns, Galloway

*For **Nancie** and **Alastair**,*

who started us on this journey.

Contents

Acknowledgments

We are indebted to many people who helped us with this book. We especially thank Historic Scotland and National Trust staff who freely shared their knowledge, time and affection for their work. We are grateful for the ideas, suggestions and stories of our Scottish friends, Ron and Helen Roberts, Ken and Hannah Crozier, and Ian and Susan Graham. Our sons, Geoff and Tim Ruzicki, occasionally traveled with us, reviewed various drafts and enthusiastically encouraged us.

We particularly appreciate the support of our friends and colleagues. While too numerous to mention all, we specifically want to thank the following: Carrie Fry and Louisa Rose for their review and comments; Ken Avery for the timeline idea; Tina Fascetti for her cover suggestions; Frank Davidson for his classic statement; and, Melvyn Phipps, Amelia Phillips, Sandy Keno, Lorri and Greg Edwards, Marcy and Lloyd Tunik for their timely advice. On a recent trip to Scotland with us, Nancy Davidson spotted standing stones and demonstrated great fortitude and humor as we searched for yet more stones.

Finally, this book could not have been completed without our professional advisors: Irene Svete, who edited an early draft and helped us with travel writing; Carla Johnson, copy editor; Michael Guilfoil, who reviewed portions of the text; Chuck Hathaway for the cover design; and, Rodger Hartman for technical assistance.

Introduction

Before our first trip to Scotland, we had formed some images about the country based on years of interest in its music, wool industry and, of course, its romantic associations with tartans, kilts and bagpipes. Although we had read guidebooks to prepare for our trip, we had no idea what we specifically wanted to see—other than the obligatory Edinburgh Castle, Royal Mile, surrounding countryside and textile mills. Only after we visited Dun Beag, Linlithgow and Cairnpapple did we fully appreciate Scotland's wealth of prehistoric and historic monuments. Returning home with our interest heightened, we studied Scotland's history. It didn't take us long to realize how much we'd overlooked on that first visit, and to decide to tour Scotland's length and breadth, searching out additional sites.

Our journeys took us to every region of Scotland, giving us intimate knowledge of the land and people, and vastly expanding our understanding of Scotland's history. Over four years and six trips, we toured famous and acclaimed attractions, as well as obscure and virtually unknown sites. We logged hundreds of miles on one-lane roads in the highlands and islands, and crossed seas and lochs on countless ferries.

Many sites covered in this book do not fall in the category of standard tourist attractions visited by tour buses and escorted groups. Located far off the beaten path, they frequently cannot be found without explicit directions and good maps. Many monuments are not staffed, and while reader boards sometimes provide information, details can be sketchy. We seek to fill the void by giving readers a historical perspective and identifying interesting architectural, geographical and archaeological features. Most importantly, we include essential directions for finding obscure sites.

We chose to include monuments that fit within a time frame from the Stone Age (about 5000 BC) to 1700 AD, when modern times began. Therefore, we left out some of the more recent events, like the Jacobite uprising and Culloden. We have not included Scotland's many stately homes and gardens or privately owned and lavishly furnished castles. We chose to focus primarily on historical ruins.

We also haven't attempted to provide an exhaustive review of Scotland's ancient sites and realize we've left out some outstanding places. However, we believe we've given a good overview and hope we've whetted our readers' appetites for seeking more.

This book is divided into two sections and an appendix. The first section explains why we keep going back and why we travel independently. It also provides many practical tips we learned through trial and error.

In the second section, we cover Scotland geographically, describing monuments in each region and starting with those closest to Edinburgh and Glasgow. We've rated sites we especially like: ★★★—outstanding, don't miss; ★★—good, worth going out of your way; ★—try to see if in the area. Many of our unrated sites warrant a visit, too, if time permits.

The appendix includes a descriptive timeline to help readers distinguish various eras, such as Stone Age and Bronze Age. A glossary of common terms used in the book, useful resources, a list of references and an index of sites complete the book.

We've written this guide to help others find enjoyment in Scotland's antiquity. It is meant for the person who only occasionally drives on the left side of the road and has never ventured off the beaten path on the single-lane tracks of Scotland.

Jerry and Dodie Ruzicki

Getting Ready

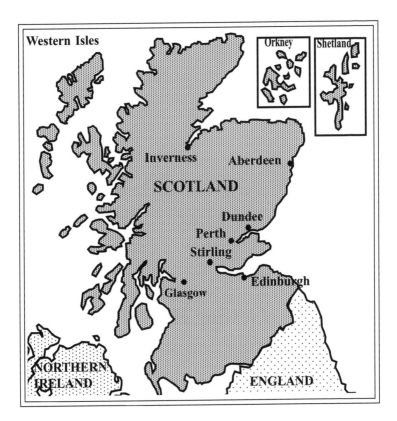

Chapter 1
Beyond Tartans and Bagpipes

Why we keep going back (Dodie's introduction)

"You're not going back to Scotland *again*, are you?" They say it incredulously—not so much a question but a statement about our sanity. We have no Scottish ancestry. We don't play golf. And, until our first trip to Scotland, we didn't like Scotch whisky. The climate didn't lure us either. As a friend from the Seattle area mused, why would he want to leave a cold, damp rainy place to go to another cold, damp rainy place? And, *he* has Scottish ancestry!

Why do we keep going back to Scotland? How did we first become interested in this wee country? Was it sheep . . .wool . . .weaving . . .spinning . . . or music? Perhaps they all influenced us. Through my handweaving and handspinning pursuits, we discovered tweed "waulking" music, the rhythmic and lively chorus music chanted by island women as they pounded the Harris tweeds. These Hebridean waulking songs introduced us to a world of Celtic music, much broader than the bagpipes we'd always associated with Scotland.

Most importantly, Jerry's lifelong interest in Britain's prehistory and history drew us into Scotland's countryside where thousands of years of history pack a region smaller than the state of Maine. Scotland's Royal Commission on Ancient and Historical Monuments estimates the country contains more than 100,000 ancient sites.

At first, I wasn't particularly impressed. Until Jerry coaxed me into remnants of a 2,000-year-old broch (a circular stone tower) on our first trip to Scotland, I considered his passion for ruins somewhat tedious and academic. I soon found that seeing and touching these structures had the power to transport me to a time far removed from our complex 20th century.

I come from the American West, where our non-Indian history is not much older than 100 years, and the vastness of our land dilutes our prehistory. In Scotland, however, both history and prehistory greet travelers at every turn. Some of the castles date back 700 years or more. Medieval Scottish King Robert the Bruce might have climbed the steps of one of these ancient strongholds. Massive standing stones, stone circles and burial cairns formed backdrops for religious rites 5,000 years ago. Sites more recent than 1700 suddenly seemed modern to me. In a small way, through Scotland's crumbling ruins, I was able to experience early lifestyles firsthand.

Why go to Scotland? (Jerry's view)

Scotland is for anyone who loves history. A country steeped in adventure, epic battles, conspiracy and intrigue, Scotland is like a time machine. Walk into an abbey, a castle, a Roman fort, a prehistoric stone circle, and step back in time.

For mystery enthusiasts, Scotland is full of puzzling questions. Who made the stone circles and erected the standing stones? Why? Were these really prehistoric computers or even calendars? Why were some prehistoric hill forts fired with such intense heat that the rock melted to create "vitrified" forts? What really went on in the castles, brochs, abbeys and crannogs? Why were the brochs built double-walled with such amazing workmanship and symmetry? What do the symbols on the Pictish stones mean?

The friendly Scots provide a warm welcome to their country and culture, similar yet so different from ours. Scotland's landscape varies from rugged, majestic mountains and gently rolling pastureland to desolate and lonely moors. In some ways, the coast of Scotland with its islands, inlets and mountains resembles our own American Pacific Northwest.

Why Independent?

We've written this guide for independent travelers, people who travel on their own rather than with group tours that make planning unnecessary. On the best tours, time-consuming mistakes don't happen, because someone else preselects worthwhile sights and arranges transportation to them. Tour guides provide running commentary and thus a wealth of information about monuments, countryside, local history and lore. Traveling independently, on the other hand, can be a little scary. There's no one else to deal with jams, and no one else to do the planning. Independent travelers tote their own luggage, negotiate local customs, contend with unfamiliar territory and, worst of all for some, drive strange roads on the wrong side. So, why endure the hassles of going alone?

We do it because part of our enjoyment of travel is planning. We find it challenging to chart our course, make our own arrangements and deal directly with the local people. This takes a lot of effort and reading, and we also leave ourselves open to making mistakes. Some places we thought would be great have not been worth the time; conversely, we've found some real gems not mentioned in guidebooks. For example, in Dunkeld, our B&B host suggested we follow the river path to a 700-year-old oak from the Birnam wood made famous in *Macbeth.* Later, in the same town, we stumbled upon Celtic musician Dougie MacLean's office tucked away on a side street. On another occasion, we explored the mountains of Harris on a twisting one-lane road with no shoulder that eventually passed the front door of an in-habited Victorian castle.

Over time, we learned traveling independently requires a mindset of great *flexibility.* This mindset helps us stay relaxed under difficult circumstances, particularly when delayed. Delays might be due to weather, slow tractors pulling farm wagons on narrow country lanes, sheep darting across the roadway or long ferry lines. We've taken wrong turns or found historic sites closed for one reason or another. While we've experienced flight delays, we've fortunately not had to deal with accommodation problems.

We especially like to travel independently because we can manage our own time, stopping when we want, exploring some places more than others. Tours have predetermined schedules to keep, limiting time to tarry. On tours we might have missed some of our most magical moments. We will always cherish the sunny afternoon we lingered on a lonely Harris beach watching the shifting clouds cast shadows over the bay's blue-green waters. The glittering white sand littered with limpet shells, the brilliant hues of the ocean, the island mounds hazy on the horizon, and the isolation of the setting imprinted this experience forever in our minds.

Traveling on our own also gives us time to talk with local folks. We've found that visiting with people on their own turf provides the best opportunity to sample their culture. Once, waiting for a ferry in an out-of-way place in Cowal, we discussed current Scottish politics over a cup of tea with the ferryman.

Most importantly, we go places tours don't. The average tour of Scotland for North Americans stops at very predictable, tourist-oriented spots. Many places we visit require a car. While Britain has excellent public transportation, traveling by bus or train requires more time and effort.

For all these reasons, we prefer independent travel. Through its flexibility, we've enjoyed a process of discovery that has led to numerous adventures.

Chapter 2
Planning is One-Third of the Trip

Our overseas adventures consist of three parts: planning, going and remembering. Over the years, we've found we like them all equally. Planning means deciding when and where and all the details in between. If the trip is carefully planned, the "going" becomes enjoyable and usually proceeds without too many problems. Remembering can be like reliving the trip. We relish rehashing our adventures and misadventures, poring over pictures and even delighting in details with bored friends. (Ah, to find those rare friends who love to hear about our travels!)

Planning is particularly important for travelers operating on the normal two- or three-week vacation cycle where time is precious. We love to plan the trip, to dream about all the possibilities, eventually narrowing them down to something reasonable and realistic for our time frame.

When to Go

Scottish weather is unpredictable. We've been in the west highlands and islands under blue December skies while friends at home were digging out from the worst snowstorm of the year. We've experienced cold, windy June weather and hot September days. We once lucked out with sunshine in the Hebrides when torrential rain drenched the rest of Britain.

The time of year we travel depends on our work vacation schedules. We prefer to avoid July and August when Scotland teems with tourists (particularly Edinburgh in August during Festival), and everything is more expensive. We've heard that the midges (tiny insects the Scots call "wee beasties") are at their worst in July and August, especially in the islands. Because Jerry teaches, his school vacation schedule limits us. Otherwise, we'd schedule more trips for late fall and spring when airfares and lodging fall to bargain rates.

Traveling to Scotland in late fall, however, can be a bit tricky. Some sites close for the winter in October and do not reopen until after Easter or May 1. Nevertheless, many ruins stay open year round. Lately, in an effort to attract more off-season tourists, some monuments have remained open until early November. Therefore, it's wise to check opening and closing times, especially between October and the end of April. (See websites for Historic Scotland and The National Trust for Scotland in "Useful Resources" at the end of the book.)

Booking the Flight

We have more difficulty finding inexpensive fares because we don't live near a hub city and can't take full advantage of some really spectacular sales. We usually have to tack on an extra $100 apiece just to get to a major city like Seattle.

We've booked our flights several ways—on our own directly with the airline, through a consolidator and through a travel agent. We got a great rate through a consolidator for our first flight to Scotland, but the well-known airline wouldn't honor our miles in their frequent-flyer program as the consolidator had promised. We learned the hard way that some airlines award frequent-flyer miles on tickets written by consolidators while others don't. We've occasionally been willing to pay a bit more for tickets when we want the miles. The miles are worth about 2 to 2½ cents apiece, so it's not too hard to check the difference. If frequent-flyer miles don't matter, a good travel agent can find the lowest priced ticket on a reputable airline, especially if departure and return dates are flexible. We subscribe to a couple of British magazines and sometimes get promotions from travel agents who specialize in travel to Britain.

Lately, we've been checking out bargains advertised

through travel companies on the Internet. For travelers not locked into specific dates, occasional sales and last minute fares available through Internet sources might save several hundred dollars per person.

Airlines frequently advertise lower fares for off-season travel—mid-October through March, with some December dates blacked out. The cheapest international flights usually leave and return Monday through Thursday. Through experience, we've learned we should be ticketed all the way through rather than negotiate separate tickets with separate airlines. That way, a missed flight or a delay on one airline won't affect the other segments. On one of our trips, bad weather delayed our international flight, cutting off one full day. To extend, we had to pay a change fee on the regional connecting airline even though the international airline waived theirs. Change fees for restricted tickets run anywhere from $30 to $75 per person on domestic flights and about $150 per person for international flights.

Renting a Car

For true independent traveling, a car is necessary (see Chapter 3: "Driving in Scotland. . ."). We've rented cars using two methods: calling international agencies and comparing prices, and having a travel agent do it for us. The travel agent got us a great price and a free upgrade from a base economy car to a compact. We saved about $200 over the previous year's car.

Most people drive small cars in Britain, because gas (petrol) is expensive. A smaller car also fits in better and manages the narrow roads more effectively. We prefer compact cars like Ford Escorts over the economy size. Economy cars contain minuscule luggage space, making it difficult to keep valuables out of sight. Not only does the larger compact have a bigger trunk (boot), it's also a bit roomier (translate "comfort").

We always rent cars with manual transmissions.

They are much more prevalent in Britain and rental fees are lower than for automatics. Although we drive manual-shift cars at home, learning to shift on the left took some adjusting.

Many car rental (car hire) agencies in Britain now require a substantial damage deposit. On most trips, we have successfully covered it with a gold Visa or Master Card. So, we were surprised when a small agency on Orkney denied our rental request. After telling us their insurance company no longer allowed them to rent cars to Americans or Canadians, the receptionist explained their worry about Americans' reputations for lawsuits and high awards. Even our gold Visa or Master Card did not make a difference, which suggested the agency probably didn't accept major credit cards either. A letter from our car-insurance company verifying collision and damage coverage would have sufficed, had we not ultimately found another agency that accepted our gold card. The company we finally used was the only one on Orkney associated with an international firm.

Where to Stay

We generally book rooms in bed-and-breakfast homes or small guesthouses instead of the more expensive hotels. Numerous throughout Britain, B&B's range all the way from elegant and expensive to homey and reasonable. We especially enjoy meeting the owners of small B&B's, who often provide a very personal overview of their region. When we return to our favorites, the special welcome we get is like a homecoming. In fact, sometimes we go back to an area just to stay at a favorite B&B.

We carefully select and book places that meet our cleanliness and comfort standards. Advance reservations also ensure that we'll not waste precious sightseeing time looking for lodging. Of course, the downside of such thorough planning means a less flexible itinerary.

We use a variety of methods to select accommodations. Sometimes, we write for brochures from the Scottish Tourist Board in Edinburgh or from tourist boards in the regions we plan to visit. We also use the Scottish Tourist Board books on hotels/guesthouses, B&B's, and self-catering accommodations. These can be ordered directly from the Scottish Tourist Board or the British Tourist Authority. Some U.S. bookstores carry them in the Scotland/Britain travel sections. A helpful legend describes lodging quality (Scottish Tourist Board ratings), features, prices (tariffs) and amenities. We look for places with private or *en suite* (in the room) bathrooms, higher ratings to guarantee cleanliness, non-smoking and rates that fit our budget. We spend in the range of 20 to 30 pounds per person per night (1999 prices). Not all good B&B's subscribe to the Tourist Board rating system, but we think it very helpful in the absence of other recommendations. Lately, we've found the Internet to be a great resource as well. (See "Useful Resources" at end of book for more information on tourist boards and accommodation websites.)

For B&B reservations, we start about two months in advance by writing or calling proprietors to check availability. Occasionally we've been able to e-mail them. Once, we called three months ahead to reserve a room in Glasgow only to discover that the whole area as far as an hour away was booked solid for a huge international convention. During June, July and August, advance reservations may be necessary, depending on location. To hold reservations, B&B proprietors may ask for a major credit card number, confirmation in writing or a deposit. We've sometimes sent a deposit check in U.S. dollars, which they return to us when we pay in cash. Other times, we've had to send an international bankers draft in British pounds.

Once made, B&B reservations must be honored or adequate advance notice of cancellation given. Most B&B's are small businesses that depend on their guests for their livelihood. Several B&B owners confided that Americans and Canadians are getting bad reputations for not showing up. Good form dictates that guests also give B&B hosts an approximate arrival time.

B&B's, guesthouses and hotels work well for traveling around the country from point to point, region to region. However, another method we like involves setting up a home base and "self-catering." Scotland is so small, it's possible to see much of the country on day trips from a central location. Self-catering is the British term for renting a self-contained holiday cottage or apartment (flat).

In Edinburgh, we rented a lovely two-bedroom flat with a sitting room, fully furnished kitchen, and a bathroom with both tub and shower. Best of all, we had a washer-dryer unit. We enjoyed the luxury of unpacking everything and leaving it all at our flat when we took day trips away!

We found our flat through the Scottish Tourist Board's book on self-catering accommodations. Most self-catering units rent for a week at a time at rates that are similar and often less than B&B prices. We also spent far less money for food, because we didn't have to dine out all the time. Compare spending $5 to $10 to fix dinner for two (not counting wine) to about $16 to $20 for an inexpensive pub meal for two. We find we get tired of eating in restaurants every night for two or three weeks at a time. When we cook for ourselves, we eat less and feel better. Then when we do dine out, the occasion is special, just like at home.

Although cooking at our flat was limited to light breakfasts and simple dinners, we thoroughly enjoyed the unanticipated cultural experience of grocery shopping in a Scottish Safeway store. Once we searched for cornstarch to make a sauce and discovered the British call it corn flour. At checkout stands similar to our own, we were surprised to see grocery checkers sitting instead of standing, and we quickly learned we were expected to bag our own groceries.

For lunches on the road, we often picnic. Cheese, bread or crackers, maybe some cold cuts, fruit and sparkling water are perfect, and can be picked up easily in markets along the way. The variety of British crackers continually amazes us. Folks must think we're crazy when we stand in the supermarket aisles eyeing shelves loaded with packages, agonizing over which crackers to sample next. We have been known to bring them home for gifts! Even the sparkling water is exotic, like the lemon and elderflower version.

What to take and how to pack

Because Scottish weather is so unpredictable, our best advice is to plan and pack accordingly. No matter what time of year, we prepare for rain. A completely clear day can suddenly cloud up. For any travel in Britain, take waterproof jackets and umbrellas.

More often than the famous rain and drizzle, we've encountered sharp, biting wind; cold, clear skies; hot, sunny weather; and cloudy, cool days. We've experienced driving rain and even snow, although the snow did not last long or stick to the roadways. We've not found the weather extreme, but temperatures can range from below freezing in winter to as hot as 80 degrees in the summer. Scotland's damp climate makes even moderately cool temperatures seem cold.

We pack for the type of weather we expect in a cool northern climate at the time of year we visit, and we take clothes to layer. Sweaters, either cardigan or pullover (jumpers as they're called in Britain), are necessities. Wool seems to be popular all year, although we've not visited Scotland during the hottest months. Cotton turtlenecks work well for cooler June and September weather. Along with a waterproof jacket, they're warm and cozy in the islands, for ferry crossings, mountains and moors.

Our number one packing rule dictates that all clothes mix and match. We stay away from items that go with nothing else. Because we tramp around on moors and hills, we pack mostly casual clothes and a jacket or blazer, skirt/dress or slacks for special occasions. We take comfortable walking shoes and one pair of dressy shoes. Some types of flat walking shoes for women double for special occasions and city walking.

We have discovered some great travel clothing. The extra pockets in the shirts, trousers ("pants" in Britain means men's underwear), skirts and vests (waistcoats in Britain) and the easy-care fabrics make them worth the extra money. (See packing books in "Useful Resources" for more tips on travel clothing.)

We don't take a lot of luggage but have never been able to leave on a two- or three-week trip with only carry-on bags, as some travel experts recommend. A small rolling carry-on for each of us, if thoughtfully packed, can hold most of what we'll wear. Then, we usually take one extra bag between us. We always manage to fill it up with treasures to bring home. Remember that compact car trunks hold minimal luggage, and hauling bags in and out means constant rearranging!

Money matters

On our first trip, we had more questions about money than answers. We wondered how much to take in cash, if our debit card would work, if traveler's checks would be accepted at B&B's. Over time, we've learned the answers and have developed a system that works for us.

The currency of Scotland, *pounds sterling*, is the same throughout the United Kingdom. However, Scotland has its own banks, so some currency will be issued as Scottish notes. This includes a one-pound paper note. Travelers who plan to go on to England should be forewarned that the English do not like to accept one-pound Scottish paper notes. Before we leave Scotland for England, we exchange any one-pound paper currency for one pound coins. Also, paper notes issued by Scottish banks may be difficult to convert back to American dollars after the trip. Our son even had trouble in a large city like New Orleans!

We always take some cash in British pounds, including a few notes in small denominations and coins for initial expenses. In our community, we have to order British money a couple of weeks in advance from a local bank. We take the remainder of our budgeted amount in American Express traveler's checks issued in British pounds because we get a good rate of exchange at our AAA. We recommend taking traveler's checks in *pounds sterling* because checks in dollars are very difficult to cash in Scotland. Most places don't want to bother with them. We've not had problems with traveler's checks in pounds at B&B's and restaurants, although very small places may not accept them. Participating banks throughout Britain also cash them. American Express traveler's checks in either pounds or dollars can be cashed at their offices in Glasgow and Edinburgh.

Most shops and restaurants take major credit cards. B&B's usually do not, so traveler's checks or cash are required. We use our Visa debit card at automatic teller machines if we get low on cash. Credit cards and debit cards probably will replace traveler's checks in the future.

Chapter 3

Driving in Scotland...
"just keep to the left and follow the person in front of you."

Jerry does all driving, so this chapter is his perspective.

The first time

My experiences are probably typical for most foreigners. I had heard a lot about driving in Britain and how hard it would be. So I worried about it. Because I am over 50, I know my reflexes aren't what they once were, which caused additional concern. Would I have to learn to drive all over again?

First trip, we arrived in Edinburgh and spent a few days sightseeing on foot, so I didn't have to contend with driving immediately. Finally, the time came to pick up our rental car. The night before, I tossed and turned and didn't get much sleep. After breakfast, we walked from our B&B to the rental agency. After filling out the paperwork, I asked the clerk if he had any driving pointers for a foreigner. He replied, "Just keep to the left and follow the person in front of you." In retrospect, that's not bad advice, but at the time, it didn't give me much comfort. The other cars on the road actually did help me learn and kept me oriented to the correct side of the road.

First, I checked out the car to find out where everything was located. This particular car had the steering wheel, clutch, brake and accelerator in the same position as our vehicles at home, but all on the right side. This meant I had to shift with my left hand, an interesting experience for those who have never done it before. One peculiarity of this car that bedeviled me the whole trip was that the turn signal arm and the windshield (windscreen in Britain) wiper arms were reversed in relation to our vehicles at home. I was forever turning on the windshield wipers when I wanted to make a turn. When I drove out into the Edinburgh traffic, I thought, "This isn't too bad." Nevertheless, I was so tense that it took me a few days before I relaxed enough to realize my arms ached. All in all, my worry was needless. Driving in Britain is very much like driving at home. The major differences are left-lane driving and the roundabouts. The signs are similar to those at home with international symbols. After a week I became quite comfortable driving. I think it helped that I'm left-handed!

Out on the road—motorways and byways

I find that drivers in Britain tend to drive fast. But I suppose people who drive the same roads day after day become familiar with them, taking them much faster than an uncertain foreigner. I have traveled the road to our home every day for years, so I drive it fairly fast. I'm sure I make the tourists who visit our fruit-growing area nervous when I come up behind them.

Our country road at home is twisty and winding like most Scottish roads. In Scotland, we seldom encounter straight stretches of road, and even then not for long. Motorways are exceptions, of course. Surprisingly, one of the straightest stretches in Scotland was the A857 northwest of Stornoway on the island of Lewis. It ran for about six miles in almost a straight line. Scottish minor roads tend to be narrow without shoulders, and they made me nervous for a while. On the other hand, the cars also tend to be small. I haven't seen many Cadillac- or Lincoln-sized cars on the roads.

British roads consist of motorways ("M" roads), through routes ("A" roads), secondary routes ("B" roads) and unclassified roads and lanes. The motorways are limited-access freeways comparable to U.S. interstates. "A" roads resemble our state highways, and "B" roads are similar to county roads. However, in the west Highlands and islands, some roads classified as "A" roads may be single lane tracks with passing places.

In Scotland (unlike England and Wales), the definition of a road generally includes footpaths, bridle paths and cycle tracks. This means that traffic laws apply to them, too.

Round and round the roundabouts

Ah, the roundabouts . . . They are neat traffic regulators but challenging at times. Roundabouts are generally marked well in advance. Large signs with diagrams showing directions to towns and roads indicate their approach.

If one could look down on a roundabout from above, it would look like a circular road with all the traffic moving one way, clockwise. From this circle, roads radiate outward like rays. Before entering the circle from one of these roads, drivers must yield to any traffic coming from the right. When certain that no traffic is coming, the driver turns left into the clockwise movement of the circle. Once in the circle, all exits are to the left. We think one of the best features of roundabouts is that if we miss our turnoff we can go around again. On some roundabouts, we've been around and around more times than we care to remember.

The first couple of trips to Scotland I thought that surely this roundabout business must be more than simply yielding to the cars from the right. I had seen some drivers use turn signals and others not. I knew I must be missing some rules, or at least some sort of roundabout etiquette. And indeed I was. I bought the Department of Transport Highway Code and read the section on Correct Procedure at Roundabouts. Here it is:

When your road is the first left in the roundabout:
  • signal left and keep to the left lane when approaching the roundabout.

• stay in the roundabout's left lane and exit left.

When your road is straight ahead or on the other side of the circle:
  • don't signal as you approach the roundabout;
  • approach in the left-hand lane on a two-lane road or center lane on a three-lane road;
  • stay in the same lane once into the roundabout;
  • just after the road prior to yours, signal left and ease into the left lane;
  • turn left onto your road.

When your exit is on the right or almost all the way around the circle:
  • approach in the right-hand lane with right turn signal on;
  • once in the roundabout, stay to the right while signaling right;
  • after the exit before yours, signal left and turn left.

The only roundabouts that still give me trouble are the occasional double roundabouts (or worse, the rare triple). A double roundabout is one where a driver enters a second roundabout immediately upon leaving the first. These types of roundabouts occur mostly in larger cities.

Mini-roundabouts might cause problems, too. Usually just a painted ball in the middle of a circle, they can easily be missed. I have found I have to be careful I don't run through them thinking I have the right of way.

Hard to believe, but true—with enough experience, most people learn to love roundabouts. In summary, stay alert and yield to any traffic already in the circle.

One car at a time—negotiating one-lane tracks

Sometimes, two-lane roads abruptly become one-lane roads. An unexpected traffic light in the road serves as the only warning of this driving hazard. If the light is red, traffic must stop at the white line on the driver's side of the road. If the light is green, traffic proceeds along the single lane. These narrow stretches occur frequently at construction sites or bridges, but sometimes on straight stretches.

Off the beaten track, single-track roads only wide enough for one vehicle are common in Scotland. On our journeys, we have traveled hundreds of miles on these roads. The only way to get to some places is by single tracks. What happens when another car appears in the opposite direction?

Specially designated passing places are located on either side of the road at varying distances. Using these passing places requires a certain road etiquette. The driver closest to a passing place must pull into a left passing place, or wait opposite a passing place if on the right. The passing driver waves acknowledgment. If the driver of the other car flashes the lights, that means that he or she will yield. Drivers should never stop or park in a passing place to take pictures or for other reasons. Cars approaching uphill should be given way, if possible.

Scottish friends told us how the natives handle one-lane roads. When approaching each other, both cars do so at a fairly good clip; each driver tries to gauge the distance in order meet the other vehicle at the same time a pullout is reached. That way both drivers swerve around each other smoothly without too much loss of speed. Unfortunately, especially with a large number of foreigners and inexperienced drivers on the road, panic can cause old habits to return. Bad accidents have happened when a driver sees an approaching car and zips into a right passing place. We have seen this, fortunately at low speed. My advice is to use caution and courtesy, and don't try to match the native drivers for speed. I generally drive slower and tend to yield more often; after all, we're the ones on vacation without the need to rush anywhere.

The worst hazards, kamikaze sheep, occur in late spring and summer when lambs abound, particularly in the highlands and islands. I once came within an inch of killing a lamb when it suddenly bolted across the road to its mother. In the highlands and islands, sheep range everywhere, even with fenced pastures. Always slow down when sheep appear, especially if a lamb is separated from its mother—the lamb on one side of the road and the mother on the other. Forever unpredictable, lambs invariably jump in front of oncoming traffic. Another sheep hazard happens at night. Sheep usually bed down (sometimes they pick the roadbed), but occasionally when they're bothered by something like midges, they wander across the road. Driving along at a good pace late at night, I have suddenly come upon dozens of sheep in the middle of the road. Should an animal be hit, either injured or killed, be sure to notify the local police.

Wayfinding

Many of the sites described in this guide are difficult to locate. Two people manage the task best, one as driver and one as navigator. Driving unfamiliar roads, I must be constantly alert to driving conditions, turning and stopping properly, all the while remembering to keep to the left. Dodie serves as my navigator/map reader. She interprets the distances and gives directions.

Signage. Scotland does not have tacky, glaring billboards. However, the signs to monuments tend to be very small and sometimes nonexistent. The authorities also have the maddening habit of placing important signs right at the entrance to a site rather than some distance before the turnoff. Many times I have been driving along only to discover I have just passed the turn. This seems to happen most when I am driving at a brisk pace to avoid being run over by vehicles behind me.

Maps. We cannot stress enough the importance of

maps. On our first trip, we missed a lot because we didn't have detailed maps. We thought all we needed was a road map like those we use at home. We would see the historic site symbol on the road map but could never find the actual site! Now, we use several different kinds of maps, depending upon what we want to see in any particular area.

Route-planning maps. We take an overall route-planning map with a scale of about nine miles to the inch. When driving, we use a motoring atlas or a handy glove box road atlas with a scale of three or four miles to the inch, convenient for general navigating. Coming from the western United States where the scale of our maps covers vast distances, using a map with only three miles to the inch was an adjustment! However, even this large scale is not adequate for searching out most ruins. The most popular sites may be shown, but not always at the exact location. We had trouble finding our first broch in Scotland for that very reason. We drove up and down the road several times without seeing it and without knowing quite where to look.

Maps for finding ancient sites. We now depend upon the outstanding British Ordnance Survey (OS), Landranger series, maps with a scale of one mile to 1 ¼ inches. More than 200 of these maps cover every part of England and Scotland. Although expensive, about $9 apiece, we've found them worth the investment in the time and trouble they save us. We buy OS maps for sections of Scotland we plan to see in depth, generally about five or six per trip. These maps show everything including farmhouses, tracks, stone circles, single stones, cairns, topography. Without these detailed maps we'd never be able to find the more obscure sites. We like them so much, we feel lost without one for every area we visit.

Trespass and courtesy

Many ancient Scottish monuments are located on private land. Visiting them requires crossing private property, something that makes North Americans uncomfortable. Our Scottish friends, surprised at this discomfort, have brushed off our concerns. They insist that everyone in Scotland has the right to go anywhere as long as they follow some general rules. These rules include latching all gates, not disturbing livestock, not harming property or causing damage in any way, not interfering in farm operations, and leaving if asked to do so. Basically, visitors should leave the property exactly as found.

These commonsense rules conform to the "country code" or, in the case of the Forestry Commission, the "forest code." The codes admonish walkers to be careful with fire, not damage vegetation or harm animals, leave things as they were, remove nothing, not litter, and not damage fences, hedges, walls, buildings and signs.

Nevertheless, visitors should always ask permission of landowners, if at all possible. Once permission is granted, they should faithfully observe the country code and protect the landowners' interests, taking special care during such times as lambing season or hunting/fishing season.

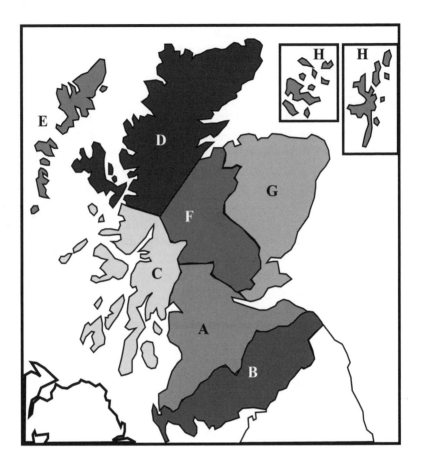

Searching

by

Region

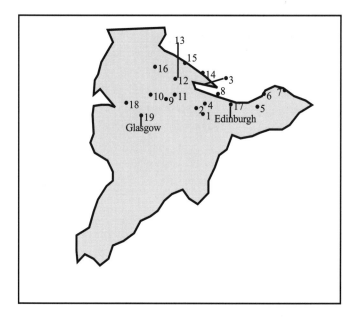

1   Cairnpapple
2   Torpichen Preceptory
3   Culross
4   Linlithgow Palace, St. Michael's Church
5   St. Mary's Church
6   Dirleton Castle
7   Tantallon Castle
8   Blackness Castle
9   Seabeg's Wood, Antonine Wall
10 Castlecary, Antonine Wall
11 Rough Castle, Antonine Wall
12 Sirling Area: Bannockburn, Stirling Castle, Old Town, Argyll's Lodging
13 Cambuskenneth Abbey
14 Castle Campbell
15 Ardoch Roman Fort
16 Doune Castle
17 Edinburgh Area: Craigmillar Castle, Edinburgh Castle, Gladstone's Land
18 Dumbarton Castle
19 Glasgow Area: Bearsden Roman Bathhouse, Glasgow Cathedral, Bothwell
    Castle

Chapter 4
Close to the Central Cities

Most first-time visitors to Scotland head directly to Edinburgh, its ancient capital. If not, they stop in Glasgow, Scotland's vibrant city of culture. Both of these popular cities offer tourists much to see in the way of museums and historic buildings, be they cathedrals or castles. Travelers who have limited time but would still like to explore some of Scotland's other prehistoric and historic monuments can still do so in easy day trips from either Edinburgh or Glasgow.

Cairnpapple ★★

Sheets of cold rain drenched Jerry and our 21-year-old son as they struggled up Cairnpapple Hill. At the top, out of the lee of the hill, the fierce March wind battered them with rain, soaking their clothes within 15 minutes. But Jerry was practically oblivious to the obstinate Scottish weather. As an undergraduate archaeology student, he'd studied Cairnpapple, never dreaming he'd someday see it. He remembered a few things—the henge, the large cairn, a chief's burial and the odd name. Now, after 30 years, he could see it for himself. Cairnpapple, used continually from about 3000 BC to 1400 BC, is considered one of the most important Neolithic and Bronze Age sites in Scotland.

Close to the populated areas of Scotland, not far from Edinburgh and very near Linlithgow, Cairnpapple is one of the more accessible ancient sites. It was also our first Scottish prehistoric monument.

What was Cairnpapple, and what did it look like before our time? According to archaeologists, events began about 5,000 years ago with the establishment of a cemetery of small pits arranged in an arc. These pits contained pieces of burnt human bone. Later, the people built a henge (circular ditch) to enclose the cemetery with entrances on the north and south. They banked soil from the ditch on the outside so it would have been difficult to see the cemetery from lower down the hill. The people who built the henge also erected 24 standing stones (or possibly timbers) in a circle inside the henge. Probably built during the Bronze Age, one very small grave near one of the standing stones contained two pots called beakers. This grave, speculation goes, belonged to an important person because it had its own stone and its own small cairn surrounded by kerb stones. The grave may have been made for a Beaker chieftain, leader of people known for their use of special red pottery. No one really knows the purpose of the henge or the standing stones. Later, another cairn was constructed to cover a second burial, not far from the first grave and also outlined by kerb stones.

Many years later, a larger mound was built over the first cairns. This new mound also had its own kerb of stones (which can be seen today), some that may have been taken from the earlier stone circle. This mound covered another important burial in a large cist that contained grave goods and two cremations. About 1,000 years later, four more cist graves were dug on the east side of the large mound. These were only a few of the changes that occurred over the several thousand years the site was used. Neolithic tools found during excavations at Cairnpapple came from as far away as the Lake District in England and from Wales.

Today, traces of the henge remain, as well as holes indicating the location of the stone circle. The huge mound was completely removed, but a stony area (with the original grave pits visible) ringed by kerb stones shows how big it once was. The initial cairns covering the first two burials were removed during excavations in 1947 but later rebuilt with interior walls of concrete. This renovated cairn is the most prominent feature today. Steps lead to the top and a hatch opens to the interior. In summer, visitors can climb inside to see the stones and graves.

The second time we visited Cairnpapple, a light snow dusted the ground, sparkling in the morning sunlight and outlining the structures. We could see all the way to the Firth of Forth. From our hilltop perch, we had spectacular views, except perhaps for the very large industrial complex off in the distance. On a clear day, it's possible to see Goat Fell on the island of Arran 150 kilometers to the west. We didn't know to look.

To get there: *Take the A706 south from Linlithgow, turn off on the B792 to Torphichen and then take an unmarked road to Cairnpapple. Or drive north from Bathgate and the A89 to the B792. Watch for small signs to Cairnpapple. A small car park large enough for one or two cars is located at the base of the hill. Steps lead to the top of the hill over 1,000 feet above sea level.*

Torpichen Preceptory

This place once served as the seat of the powerful Knights Hospitallers of the Order of St. John of Jerusalem. These soldier-knights belonged to a religious order that fought for their beliefs. Torpichen, dating from the 12th to the 15th centuries, was their only center in Scotland. Torpichen stands in a pleasant little valley not far from Linlithgow and on the route to Cairnpapple.

The graveyard contains an odd-looking short, squarish stone with cup mark on the top. Some speculate this stone may have come from Cairnpapple, or could possibly have been one of the boundary markers. Criminals and others seeking sanctuary often tried to reach the preceptory's boundary located some distance from the building.

Only the preceptory tower and transepts remain while the nave and choir have mostly disappeared. We visited on a weekday when the preceptory was closed so we couldn't see the 14th century turnpike stair that leads from the north transept to the 13th century tower. The site is cared for by Historic Scotland and open on weekends for a limited number of hours.

To get there: *Follow the B792 to the village of Torpichen located between Bathgate and Linlithgow.*

Culross ★★

Anyone who has ever wanted to step into a 16th or early 17th century village should see Culross (pronounced "cyoo russ"). Restored by the National Trust for Scotland over a 50-year period, some of the earliest houses date from the late 1500s. The town isn't large, with only about a half-dozen steep, cobbled streets lined with tiny houses. The oldest house in Culross, appropriately called "The Oldest House," was built in the square facing the Mercat Cross. Many other buildings date from the late 1500s, 1600s and into the 1700s.

Culross served as an important Celtic religious center in the 6th century. According to legend, the monks saved the life of Thenew, a Celtic princess. Her father, King of Lothian, set her adrift in an open boat after he learned she was pregnant. Her name later became Enoch, hence St. Enoch's square in Glasgow. She gave birth to St. Mungo, patron saint of Glasgow.

Cistercian monks, who founded Culross Abbey in 1217, eventually replaced these early Celtic monks. The abbey ruins sit above the town, a short uphill walk through narrow streets. In 1633 the nave or lay brothers' choir was converted into the local church, a common occurrence in Scotland. Not much remains of the cloister buildings, although it's possible to climb around in the vaults. Care is required, as some high places have no safety railings.

In 1490, the abbey granted Culross a charter to make it a Burgh of Barony. That meant the town could have a weekly market inside the town limits. Since the time of the earliest monks, coal has been mined here, which assured the town's future. In the late 1500s, Sir George Bruce, a descendant of King Robert the Bruce, bought the mine from the abbey. He was able to dig much deeper than the monks, even tunneling under the Firth to a tower he built in the water.

King James VI, a friend of Sir George Bruce, granted Royal Burgh status to Culross in 1592 to help increase royal income. Bruce, successful in business, constructed a fine home in 1597 and King James stayed with him several times. In an amusing story, the king was taken on a tour through the mine to the tower, via the underwater tunnel. When he came up and saw water all around, he thought he'd been tricked in a treasonous plot.

Unique Culross can be quite popular during tourist season. We think the best times to go might be late spring or early fall. We first visited in March when all Trust buildings were closed. We used that time to explore the abbey and streets. We next visited in early September and saw the historic buildings: George Bruce's house now called the Palace, the Town House and the Study. The Palace gardens have been planted with flora common to the time.

<u>To get there:</u> *Culross is located on the north shore of the Firth of Forth just off the A985 between Dunfermline and Kincardine. Take the Forth Bridge from Edinburgh.*

<u>Linlithgow Palace</u> ★★★

Mary Queen of Scots was born at Linlithgow Palace on the third floor in the queen's quarters just above the king's in the west range's royal apartments. Mary's grandmother watched in vain for her husband, James IV, to return from battling the English at Flodden Field from Queen Margaret's Bower, at the top of the northwest tower. An impressive ruin, Linlithgow Palace played a big role in Scottish history, particularly during the Stewart dynasty.

Linlithgow is a palace, not a castle. A palace served as a royal home whereas a castle was built for defensive purposes, although castles often contained palaces. Edward I of England used early Linlithgow as a castle, but Scotland's kings later rebuilt it as a palace.

Today, Linlithgow Palace is an enchanting ruin, still evoking the lavish lifestyle of royalty. Historic Scotland interpretive signs explain the uses of the various rooms and palace features. We recommend at least two hours to explore Linlithgow.

The size of the cellars, kitchens, storerooms and other rooms under the four living ranges surrounding the central courtyard underscore its royal palace status. Both numerous as well as large, these lower rooms include guardrooms and a prison. Passages wind everywhere. The wine cellar in the northeast corner has figures drinking from flagons on the ceiling corbels. The great hall on the second floor (first floor in Britain) is likely the most impressive room, measuring 100 feet long by 30 feet wide, once covered by a beamed wooden roof like the one at Edinburgh and Stirling castles. The hall's massive fireplace, located at the south end, almost extends the width of the room. A large minstrel gallery runs the whole length of the hall. Imagine the hall lined with tapestries, minstrels playing above and a huge fire crackling in the fireplace. A great window allowed light to fall on royalty dining at the head table.

Remarkable turnpike stairs lead to the roof in each of the four corner towers. Visitors can climb the northwest tower stairs all the way to the top for views of the surrounding area and some great photo opportunities. Although Historic Scotland has installed protective railings, this climb is not for people afraid of heights.

James V gave Mary of Guise (mother of Mary Queen of Scots) the ornate Gothic/Renaissance octagonal fountain in the center of the courtyard as a wedding gift. When Bonnie Prince Charlie stayed at the palace, the fountain supposedly flowed with wine.

Linlithgow Palace and its site have long been part of Scotland's history. A Roman way station stood here along the Roman road that connected to the Antonine wall farther to the north. In the time of King David I, a royal house or residence was located here. Following this, Edward I of England built a pele (wall) with a castle inside, where he stayed for three months in the winter of 1300. Bruce destroyed Edward's castle in 1313 in a maneuver not unlike the Trojan Horse. The wily Scots used a farmer who regularly delivered hay for the horses to the castle. One delivery day, he concealed some Scots soldiers in the wagon. Other soldiers hid just outside the walls. When the farmer got his wagon inside under the raised portcullis, he stopped, released his horses, and the Scots jumped out. Then the rest of Bruce's soldiers rushed in to surprise and overtake the garrison.

King David II restored the residence, but fire destroyed his efforts in 1424. James I rebuilt it, and other Stewart kings used the palace. Both James IV and his father, James III, were fond of Linlithgow. James IV continued to make major additions to the palace. James V erected the gatehouse visitors enter today and also completed the palace. His queen, Mary of Guise, declared that she had not beheld a more princely palace although she had seen many noble structures in France. Charles I stayed at Linlithgow as did his successor Oliver Cromwell, during the winter of 1650. After the Restoration, future King James VII of Scotland (brother of Charles II) lived at Linlithgow for a while as did Bonnie Prince Charlie during the last Jacobite Rebellion in 1745. In 1746, the Duke of Cumberland's army left fires burning that razed the interior. Linlithgow has remained a roofless ruin ever since.

While we might wish the palace had survived, at least in ruins it gives us a sense of its previous magnificence.

Continuously occupied ancient buildings have undergone so many changes and supposed improvements that they often lose much of their medieval character.

St. Michael's Church

Just south and next to Linlithgow Palace stands what may be one of the largest pre-Reformation churches in Scotland. Also an excellent example of a medieval Scottish parish church, St. Michael's was built between 1424 and 1535, about the same time as Linlithgow. In the south transept, King James IV saw an apparition that warned him of his death at Flodden Field. He ignored the warning and rode to his death anyway. Cromwell used the church as a stable for his horses.

The tower's modern spire was placed by helicopter in 1964, sparking a great deal of controversy. Look for the Gothic window tracery, St. Michael's most striking feature. The stained glass is modern.

Both the palace and the church stand in the center of the charming village of Linlithgow. We stopped for a pub lunch at The Four Marys, known for its good ale, just down from the palace.

To get there: *Linlithgow Palace and St. Michael's Church are easy to reach, close to Edinburgh on the way to Stirling just off the M9. The palace can be clearly seen from the motorway if you miss the first exit on the motorway from Edinburgh.*

St. Mary's Church, Haddington *

St. Mary's Church is the largest parish church in Scotland. Located in the appealing East Lothian town of Haddington, it contains a number of unusual artifacts. These include a scallop shell carved into a pillar that records a pilgrimage to Compostella, Spain; two Green Men; the Lauderdale Aisle with the ornate Maitland family tombs; a 500-year-old carved consecration cross; the grave of Jane Carlyle; flags of the Napoleonic wars; and the medieval Haddington Goat.

Church members serve as knowledgeable guides. Our guide pointed out things we would have missed and graciously answered our many questions. The carved Green Men heads with flowing greenery for hair derive from Celtic pre-Christian origin and represent the tie between humans and nature. The consecration cross was carved when the bishop blessed the completed church, probably around 1350 or 1360.

The Maitland coat of arms on the Lauderdale Aisle tomb bears an unusual lion rampant. Looking closely, we could tell that it differed from Scotland's rearing red lion symbol, because the paws were detached from the body. Our guide explained that the Lauderdale lion was purposely contrived to distinguish it from the king's. Only the king could display the real lion rampant.

Historically, St. Mary's served as a collegiate church, meaning that it housed a college of priests and ministers. They attempted to revive worship in pre-Reformation days by introducing the music and ceremonies of great cathedrals to parish churches.

The church building itself illustrates both conservation and restoration. Inside, the east end of the church beyond the crossing looks far more weathered than the west or nave end. This portion lay in ruins from 1547-48, when Henry VIII razed the church roof during his rough wooing of Mary. The church's west end was saved by John Knox who advised that it be partitioned off to function as a parish church. After 400 years, a masterful restoration of the east end in the 1970s finally made the church whole again. Our guide explained that the restored roof was made of lightweight fiberglass because the weathered walls could not support stone.

To get there: *We could not find any signs to the church and only stumbled on it driving through town. After end-*

ing up on the River Walk turn-off at the southern edge of High Street, we came to Church Street. Because that sounded like we were on the right track, we followed it past an Episcopal church. Suddenly, St. Mary's rose up in front of us.

Dirleton Castle ★★★

Imposing Dirleton looks like a castle. With its ancient drum tower, a bridge over a dry moat, and its myriad nooks and crannies, we rank it as one of our favorites. Its grounds delight the senses. The flower border is supposedly the longest in the world.

Dirleton Castle has stood on its pedestal of rock for more than 700 years. In its 300 years of occupation, three different powerful families lived here. The castle wall construction demarcates each family's occupation. The oldest part of the castle, built in 1220 by the de Vaux family, stands out clearly because the earliest builders used square stone blocks for the walls. The drum tower, lesser towers, and walls to the left of the entrance date from this time.

In the 14th century, a second family, the Halyburtons, moved in and built the great hall wing using the rubble technique. This method placed stones inside the walls and only the stones on wall faces were smoothed. Some decoration appears on stones around doorways and windows. The gatehouse at the entrance provides a good example of the rubble technique.

The Ruthven family took over in the 16th century and also used the rubble technique. However, these walls have horizontal strips of finely carved stone that decorate the walls. This work can be seen inside the old 13th century walls just to the left of the entrance.

Dirleton, a castle to get lost in, includes such structures as the old lord's hall, the more modern great hall, and the gruesome pit prison below the main prison. In the lord's quarters, we could visualize its window seats

Dirleton Castle close

lined with cushions, tapestries on the walls and fires crackling in the huge fireplaces.

If the castle walls could talk, they would tell of a violent history. Dirleton was besieged and taken in 1298 by Edward I, retaken by the Scots in 1306, taken again by the English, and finally captured and destroyed by the Scots after Bannockburn in 1314. In 1649, some unfortunate women were interred in the main prison before they were strangled and burnt as witches. The last siege occurred in 1650 by Cromwell against loyalist "Moss-troopers" who used the castle as a stronghold. The castle was captured and once again destroyed.

At Dirleton Castle, we met Andrew, a Historic Scotland custodian, who readily shared his vast knowledge of castles with us. A keen historian, he has studied East Lothian castles, publishing his work in a regional magazine.

To get there: *The castle is easy to find in the neat village of Dirleton, just off the A198 coast road. The large car park also serves a park near the entrance.*

Tantallon Castle ★★

Tantallon screams defense. From a distance, its walls soar out of the rocky headland like a monster fortification. A single line of huge wall was all that was necessary to defend this promontory from the land. Sea cliffs fall away precipitously from all sides except the front. Behind the castle, picturesque Bass Rock juts out of the Firth of Forth. Not only does Tantallon occupy a dramatic location, it served as a strategic stronghold in Scotland's turbulent history.

Closer to the castle, the extent of the defenses becomes more apparent. A series of three ditches leads to the castle. Anyone attempting to reach the gate would have to cross these ditches in full view of the castle walls. The great outer ditch was protected by a short stretch of wall and a gun tower built in 1520. The outer ward contains a 17th century dovecot. The huge main ditch, crossed by a modern bridge, protects the front of the castle and leads into the massive gatehouse.

The castle was built to withstand attack before the threat of artillery. Artillery proved its undoing, evidenced by the scarred face of the castle walls. Fierce winds and storms that strike this area also took their toll. Remnants of what were once enormous towers protect either side of the entrance, and in the center stands the great tower that includes the gatehouse, still in good condition.

We didn't realize that the castle was just a single huge wall until we walked through the central tower and into the close, the open grassy area leading to the cliffs. This is why the wall is called a curtain wall, as though a curtain (of stone) bisects the neck of the promontory. The only other walls consist of the remains of the two-story hall block to the left of the close.

For a real treat, climb to the ramparts by way of stairs in the wall. When we visited, Historic Scotland had closed the north end of the wall due to work by stone masons, but most of the wall, including the central tower was open to exploration. Once on the ramparts, we had superb views of the Firth of Forth and the countryside including the steep drop to the sea.

Lord Douglas, of the Douglas family that supported Robert the Bruce, built Tantallon in 1350. He did a good job because much of what remains dates from that time, even though the castle experienced many attacks. After the Douglas family split into two factions, Tantallon became a center of power for the "Red" Douglasses. During its long history, it was besieged at least three times, once by the King James IV in 1491, again by his successor King James V in 1528, and finally by Cromwell in 1651. In 1548, the castle guns fired on English ships engaged in a sea battle with a French fleet.

To get there: *The castle stands a little less than four miles east of North Berwick just off the A198 coast road.*

Blackness Castle ★★

Blackness Castle deserves its reputation as one of the strongest fortresses in Scotland. Not far from Edinburgh to the west, the castle juts out into the Forth, resembling a ship. Its pointed "bow" projects into the water to the northeast and the "stern" southwest toward the land. Although not present now, water and marsh originally would have surrounded three sides of the castle.

Blackness Castle contains many structures built into the walls and on its rock "yard." The castle's stark appearance gives mute testimony to the years it served as an impregnable prison.

The North Tower stands in the "ship's" bow and readily demonstrates how prisoners were provided for according to social status. Now only a little over two stories high, its first two floors housed prisons for lesser folk. The reasonably comfortable and ventilated top floor contained a fireplace and latrine for more important inmates. The pit prison at the very bottom interred prisoners on the lowest rung of the social ladder. Anyone held in the pit prison probably did not come out alive. The tide flushing it out twice a day served as a questionable amenity.

The South tower stands at the stern of this rocky ship. In the castle's earliest rendition, the great hall was likely located here. Starting in 1537, work began to make the tower as high as it is today and to strengthen the walls. The crenellations of the earlier wall are visible a little over halfway up when viewed from outside the walls.

The strong spur attached to the south tower was built during Queen Mary's time to house a new entrance originally in the east curtain wall. The parapets of spur are still in good condition. The yett or iron gate in the entrance dates from 1693.

The central tower most likely dates from the 1400s. Very early on, this served as a prison for high status prisoners. Cardinal Beaton was probably imprisoned here in one of the spacious rooms. A stair tower built in 1667, when Covenanters were held at the castle, connects the floors.

The powerful Sir George Crichton, who was governor of Stirling and Edinburgh and chancellor to the young King James II, likely began constructing Blackness Castle in the 1440s for use as a residence and a prison. The Crichtons kept the castle only until 1453, when King James II annexed to the Crown all the land owned by Sir George.

Because of its strength, Blackness was successfully besieged only once. Oliver Cromwell secured powerful new guns in 1650 and battered the castle into surrender.

More recently, the castle served as a backwater garrison and a munitions depot. Buildings outside the castle, such as the officer's quarters, date from its depot days in the 1800s.

To get there: *Take exit 2 off the M9 out of Edinburgh to the village of Blackness. Signs give good directions to the castle.*

Antonine Wall

To keep the ferocious Picts contained, in 142 AD Roman emperor Antoninus Pius built a 37-mile wall across the narrowest section of central Scotland from the Firth of Forth to the Firth of Clyde. Although not completely constructed of stone, this wall was Scotland's equivalent of Hadrian's Wall to the south. It consisted of a 14-foot-wide stone base with drainage culverts regularly spaced along its length. Above this, the Roman legionaries laid thin layers of turf to about 10 feet tall, and topped this with a timber wall. A large ditch in front completed the defenses. Even today after nearly 2,000 years of erosion and destruction, parts of this massive wall still exist.

Historic Scotland has made several sections of the Antonine Wall accessible to the public. We visited Bearsden Roman Bathhouse (see Glasgow Area), Castlecary, Seabegs Wood, and Rough Castle.

Seabegs Wood

At Seabegs Wood, the ditch, rampart, and military way, or Roman road, behind it are all visible. This is supposed to be the best-preserved stretch of Roman road.

To get there: *Follow the signs from Bonnybridge. The wall lies about a mile west of Bonnybridge, south of the B816. The wood lies between Castlecary and Bonnybridge. We found space to park off the B816 at the eastern end of the wood. A small roundabout from Bonnybridge has one exit leading south to High Bonnybridge. Following this road south, the first right turn led to the Seabegs Wood site.*

Castlecary

At Castlecary we saw a much eroded section of wall and didn't visit the remains of the fort. A couple of vandalized but still legible information boards stand on the approach to the wall.

To get there: *The section we saw lies west of the A80 at Castlecary. A much-weathered sign points toward the wall. We entered an industrial yard and parked off to one side.*

Rough Castle ★★

In addition to Bearsden, Rough Castle is by far the most impressive and best-preserved section of the Antonine Wall. The Roman fort stands out clearly, while the wall and massive ditch demonstrate the wall's purpose as a formidable barrier. We liked it a lot.

In comparison to other forts along the wall, Rough Castle was a small one, manned by about 500 auxiliary troops not as well trained as the regular legionaries. Excavation of the fort in the early 1920s revealed the foundations of stone buildings and bathhouse. These have all been reburied, so are not visible today.

Rough Castle defensive pits, Antonine Wall

Part of Rough Castle's defenses included the pits located on the north side of the ditch near the causeway. The Romans called these lilia (or lilies). They were dug out in a precise pattern and lined with sharp stakes to create a formidable barrier to anyone charging the wall and fort. Today, the park-like setting belies the military purpose of the huge bank and ditch arrangement. On a sunny day, local people walk their dogs, stroll or picnic. A burn runs alongside the fort.

To get there: *Follow the same route out of Bonnybridge taken for Seabegs Wood. Instead of turning right, continue straight south to High Bonnybridge where a sign points to a road to the left and the fort. This road leads through an industrial area toward Bonnybridge Farm. It eventually turns into a rough track for about a quarter of a mile until crossing a cattle grid into a park and large car park for Rough Castle.*

Stirling Area

Anyone traveling to Scotland's north probably will drive around or close to the historically significant town of Stirling, made recently more famous by the movie, *Braveheart.* (A Glasgow taxi driver told us that people arrive in Glasgow and ask to be taken to *Braveheart* country!) The Stirling area has so much to see at least a day or more there is necessary. On the motorways, getting to Stirling from either Glasgow or Edinburgh requires less than an hour's drive.

Bannockburn ★★

At Bannockburn on June 24, 1314, Robert the Bruce with only 5,000 men defeated and destroyed an English army of 20,000 soldiers commanded by Edward II. History documents this event as a critical turning point in

Scottish independence. The Scots finally succeeded in driving out the English to regain their freedom. Not much is left of the battlefield—only 58 acres surrounded by homes. Even this was narrowly saved in 1930 when developers threatened to build more houses. The 10th Earl of Elgin, head of the Bruce family at the time, raised enough money through a national committee to buy the site. The National Trust runs the Bannockburn site, which includes a visitor center, a large rotunda display on the battlefield and the famous bronze statue of Bruce on his horse. Although we'd seen pictures of this statue many times, we were amazed at its huge size. The base alone is twice as tall as most people.

The visitor center contains an exhibition called the Kingdom of the Scots tracing Scottish history from the Wars of Independence to the Union of the Crowns in 1603. An excellent audiovisual program in the small theater sets the stage for a tour of the battlefield.

On the battlefield, the rotunda and statue stand on the hill that was thought to have been Bruce's headquarters. The rotunda exhibit explains the details of the battle, documents important events and specifies the locations they occurred. Even today, major battle landmarks are visible. The modern A872, built right over the ancient Roman road, marks the approach route of the English army.

Stirling Bridge, where William Wallace defeated Edward I in 1297 is close to Bannockburn, just under the walls of Stirling Castle. The castle can be seen from the battlefield.

To get there: *Getting to Bannockburn is not too difficult, except for the roundabouts. On our first visit to Stirling and Bannockburn we saw the same roundabouts far too often! Bannockburn is on the south side of Stirling, so if you approach it from the motorway (M9) on your way to Stirling, you'll probably have more success than if you approach it from Stirling. Since* Braveheart *and resulting publicity, we've noticed better signage to sites around Stirling. Bannockburn is just off the A872 on the way into Stirling. Look for the visitor center on the west side of the road. Also, don't get confused by the town of Bannockburn. Look for the Bannockburn National Trust site.*

Stirling Castle ★★★

Like Edinburgh, the castle is Stirling's most impressive landmark. Nestled 400 feet high on its immense volcanic rock, Stirling Castle dominates the area. In fact, we've often used it to orient ourselves to direction when we've gotten mixed up on the roads in and around Stirling!

We highly recommend a visit to Stirling Castle for tourists who only have time to see one castle in all Scotland. Yes, we know it's practically heresy to prefer Stirling to Edinburgh Castle, the most visited Scottish tourist attraction. Edinburgh Castle is magnificent, but Stirling Castle is more so. In the past few years, Historic Scotland has been busy restoring the castle after years of abuse and use as a military post. Its palace has been renovated, and when workers removed the Great Hall's wall coverings to the original masonry, they discovered seven massive fireplaces. Larger than Edinburgh Castle's, the immensity of Stirling's Great Hall with its seven fireplaces documented the castle's importance as a royal residence. Throughout the castle grounds, outstanding exhibitions depict castle life. We especially like the reconstructed kitchens, complete with workers, food and medieval recipes!

The unique location of Stirling Castle destined it to be one of the most important fortifications in Scotland. Guarding the north-south and east-west routes of Scotland, anyone who held Stirling controlled the country. What's more, the castle presided over the Forth River at the highest maneuverable point for sea vessels. Like

Edinburgh's rock, Stirling's glacial crag was probably fortified for centuries. The castle walls on all sides provide superb views of the farmlands and highlands to the west and north, the river and town to the east, and the Bannockburn battlefield to the south. The Wallace Monument, easily recognized, rises out of the crags to the east.

To get there: *Follow the signs through the old town to the car park at the top of the hill.*

The Old Town of Stirling

A visit to Stirling Castle is only a beginning, because the charming old town lying below the castle on the rock's glacial tail has more to discover. We strongly recommend buying one of the local guidebooks about the old town. We completed a walking tour in about an hour, although we were a bit pressed for time and suggest a more leisurely tour. Some of the sights include 17th century Argyll's Lodging (below), the Church of the Holy Rude where King James VI was christened, and Lord Darnley's house where he stayed when Mary was in residence at the castle. The crow-stepped gables on the old buildings are a unique Scottish architectural feature.

Argyll's Lodging ★★

Imagine walking through a door and into 1670. We felt as if that happened to us at Argyll's Lodging. This one-of-a-kind town house once belonged to the earls who later became the dukes of Argyll. The family owned the house until 1764. The house's location was convenient for nobility expected to be at court. Nearby Mars Wark, started in 1570 but never finished, exemplifies another such home.

The house has been restored to appear as it did in the time of the ninth Earl of Argyll, who acquired it in the 1660s. Argyll was Protestant and fell out with King Charles II's brother who later became James VII, II (James the Seventh of Scotland, Second of England). He escaped imprisonment in Edinburgh Castle by posing as his stepdaughter's page and fled to Holland. He later returned only to be executed after leading an unsuccessful revolt against King James VII, II.

The house has a varied history. Records indicate that Sir William Alexander, who became the first Earl of Stirling, owned it in 1633. He remodeled an existing structure dating from the late 16th century. Sir William traveled widely and received his education at the University of Glasgow as well as Lieden in Holland. He was a poet and friend of Ben Johnson.

After the Argylls, the house fell on difficult times. It was sold to the government around 1800 and became a military hospital. In 1964, it was transformed into a youth hostel. The house languished until Historic Scotland acquired it, restoring and opening some of the main rooms to the public in 1996.

The earliest section of the house, the range to the left upon entering the courtyard, was built in the 1500s. In Argyll's day, it accommodated the kitchens. Laigh Hall, the main entrance to the house, stands directly in front. It primarily consists of two reception rooms, a more common hall below and the important one above. The building to the right contained the lord's private living quarters.

Argyll's Lodging is one of few properties that Historic Scotland has restored to a specific period of time. The lord's living area serves as entrance to the exhibit and includes a computerized video history of the house. Lord and Lady Argyll's chambers and the two reception halls were reconstructed using detailed inventories from 1680 and 1682. Fortunately, many original fixtures remained. These included wall paintings, the main wooden staircase, and the dining room and drawing room fireplaces. One wall of the main reception room retained original painted designs that allowed the curators to faithfully match the rest of the room.

We had a definite sense of visiting a real home and almost expected to meet the earl or countess around the next corner. The heavy wall hangings, the wooden commode, the four-poster bed, wooden chairs and other furniture clearly illustrate the decorating style of a noble family in the late 1600s.

To get there: *Argyll's Lodging is located right below Stirling Castle. In fact, you have to pass by it in order to reach the castle parking lot.*

Cambuskenneth Abbey

After soundly defeating Edward II at Bannockburn, King Robert the Bruce held a parliament at Cambuskenneth Abbey, about two miles from the battlefield. This parliament punished Scots who had fought for the English. Today, little from Bruce's time is left. In fact, except for the well-preserved bell tower, very little remains at all.

Founded by King David in 1147 and first known as the Abbey of St. Mary of Stirling, Cambuskenneth became a renowned Augustinian house. Most abbey construction occurred in the late 1200s. Today, only the foundations of the church and the tower remain. The rest ended up in Mar's Wark and other structures in Stirling. The tower, although original, has been restored. It is the only surviving example of a freestanding medieval belfry in Scotland, a style more characteristic of Italy.

The site has other associations with royalty. Edward I visited in 1303-4. Robert the Bruce held another parliament at Cambuskenneth in 1326. The coffins of King James III and his queen, Margaret of Denmark, discovered near the high altar, were reburied here in a fine tomb dedicated by Queen Victoria.

To get there: *The abbey site is one mile east of Stirling just off the A91. Drive through the small village of Cumbuskenneth and park at the end of the village road where a cow pasture begins. The abbey and tower are visible at this point. Historic Scotland maintains the abbey. A fence surrounds it.*

Castle Campbell ★

Once called Castle Gloom, this castle was anything but gloomy on the bright June day we visited. Flowers bloomed in the castle gardens and foliage covered the grounds. The castle lies at the head of Dollar Glen owned by the National Trust and overlooks the town of Dollar with dramatic views stretching south toward the Pentland Hills. Castle Campbell is worth visiting for its serenely beautiful surroundings as well as its history.

A visit requires a fairly strenuous and steep uphill walk when returning to the car park from the castle (although handicap access is possible by vehicle). Given enough time and decent weather, an alternate scenic trail leads up to the castle through Dollar Glen. Approaching from either route, the castle's stone walls rise out of the thick woodland from a narrow finger of land between two streams, called the Burn of Sorrow and the Burn of Care.

Some sort of fortification has stood on this site since 1466 and most likely earlier. The earliest structure was probably a motte and bailey style castle. Stewarts owned these lands until one of their three last heiresses married Colin Campbell of Argyll in the late 1400s. Through this liaison the Campbells acquired land and castle, and Colin probably started building the present tower house at that time. In 1489-90 Parliament changed the name from Gloom to Castle Campbell.

A later Campbell, Archibald, became the first nobleman in Scotland to adopt the Protestant religion. He invited John Knox to live at the castle and preach. According to legend, Knox preached to a large crowd on a rocky knoll just below the castle garden.

In keeping with their Protestant tradition, later Campbells joined the Covenanters against Charles I, and Castle Campbell became a center of power for them. The Marquis of Montrose passed through Dollar, sacking and burning the countryside but didn't harm the castle. Nine years later, in 1654, Oliver Cromwell garrisoned the castle with English troops until opposing forces captured and burned it. Although the Campbells kept the lands, they forsook the castle.

Overall, the tower house remains in excellent condition. Some of the flooring has been restored, allowing visitors to explore the tower house interior. Few original interior features remain with the exception of some grotesque carved heads that once held hanging lamps from the ceiling of a vaulted upper room. The lower floor had a special hall that served as a prison complete with a pit. The castle courtyard still retains its walls. Unfortunately, the hall range on the south side of the courtyard reflects damage caused by the fire. While not much is left of the great hall, the basement and the south wall give an idea of its previous grandeur. The National Trust for Scotland and Historic Scotland jointly administer the castle, and the National Trust maintains a tearoom on the lower level of the tower house. We enjoyed that respite after the hike to the castle.

To get there: *Take the A91 north and east of Stirling to the town of Dollar where signs give directions to the castle parking lot. Then it is a fairly long hike down a steep hill and over a small stream (burn) to the castle on a mostly asphalt path.*

Ardoch Roman Fort ★

Ardoch provides the opportunity to see a fine example of the might of the Roman army in Scotland around 150

AD. The fort's earthworks are massive. It's hard to believe soldiers of the Roman army created these ditches and ramparts when it looks as though giant machinery would be necessary.

Today, a huge grass-covered complex of banks and ditches masks the once busy fort. Time has erased any evidence of streets and buildings. The slight indentation in the center of the fort was possibly a medieval hospice. The locations of the four gates are still easy to find. From each gate, causeways lead from the rampart out across the defensive ditches. After 2,000 years, the rampart remains about six feet high. The fort's five ditches stand out vividly on the north and east sides.

Ardoch, occupied and abandoned a number of times, served as an outpost of the Antonine Wall 20 miles south. The longest period of the army's occupation was 20 years. Six Roman marching camps, all larger than Ardoch, were situated just north. The old Roman road ran past the fort on the east, heading northeast to another fort at Strageath.

To get there: *Ardoch lies on the east side of the A822, within walking distance of the village of Braco in Perthshire. Since parking at the site is restricted, leave your car just north of the village and walk to the site. A very weathered sign at the gate was hard to read.*

Doune Castle ★★

Imagine Ivanhoe charging out from a castle gate. That castle could have been Doune Castle, because part of a BBC special on Ivanhoe was actually filmed at Doune.

Doune Castle looks like everyone's idea of a castle. A huge tower, complete with turrets, soars above the entry. To the right of the tower and gate, a massive block contains the great hall and stretches a long distance before ending in the smaller kitchen tower. These structures also sport turrets and high windows. A huge, intact curtain wall runs around the remaining part of the large castle mound. This entire enormous structure rests on an easily defended narrow strip of land between the River Teith and Ardoch Burn.

Robert Stewart, first duke of Albany and earl of Mentieth and Fife, built Doune around 1361. The castle eventually became a royal castle for all of Scotland's kings named James, up to and including James VI. It also counted as property of several Scottish queens. Later, the castle belonged to a long succession of earls of Moray until 1984 when the 20th earl placed it in the care of the government. During its long life, Doune Castle suffered one siege in 1570 lasting only three days.

Doune Castle's excellent condition is due to a number of repair and reconstruction projects over the centuries. When we visited, work progressed to stabilize and safeguard some of the weaker parts, although we could still tour much of the castle.

Inside the courtyard, stairs give access to the great hall and kitchen tower as well as the gate tower. The curtain walls appear even more impressive here because their thickness is more evident. Windows in the east wall show that an intended building was never completed. Passages lead to the curtain wall battlements from the kitchen tower and the gate tower.

Much of the current castle interior resulted from the 1883 restoration by the 14th earl. The floor, furniture, lights and other features show just how well nobility lived. The second floor of the gate tower contained the lord's hall, a comfortable and well-appointed room. The great hall or outer hall measures about 25 by 61 feet and connects the gatehouse to the kitchen tower. It has no fireplace, just a hearth in the center of the room with a vent in the roof to allow the smoke to escape. Nowadays, parties and other events are held in this hall.

The kitchen tower contains a massive fireplace. Serving hatches between the kitchen and servery are so large they resemble small closets. Rooms at the top of this tower were probably used for guests, although some of Doune Castle's guests were not voluntary. Author John Home described his daring escape from one of these upper rooms in 1746 using knotted bed sheets. A nephew of Rob Roy held the castle for Bonnie Prince Charlie at the time.

To get there: *The castle is just off the A84 in the small town of Doune, near Dunblane.*

Edinburgh Area

Many tourists spend what little time they have in Scotland in Edinburgh, a city rich in history and legend. If numerous tourist shops and vehicles didn't line the Royal Mile, it could easily appear 18th century—albeit without the buckets of muck splashing out windows and sewage running in the streets!

Even visitors who stay only in Edinburgh can experience much of Scotland's history in the city. Plan to invest in both an Edinburgh guidebook and a city map. Here, we've highlighted just a very few of Edinburgh's many historical attractions. A map is essential for walking or driving, because like many British cities, streets often change names at every block.

Museum of Scotland ★★★

For starters, we suggest a day at the modern, new Museum of Scotland. Connected to the old Royal Museum, its entrance faces Edinburgh's Chambers Street, two to three blocks south of the Royal Mile. Clearly, more than one day is required to do the museum justice, but even a few hours can give a good overview of Scotland's heritage. We especially enjoyed the exhibits on early people on Level 0 and "The Kingdom of the Scots" on Level 1.

Craigmillar Castle ★★★

Craigmillar Castle, not nearly as famous as its Edinburgh counterpart, is a little-known treasure. Located on Edinburgh's outskirts, Craigmillar remains one of the best-preserved medieval castles in Scotland with a complete outer bailey containing farm buildings, chapel, and gardens. A number of major events took place at Craigmillar, making it a significant historical landmark.

The Preston family, lairds of Craigmillar for about 300 years, started construction on Craigmillar Castle sometime in the 15th century. A later Preston, Sir William Preston, brought the arm bone of St. Giles from France and gave it to the high kirk of Edinburgh. Preston is buried in the Lady Aisle of Edinburgh's St. Giles Cathedral, and a chapel was built in his honor at the kirk.

The castle has long been associated with Scotland's royalty, especially Mary Queen of Scots. When the Scots refused Henry VIII's offer to marry his young son to the child Mary, he retaliated with his so-called "rough wooing." This resulted in much destruction and loss of life in Scotland. Craigmillar fell victim, suffering capture and

Machicolations,
Craigmillar Castle
Edinburgh

Caerlaverock Castle near Dumfries

Standing stone, Machrie Moor, Arran

Tarbert Castle
Kintyre
Argyll

View of River Add from Dunadd Fort

Footprint, Dunadd Fort, Argyll

Basin, Dunadd Fort, Argyll

Front entrance, Castle Sween, Argyll

Loch Sween and Castle Sween

Dun Grugaig, Isle of Skye

View from Duntulm Castle, Skye

View from St. Michael's Chapel, Grimsay near North Uist

Dun Bharabhat, Great Bernera, Lewis

burning in 1544. In 1549 Sir Simon Preston IV completely rebuilt the castle. Sir Simon supported Mary when she returned to Scotland as an adult, and she rewarded him by making him provost of Edinburgh. In September of 1563, Mary spent a week at Craigmillar where she received Queen Elizabeth's ambassador who informed her she had to marry. After the birth of her son, James VI, she became quite sick and spent time convalescing at Craigmillar. During this stay, a group of her advisors made a pact to kill her husband, Darnley. Mary's room is in the south wing of the keep on the fourth floor. Only seven by five feet, the room contains a fireplace and two windows.

The oldest part of the castle is the L-shaped tower, four stories tall with massive walls over nine feet thick. With the exception of the south wall of the south wing, the tower is surrounded by the huge inner curtain wall of later 15th century date. The formidable walls have towers at the four corners. Both towers and walls are corbelled out for a rampart that has machicolations used to throw spears and whatnot down on anyone foolish enough to try to scale them.

Apartments for guests and other domestic rooms such as kitchens, storage and sitting rooms were located inside the walls along the east and west sides. These rooms also probably served as barracks for the garrison. In most other castles, such rooms were built of wood, and therefore have not survived. A basement, partly cut into the rock, housed the bakehouse as well as what might have been the prison in the southeast corner. During work on this room in 1813, an upright skeleton was found in the wall.

A walled garden in the southeast section contains a pre-Reformation chapel. A terraced garden lies outside the walls to the southwest and leads to the huge fishpond in the shape of a P for Preston.

On one of our visits to Craigmillar, the castle was filled with people in medieval costume. Medieval music wafted through the great hall furnished with tapestries and pillows. In marked contrast, 20th century stage lights illuminated the hall. Perhaps, a movie was being filmed.

To get there: *The castle is situated just three miles south-east of Edinburgh on top of a low hill. Edinburgh Castle and the pastoral surrounding countryside can be seen from the walls. To get to Craigmillar Castle from central Edinburgh, go south on South Bridge Road (it becomes several other roads in the process) to any road east, such as Preston, that will get you to Dalkeith Road. Follow Dalkeith Road to the roundabout where it becomes Old Dalkeith Road. Old Dalkeith Road goes right by the Craigmillar Castle Road. Going south, it's on the left. Alternatively, you can take South Bridge Road south until it becomes Craigmillar Park; then watch for a large round-about with Lady Road as the first left. Take Lady Road to Old Dalkeith Road and proceed south to Craigmillar Castle Road. If you reach the motorway, you've gone too far.*

Edinburgh Castle ★★★

No trip to Scotland would be complete without a tour of Edinburgh Castle, Scotland's ancient and beloved citadel. While the modern castle is still used by the military, its history goes back to Dunedin, an Iron Age fort. This natural defensive position at the top of a massive volcanic rock has been fortified for centuries. The old town of Edinburgh developed along a craggy tail sculpted by glaciers.

Masses of tourists throng Edinburgh Castle most times of the year. Must-see sights include the Scottish Crown Jewels (Europe's oldest regalia) in their case alongside the returned Stone of Destiny, St. Margaret's Chapel (the oldest building on the site), the Great Hall, and the small room in the Palace where Mary gave birth to future James VI of Scotland. Historic Scotland recently restored two of the castle's royal apartments to appear as they did for the 1617 "hamecoming" of James VI.

To get there: *Impossible to miss, Edinburgh Castle stands at the top of the Royal Mile in the old town. We recommend parking in a car park away from the old town and walking up the Royal Mile.*

Gladstone's Land ★

A few steps down the Royal Mile (High Street) from Edinburgh Castle stands a house called Gladstone's Land that looks just as it did in the 1600s. This house, presently owned by the National Trust, gives visitors a taste of the lives of affluent Edinburgh merchants of that era.

The prosperous merchant, Thomas Gledstanes (modern spelling is Gladstones), built his house, or land, after he and his wife bought the property in 1617. His multistory house along High Street was referred to as "land" because it occupied a narrow strip of land that stretched back from the street; the ground itself was described as a "tenement." A building already stood on the site, but Gledstanes added larger rooms to each floor extending the front of a building. He then leased most of it out to tenants while he and his family probably lived on the fourth floor (third floor in Britain). The painted ceiling of that floor displays a *gled* (Scottish for hawk).

Shops occupied the ground floor front of the building, with stalls under the arched arcade. The arcade sheltered customers who patronized the shopping space. In front of the house, a surviving curved outside stair provided access to a turnpike stair leading to the rooms above. A pig or other livestock was likely kept beneath the stair.

The National Trust has decorated the various rooms with 17th century furniture and artifacts to give visitors an idea of how it may have appeared. The half-glass, half-wooden windows visible today are exact replicas of the original windows. The painted chamber retains its original Scandinavian-style painted ceiling.

To get there: *The house is located on High Street, a block
or so down from the castle on the north side of the street.
A blue sign, "Gladstones Land—1617," hangs on the wall
outside the arcade. We had to look closely, because it is
easy to miss in the bustle and color of the Royal Mile.
Lady Stair's House is located right behind.*

Glasgow Area

Glasgow is a city with a bad rap. Most Americans,
who've heard of it, think of Glasgow as a big, dirty industrial city. We were pleasantly surprised to find that
Glasgow has undergone a metamorphosis in recent
years, becoming a major European cultural city. Glasgow
is especially noted for its museums, architecture and
entertainment, as well as a reputation for friendliness.
Although not described here because the exhibits don't
fall within our historic timeline, we've enjoyed visiting
Glasgow-area heritage sites like the Tenement House in
the city, Charles Rennie Mackintosh buildings, and the
Weaver's Cottage in nearby Kilbarchan.

Dumbarton Castle ✳

Dumbarton Castle stands just outside Glasgow in
the small community of Dumbarton. The fortress may
have the longest recorded history of any stronghold in
Scotland because of its strategic location on the Clyde.

When we visited the castle, we were functioning on
pure adrenaline. We had just flown into Glasgow after a
sleepless overseas flight and a long, unplanned layover
at Gatwick. Glasgow and the surrounding area were
booked up tight with a convention of 20,000 Rotarians.
So, we picked up our rental car at the airport and drove
straight to Dumbarton. Getting off an international over-
night flight with no sleep, renting a car and then negoti-

ating left-side traffic, roundabouts and motorways near a major city are tourist activities we don't recommend. However, we had no choice. Our B&B was located about 1 and ½ hours west of Glasgow, and because Dumbarton Castle was on the way, we decided to stop. Although rummy from lack of sleep, climbing around Dumbarton Castle in the afternoon sun re-energized us. The best way to combat jet lag is sun, air and exercise.

While most of what currently exists was built after the 16th century, the story of Dumbarton Rock is an important one reaching back to the Iron Age, if not before. The current entryway to the castle and the walls, as well as the castle's Governor's House are all essentially 18th century structures, built to keep rebellious Scots in line.

Archaeological evidence revealed the site held an Iron Age fortress. Written records documented Dumbarton Rock as a winter port for the Roman fleet and the last fort of the Antonine Wall. The Romans called it Theodosia. In 450 AD, St. Patrick mentioned the rock in a letter he wrote to soldiers of the king who had committed a raid on some of his Irish converts. During the Dark Ages, Bede wrote about Alcluyd or rock on the Clyde. Later, as the capital of the British kingdom of Strathclyde, it was called Dun Breatann, fort of the Britons. The modern name, Dumbarton, derives from Dun Breatann.

The fortress was besieged repeatedly. In 756, an army of Picts and Northumbrians briefly captured it. Another attack may have occurred in 780. In 870, Vikings besieged it for four months before finally capturing it by cutting off the water supply. Two hundred longships carried slaves and treasures back to Dublin, a Viking stronghold of the time. This conquest destroyed Strathclyde until the kingdom became a power again in the 10th century. Subjects of Strathclyde killed a king of Scotland in battle in 971. In 1018, Malcolm II's grandson, Duncan, became king of Strathclyde. When his grandfather died, Duncan became king of Scotland as well, and the kingdom of Strathclyde disappeared. This was the Duncan eventually killed by Macbeth.

As a medieval royal stronghold, Dumbarton played a part in the struggles between the English and the Scots during the wars of independence. The remains of one of the castle structures is called Wallace Tower. It has been suggested that William Wallace was imprisoned in the castle before being sent to London for execution, but a Historic Scotland pamphlet calls this "improbable." After Wallace's victory at Stirling Bridge, Dumbarton incarcerated English enemies. Until the early 1800s, it continued as a French prison through Britain's wars with France, ironic because Dumbarton had been a gateway to France during Scotland's Auld Alliance with France against the English. French ships and fleets arrived and departed at Dumbarton, which was once even garrisoned by the French.

Dumbarton played a large role in the affairs of the Stewart monarchs, including Mary Queen of Scots, safeguarded here for five months as a child before being taken to France. In 1571, 100 men captured the castle in a surprise, daring raid while it was held for the adult, exiled Mary. It served as a military post until the Second World War and was even bombed.

Evidence of early occupation has been found throughout the site. Earliest artifacts included fragments of Mediterranean pottery from about the 400s. Archaeological excavations in the 1970s discovered a rampart destroyed by fire, most likely from the Viking attack in 870. Two stone slabs of Celtic Christian design dating from the 900s are displayed in the Governor's House. Not much is left of the medieval castle. The most ancient structure on the rock is the Portcullis Arch built in the 1300s. It is wedged in the cleft between the two peaks of the rock. We could clearly see the groves inside the arch to raise and lower the portcullis. Probably the next oldest structure is the 16th century Guard House between the Portcullis Gate and the Governor's House. The spur battery built in 1680 is located west of the Governor's House. An ancient walnut tree grows above the battery. Most of the remaining defenses were built in the 1700s and later.

Any visit to Dumbarton requires climbing around steep hillsides. The arduous climb affords superb views of Glasgow, the Clyde and the surrounding countryside from either of the two summits. The tallest, White Tower Crag, gives the best view.

To get there: *The town of Dumbarton is just off the A814, which in turn leads off the A82 heading northwest out of Glasgow. The way to the castle is signposted so it is fairly easy to follow the route through town. If you miss a turn, don't despair because Dumbarton Rock with the castle is impossible to miss. Just keep heading toward it, and eventually you'll get there. There's a small car park at the lawn bowling club right in front of the castle entrance.*

Bearsden Roman Bathhouse ★★

The Romans advanced far north into Scotland, and Bearsden provides tangible evidence of their vast empire. The Bearsden (bear's den) Roman Bathhouse is located in one of the most improbable places imaginable—right off a busy street in a housing project!

The Bearsden Bathhouse is the best preserved and most impressive Roman structure along the Antonine Wall, a 39-mile, 10-foot-high earthen defensive barrier built between the Forth and the Clyde. The bathhouse is all that remains of the fort, one of the 20 Roman forts lining the wall.

The modern street aptly named Roman Road lies over the old Roman road that cuts through what was once the fort's center. The bathhouse is located in the fort's northeast section in the "annexe," or enclosure, separated from the main part of the fort. Antonine's Wall would have formed a wall of the fort and annexe just north of the bathhouse where the modern wall and iron

Bearsden Roman Bathhouse

gate are located.

Bearsden is a success story of cooperation between the Ancient Monuments Board for Scotland and private developers. Since the 1700s, antiquarians knew a Roman fort existed here. The site was presumed lost when Glasgow's suburbs expanded with Victorian villas constructed over the fort. In 1973, a developer announced his company would level the villas to erect modern flats. At that time, the Ancient Monuments Division received permission to excavate the area and discovered the fort and bathhouse. The developers allowed the Division to work at the site for five years before the project was sold to another firm that constructed the flats. The bathhouse and surrounding land were donated to the state and became the first Roman building made of stone in Scotland to open to the public.

Bearsden Roman Bathhouse is comparable to the bathhouse and structures at Housesteads Roman Fort on Hadrian's Wall. The main part of the building is aligned east and west. Posts in the ground mark the wooden entry and changing room on the far west side. The central or cold room came after the changing room.

The bather then could enter the hot dry room (like a sauna) to the north, or go to the steam range on the east. The round cold water plunge bath with its red plaster (the original plaster was removed and replaced with a modern equivalent) is located to the south. The remains of the furnaces are easy to see as well as the heat ducts under the flooring slabs. In Roman times, running water flushed the latrine in the southeastern corner of the site. Historic Scotland interpretive signs provide information.

Recognizing the relationship between filth and disease, bathing and cleanliness were very important to the Roman army and citizens. Physicians, stationed at the larger Roman forts, cared for ill soldiers. Housesteads Roman Fort on Hadrian's Wall has remains of a hospital. When the Romans left Britain, inhabitants abandoned bathing until the medieval monasteries adopted the practice of washing before meals and using running water for toilets. The period after the Roman occupation is called the Dark Ages, not surprising because of the filth, disease and regression. In fact, bathing did not come back into style until Victorian times, more than 1,300 years later. We visited Bearsden on a damp rainy day and could easily appreciate the appeal of hot baths in Britain!

In addition to the bathhouse, parts of the Antonine Wall can be seen in and around Bearsden. Stretches have been left and in a few places the stone base of the wall was exposed so people can see it. One of these is on the nearby golf course!

To get there: *The site is in the Glasgow suburb of Bearsden, on the north side of Roman Road a short way east of where it joins the A809. The bathhouse is surrounded by wrought iron fence with a wall and a gate facing Roman Road. Just west of the site, signs direct visitors to parking. Toilets are available at the car park.*

Glasgow Cathedral ✱

While medieval cathedrals abound in England, Glasgow Cathedral is the only one left intact in Scotland. Very little has been altered, changed or damaged. Most of the current structure was built in the 1200s, although the Lower Church contains parts of the 1197 cathedral in their original positions. A unique and rare "painted stone" from this earlier structure can be seen in a glass case in the nave. It is a *voussoir*, or wedge-shaped stone from an arch. Only two other examples of church wall painting still exist in Scotland.

The cathedral site's long history began when St. Kentigern (popularly known as St. Mungo) came from Culross to what is now Glasgow. Kentigern, the patron saint of Glasgow, died about 612 AD. He supposedly established a Celtic church and monastery on the site of the present cathedral. His tomb and shrine are located in the Lower Church. In one of the lower chapels, remnants of the earlier shrine are on display, as well as stones from the now vanished Bishop's Castle, that once stood where Cathedral Square is today. In 1451, the pope decreed that a pilgrimage here equaled going to Rome.

Glasgow Cathedral was constructed as a rectangle, not the usual cruciform shape. The transepts don't project from the sides as they do in most cathedrals; instead they are incorporated into the rectangle and only the roofline indicates their position. The building was also built with its east-end on a slope, so the under or "lower" church is above ground and not called a crypt.

The cathedral contains a rare pre-Reformation choir (or quire as spelled in some guidebooks) with seven pairs of carved figures at the top. Most of the wood of the open timber roof of the nave is 14th century. The wood-and-tile roof was lighter than stone and didn't require flying buttresses for support. Note the oak board ceiling in the choir with its painted wooden bosses. The wood was renewed in 1910-1912. In the most northeastern area of the upper church, an original door leads into the chapter house. Bullet holes and lead bullets in the door verify that the cathedral didn't altogether escape violence. This upper portion of the chapter house was rebuilt in the 1430s to 1440s.

During excavation work on the cathedral, workers unearthed two bronze mortars and an iron pestle. Secretly buried at the time of the Reformation, one of the mortars had the name of Bishop Wishart on it. The cathedral stands intact today, thanks in part to the citizens (in the form of militias made of workers' guilds) of Glasgow who took up arms to save it.

The volunteer guides at Glasgow Cathedral love to share their extensive knowledge of the cathedral. We learned a lot about the cathedral by talking with them.

To get there: *Glasgow Cathedral is not difficult to find. It is located on the east side of downtown, on the far side of the new Strathclyde University. Our advice would be to walk to the cathedral unless you're very short of time or can't walk far. We estimate the walk to be about ¾ of a mile from downtown. From Buchanan Street, walk east on George Street to High Street; turn left on High Street (it eventually becomes Castle Street), walk a bit farther and you'll come to the cathedral on your right. A slightly shorter alternative and perhaps a more direct route might be to take Cathedral Street from the Glasgow Royal Concert Hall at the top of Buchanan Street to Castle Street where you'll see the cathedral directly ahead. If you decide to drive to the cathedral, be aware that parking is limited. A few small car parks can be found near the cathedral. Signs are posted to alert users to secure their cars and belongings against theft. Because we only visited the cathedral, we had our car and thus wasted precious time finding parking.*

Bothwell Castle

Considered by many to be one of the best examples of castle architecture in Scotland, Bothwell Castle with its massive round tower (donjon) conveys an impression of immense strength. Mighty fortress aptly describes this early medieval stone structure located in a suburb of Glasgow. Today, a tranquil, pastoral setting disguises the castle's violent past and place in Scottish history.

Walter of Moray or his son, William, started building Bothwell Castle in the late 1200s. The donjon is the only surviving portion of the initial castle except for some incomplete foundations outside the wall.

Bothwell Castle featured prominently in the wars of independence. Edward I besieged it twice, the first time in 1296 when he captured William and the castle. The Scots won it back after 14 months, but in 1301 Edward besieged it again, capturing it in a month with 7,000 men and a siege engine. Following their success against the English at Bannockburn, the Scots pursued Humphrey de Bohun and other English nobles to Bothwell. When the Scots arrived, the castle governor, thought to be sympathetic to the English, delivered the fugitives to Bruce. Bruce later traded these important prisoners for his queen, sister, daughter and nephew. To keep the castle from English hands, Bruce destroyed it.

The English returned in 1336-37 and rebuilt it, allowing Edward III to stay at Bothwell for a couple of months. To prevent further English occupation, Sir Andrew Moray of Bothwell attacked and destroyed his own ancestral seat. His handiwork is visible today in the half-demolished shell of the huge donjon.

Some years later in about 1392, Archibald Douglas "the Grim" acquired the castle and lands through marriage. Because he also was called "black Archibald," his branch of the family became known as the "black Douglasses." He initiated a rebuilding program continued by his son. They left the donjon untouched but constructed a new wall around a courtyard and the living range visible today. With the downfall of the Douglasses the castle changed ownership in the early 1400s. The last owner, the first earl of Forfar, dismantled some of the black Douglas' work to use the stone to build a new house. The huge partially ruined donjon dominating the entire structure is clearly the focal point of any castle tour. The donjon actually forms the west wall of the newer castle built by the black Douglasses. Visitors enter the donjon by way of a modern wooden bridge over a dry moat. The River Clyde flowing through a peaceful wooded area can be seen from the windows of the donjon.

The remainder of the castle built by the Douglasses includes a kitchen range on the north wall, a badly ruined south range and latrine tower, and the walls of the great hall. Two additional towers complete the castle—a fairly intact tower in the southeast corner and the remains of a square tower in the northeast corner.

To get there: *We had some difficulty finding our way around the suburbs of Glasgow. The best way to get to Bothwell, we think, is to head toward Uddingston. The most direct route would be to approach it from the interchange of the M74 and M73 located north of Uddingston. Then near the south end of Uddingston, take the B7071, the Bothwell Road, and follow signs to the castle.*

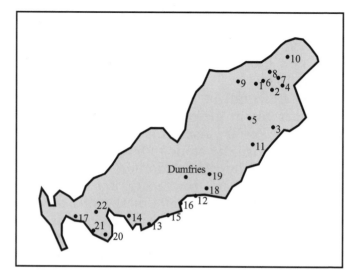

1   Melrose Abbey
2   Dryburgh Abbey
3   Jedburgh Abbey
4   Kelso Abbey
5   Hawick Motte
6   Trimontium
7   Smailholm Tower House
8   Greenknowe Tower House
9   Traquair
10   Edin's Hall Broch
11   Hermitage Castle
12   Caerlaverock Castle
13   Dundrennan Abbey
14   Cairnholy Chambered Cairns
15   Mote of Mark
16   Sweetheart Abbey
17   Glenluce Abbey
18   Ruthwell Cross
19   Burnswark Hill, Fort, Roman Camps
20   Whithorn Priory
21   Rispain Fort
22   Torhouse Stone Circle

Chapter 5
Toward the English Border

The Borders

The Borders comprise a lovely section of Scotland. Driving through their gently rolling hills and peaceful towns, it is hard to believe that so much violence took place on this soil. For centuries the Borders served as a battleground between England and Scotland, ravaged mercilessly by both sides in an effort to keep the other from advancing. Without food, armies couldn't move, so the Borders were subjected to countless episodes of burning, pillaging and fighting. The Border abbeys exemplify the destruction leveled on this region. They were built and rebuilt; their final chapter occurred during the so-called "rough wooing" of Henry the VIII in his attempt to convince the Scots to support a marriage between infant Mary, Queen of Scots, and his son, Edward, in order to consolidate the kingdoms.

Unfortunately, most tourists miss the beauty and history of the Borders in their mad dash to get to Glasgow, Edinburgh or the Highlands. Jedburgh Abbey is the exception, standing on a main route from England, where organized coach tours regularly stop.

The Border Abbeys

Relatively few tourists spend much time in the Borders, so the four great abbeys nestled in their heart are not mobbed with people. The ruins of Dryburgh, Jedburgh, Kelso and Melrose Abbey lie within 12 miles of each other in green, pastoral countryside, close to the River Tweed. All were founded in the 12th century with three built by King David I. Nearby towns include Galashiels, Selkirk and Hawick (pronounced Hoyk). Melrose Abbey, Jedburgh Abbey and Kelso Abbey are located in towns that carry their names.

Melrose Abbey ★★

Melrose Abbey was a Cistercian abbey built by David in 1136 making it the oldest Cistercian monastery in Scotland. All told, it was destroyed and rebuilt about nine times. Although the English nearly finished it off in 1545, monks lived in the abbey for a long time after that. They were only able to stay because they renounced monasticism and joined the Reformed Church. Up until 1590, when the last monk died off, the records document complaints by the monks about people stealing rock and other materials from the abbey.

Melrose Abbey once must have looked similar to English abbeys and cathedrals like Durham. In its heyday, this huge structure could probably be seen far away. The stonework is graceful but imposing. Even on a gray, cold, misty morning in March, we immediately noticed the dramatic flying buttresses and elegant windows. Many stone carvings adorn the walls, a few of them whimsical, like a pig playing the bagpipe. We'd seen a picture of this pig in a book but couldn't find it on two different visits.

Parts of abbeys were frequently used for parish churches. Sadly, an ugly stone wall stands in the monk's choir. Made of rubble taken from the abbey structure, this wall is a remnant of the post-Reformation parish kirk torn down in 1810.

Very little remains of other abbey structures. Only foundation walls demarcate the monk's range and cloister. The chapter house featured tiled floors, one of only two abbeys in Scotland. The other, Glenluce Abbey in Galloway, still contains some floor tiles.

The heart of Robert the Bruce is believed buried at Melrose Abbey. Prior to his death, he asked his trusted friend, James Douglas, to take his heart on a crusade to the Holy Land. After Douglas was killed in Spain, Bruce's heart was returned to Scotland and presumed buried at Melrose. In 1921, archaeologists discovered a mummi-

Melrose Abbey at night

Excavations of the Chapter House, Melrose Abbey

fied human heart beneath the ground of the Chapter House. They reburied it. In 1996, archaeologists surveying the Chapter House rediscovered the heart in its lead container. This momentous event made headline news in British papers and on TV. We chanced to visit Melrose the day of the discovery and experienced some of the excitement.

Another famous person, Michael Scot the wizard, is believed buried in the south transept in a grave set into the floor with a cross on it. Michael Scot lived in the 13th century. He denounced magic but loved science and astrology. His exploits fostered a large body of Scottish legend.

Historic Scotland manages Melrose Abbey with a gift shop on premises. Signs mark the various abbey structures. At night, floodlights produce dramatic scenes and provide good photo opportunities.

To get there: *Melrose is located off the A6091 close to Galashiels between the A7 and the A68. The area is richly associated with Sir Walter Scott. His museum-like home, Abbotsford, occupies a pastoral spot on the nearby Tweed River.*

Dryburgh Abbey ★★

Dryburgh Abbey occupies an idyllic and peaceful park on the Tweed River between St. Boswells and Newtown St. Boswells. Small wonder the abbey once served as a garden ornament! David Erskine, Earl of Buchan, the man largely responsible for preserving Dryburgh Abbey, built a grand garden in the 1780s using the abbey buildings as the garden's centerpiece. The garden has since been removed.

Dryburgh was the only abbey of the four not commissioned by King David. Instead, Hugh de Moreville, David's constable, brought the Premonstratensian order here from Alnwick. The word Premonstratensian derives from a location in France where the order began. The Premonstratensians were canons or priests, not monks.

Although the abbey church has largely been demolished, Dryburgh provides a good example of early medieval building. Much of the 12th and 13th century stonework survives and the living areas remain remarkably well preserved, including the cloister. The upper floors, where the dormitory once existed, now hold the remains of the commendator's house. The night stair the monks took from their dormitory to the cathedral still exists. The sacristy, parlor, warming house and chapter house located under the dormitory look very much as they did in the abbey's prime. Even traces of original paint and plaster can be detected.

The crisp stonework appears new. In fact, in the north wall of the church early masons fitted a rock that previously had been used for a game. The rock has been scratched with a Merelles Board. Very few of these game boards survive in Scotland, and those that do are associated with religious structures.

The stones on the north wall of the dormitory show cracks from heat. Retreating south after a defeat by the Scots in 1322, the English may have started a fire out of spite. Of course, like all Border abbeys, Dryburgh endured many attacks.

The south range of the cloister housed the refectory and kitchen. Not much is left of these, but the arched recess seen in the southwest corner of the cloister served as a sink where canons washed before meals. Monks and canons valued cleanliness, and, as a result, they probably suffered fewer diseases and ailments than the general population. All religious houses had toilets (reredorter) with running water to wash sewage away.

After the Reformation in 1560, the commendator and nine remaining canons joined the new religion and were allowed to remain. By 1600, all had died. Later, influential families appropriated parts of the church for their family burial plots. Graves of Sir Walter Scott and Earl Haig, former commander-in-chief of the British Expeditionary Forces in France during World War I, lie in the north transept of the church.

Historic Scotland staffs the abbey with a custodian who runs the small gift shop. Like most, he was most friendly and informative. We learned that we had met his wife earlier in the day when visiting Melrose Abbey, where she worked.

To get there: Dryburgh in its isolated setting is more difficult to find than the other three town-based abbeys. It's best reached by driving through St. Boswells on the B6404. Don't be confused by the town called Newtown St. Boswells.

Jedburgh Abbey ★★

David I founded the Augustinian Jedburgh Abbey in 1138, to the southeast of Melrose and Dryburgh in the town of Jedburgh. Saxon Christian stones from the 8th and 9th centuries discovered at the abbey suggest the site was probably a previous Saxon church. Abbeys were frequently built on previously sanctified places, such as older Culdee (Celtic Church) sites.

Attacked and damaged six times, the abbey church is amazingly well preserved. On the other hand, not much except the foundations and low walls remain of the monks' living areas or claustral buildings. The cloister, west range, east range with chapter house, and the south range with refectory or dining hall show typical features. A guided path describes the layout.

At the west end of the nave, two doorways on either side of the arched main entrance contain narrow turnpike stairs. These lead to the second level of the church where visitors can view the entire nave, the crossing under the tower and the presbytery. The north entry conceals something quite special. A Roman altar stone complete with Latin inscription has been reused and built into the top of the doorway. A detachment of Raetian spearmen who were under the command of a tribune named Julius Severus dedicated the altar to Jupiter.

Jedburgh Abbey has served as a site for a lot of archaeological work. Therefore, a good deal is known about it. For example, excavation of the drainage ditches showed high concentrations of lead and pollen, indicating that lead pipes diverted the drinking and washing water obtained from open streams. Some lead pipes have been recovered at other abbeys. Archaeologists love to be able to dig up ancient latrines and sewage ditches because of what people threw in them! Besides artifacts, archaeologists discovered human gut parasites (which tells a lot right there), lead deposits, and pollen of a plant with astringent value called tormentil.

A ghost or two may even haunt the ruin. In the same sewage ditch mentioned above, archaeologists found remains of a human torso with an expensive ivory comb, pendant, horn buckle and a whetstone. All of these items would have belonged to an important person. Perhaps, as the victim of bungled robbery, the poor person was killed, his body cut up, and then dumped along with the loot—all before 1170. A coin dug up in the ditch fill verifies the date.

To get there: *The town of Jedburgh is right on the A68, a main route into Scotland from England. The prominent abbey is difficult to miss.*

Kelso Abbey

King David founded Kelso Abbey for the Benedictine monks in 1128. Built on the left bank of the Tweed, the abbey now stands almost in the heart of modern Kelso. Only the west end is left, conveying an impression of how grand it must have been. Because of their wealth, the major abbeys endured repeated raids. About 1200 AD, Kelso Abbey's farm (called a grange) owned 1,400 sheep, 16 shepherd cottages, and 250 acres of tillable land.

To get there: *The major market town of Kelso sits at the crossroads of the A698, the A699 and the A6089. The abbey remains stand in a small park close the center of town.*

Hawick Motte

In the town of Hawick, we had yet another lesson on Scotland's difficult local and regional pronunciations. We were looking for Hawick Motte and felt a little smug that we knew how to pronounce Hawick ("Hoyk"). We thought the motte was located in the center of town but couldn't find it (again, a good map would have saved us trouble). After driving around, we stopped to ask directions to the "mot." Our informant graciously replied that the local people call it "moat," as in a castle moat. We have since heard a well-known travel show host talk about a "mot."

Mottes functioned as early fortifications, precursors of the motte and bailey design of castle construction. When the Scottish kings invited the Norman knights to settle in Scotland, they built mounds or mottes with palisades of wooden posts. Hawick Motte stands about 24 feet high with a set of stairs leading to the top. The flat top extends more than 30 feet in diameter. A ditch, difficult to detect now, once surrounded the motte.

To get there: *The town of Hawick is right on the A7, a major highway into Scotland from Carlisle, England. Hawick Motte is located in Motte Park on a street called Loan to the southeast of Drumlanrig Square in Hawick.*

Trimontium

Our Scottish B&B host chuckled when he told us Trimontium was likely the biggest brothel in Scotland! In addition to serving as a major command center for the Roman army in Scotland, Trimontium also may have provided rest and relaxation for Roman troops posted in the north.

Trimontium proves that the Roman presence in Scotland was far greater than once thought. Just outside of Melrose and partly in the village of Newstead lies evidence of this 1,800-year-old Roman fort. Trimontium was vast and complex, almost like a city with a castle at its center. Some think that as many as 5,000 Roman soldiers lived at the fort. These troops, along with a sizable civilian population of traders, blacksmiths, bakers, sandlemakers, potters and glassworkers would have made Trimontium one of the larger cities in Britain. Archaeological evidence indicates that a huge iron-making industrial center stood outside the fort. Trimontium probably served as the supply and service center for the entire Roman army in Scotland. The fort's *annexe* and civilian areas, an amphitheater and what may have been a villa have also been discovered.

Trimontium was positioned along the route of Dere Street, the main Roman road leading from Hadrian's wall. Parts of the modern A68 use this well-built road as foundation.

Unfortunately, not much can be seen at the site, except perhaps for archaeologists working in different sections. However, a walk around the site gives an idea of its size. Waterlogged pits preserved the artifacts amazingly well. These included complete Roman helmets, bronze wine jugs, wooden tent pegs, sandals (undamaged), pottery, bronze and glass bowls and other dishes, and tools of the various workers. The carpenters' tools are supposed to be in such good condition they can be used today. These superb Newstead artifacts form a major part of the Roman exhibits at the new Museum of Scotland in Edinburgh.

Finally, to get the most out of a visit, we suggest a tour of the Trimontium Museum in Melrose, small but worth the nominal admission fee. The museum provides information about the fort and a listing of events. About once a week, the local Trimontium Trust in Melrose conducts tours to the site.

To get there: *The village of Newstead, thought to be the oldest continuously inhabited village in Scotland, lies just outside of Melrose on a minor road heading toward the A68. However, we suggest the best way to find out how to get to the site is to ask directions at the Trimontium Museum in Melrose. On two different occasions, we had problems because it doesn't look like much more than a grassy hill.*

Smailholm Tower House ★★

Tower houses date to a time of continual warfare, thieving and marauding on the constantly shifting border between Scotland and England. These forbidding structures served as fortified homes. Border life often was filled with danger, and these towers were built to protect the area's leading families. To shield the inhabitants, tower houses usually had only one door guarded by an iron gate called a "yett" opening outward and a strong wooden door that opened inward.

The first tower we visited, Smailholm (pronounced "Smailem"), was built sometime after 1495 by a local laird, David Pringle. Historic Scotland staffs the tower in summer when it's possible to tour the interior.

Smailholm, a tall square stone building not unlike a castle keep, can be seen from quite a distance. A long one-lane farm road with no pullouts leads to it. The tower stands just beyond Sandyknowe farm (most farms and houses in Scotland have names), so it's necessary to drive right through the farmyard.

Four-story Smailholm soars 57 feet high on an outcrop of rock. It remains in great shape considering how many times it was attacked. The English attacked it in 1543, 1544, 1546 and once again in 1640. The tower looks severe and forbidding with a few small windows and only one door. On a clear day, visitors are rewarded with panoramic views of the countryside from the top of the tower.

Smailholm very much influenced Sir Walter Scott. As a boy, he lived for a while with his grandfather at Sandyknowe farm. The tower appears in some of his novels. Scott is credited with saving Smailholm from destruction by pleading with its owner.

To get there: Smailholm *is located close to Dryburgh on a one-lane road just off the B6404. You also can approach it driving south from the small village of Smailholm.*

Greenknowe Tower House

The contrast of Greenknowe to Smailholm is striking. While Smailholm is harsh looking, Greenknowe resembles a home with more windows and bigger windows. Greenknowe also sports turrets. Although appearing friendlier than Smailholm, it was clearly built with security in mind (note the gun ports).

James Seton of Touch and his wife, Janet Edmonstone, built Greenknowe Tower House. Their marriage lintel just above the entry door contains their initials, family coats of arms and the date of 1581, nearly 100 years after Smailholm was built. The yett is original and in almost as good condition as when it was first made. The yett was locked, so we couldn't go in, but we could see stairs and other interior details through the door. The "L" building plan allows for larger and more spacious rooms, while Smailholm is nearly square.

To get there: *Greenknowe Tower is not far from Smailholm, about six miles north/northeast as the crow flies. It is located on the A6105, close to the junction with the A6089. It sits on the north side of the road in a romantic, secluded area with trees all around. Unlike Smailholm, Greenknowe is not staffed. An interpretive sign at the car park describes it. Greenknowe is seldom mentioned in guidebooks, but it is worth a visit, especially after you have seen Smailholm.*

Traquair ★★★

Romantic Traquair has the distinction of being the oldest continuously inhabited house in Scotland. Parts of the house have witnessed action for more than 1,000 years. King Alexander I granted its first charter in 1107. Over the years, the house has undergone many modifications, additions and structural changes. However, it still looks about the same as in the early 1700s because Louisa, sister of the 8th Earl didn't change anything during her long life. Twenty-seven monarchs visited Traquair from Alexander on, including both Edwards I and II of England and Mary Queen of Scots. Bonnie Prince Charlie also stayed at Traquair.

Traquair continues in private ownership, inhabited by the Stuart family since 1491. (Note: this family uses "Stuart," a variation of the Stewart name, originally derived from "steward.") We were delighted to discover Traquair was the model for the Scottish baron's estate described in Sir Walter Scott's *Waverley*, complete with the famous bear trappings (bear statues everywhere— be sure to look for them in odd places like the roofs of the outbuildings) and Bear Gates. As staunchly Catholic Jacobite supporters, the family decreed that the Bear Gates would stay closed until a Stuart/Stewart occupied the British throne.

Because family members still live in the house, Traquair is accessible only during tourist season, generally after Easter and into September. On our first visit in March, we looked at the house from the closed Bear Gates down the long driveway that lies parallel to the original drive. On the next visit, in early September, we thoroughly enjoyed our tour of this unique building. The house contains many artifacts, some dating to the time of Mary Queen of Scots and the Jacobite period. These include the bed Mary slept on and a hand-stitched silk quilt made by Mary and her four ladies-in-waiting. The cradle used for Mary's son, the future James VI of Scotland, rests at the foot of the bed. The drawing room contains a harpsichord made in 1651, the only harpsichord in Scotland with its original Belgian decoration. Items in the museum room looked dusty to us and a little worse for wear. We saw old clothing, Mary's rosary and crucifix, documents signed by Mary and other famous people. This room displays a mural on one wall discovered under some wallpaper in 1900. Painted in 1530, the mural once covered the whole room.

The owners threw nothing away, so all original documents, papers and correspondence remain in the house. These include recorded deeds of owners prior to the Stuarts: Douglas, Maitland, Keith, Haliwell, Craig, Lindesay, Watson and Murray. So many documents exist that the family received a state grant to hire a part-time archivist to research and catalog the material.

The house also witnessed years of religious persecution. Practicing Catholicism was illegal in Scotland after the Reformation, and this devout Catholic family suffered greatly for their beliefs. Throughout the house, but especially in the priest's room, the anguish caused by religious persecution and intolerance was most apparent. Vestments were disguised as linens. A tiny secret stairway, hidden in a cupboard, provided an escape route for the priest when the house was searched. In fact, the Catholic chapel attached to the house wasn't built until after the Catholic Emancipation Act of 1829. This tiny chapel seems oddly out of place in staunchly

Protestant Scotland. We thought it appropriate to pause for a moment of silence to remember victims of religious persecution throughout the world.

To get there: *Traquair is located between Peebles and Galashiels just off the A72 near Innerleithen. It is well signposted.*

Edin's Hall Broch ★

A visit to Edin's Hall Broch necessitates extensive and serious hill walking. In addition to its remote and scenic location, Edin's Hall has other features that make the trek worthwhile. First of all, it is one of the few brochs found in southern Scotland. Most are located in the north and on Scotland's islands. Secondly, this broch is especially large. Although its walls don't reach the height of other brochs, the interior is unusually spacious.

When we started our walk to Edin's Hall, we had no idea what lay ahead. We read that the broch was located about a mile and a half off the road. In retrospect, we think it was farther. To reach the broch, we crossed

Edin's Hall Broch

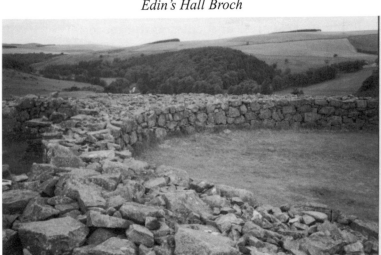

a river called the Whiteadder Water on a narrow suspension bridge, climbed over two stone walls, passed several cottages, traversed fields riddled with rabbit holes and hiked up, down and over steep hills. When the path existed, it varied between dry, muddy and marshy. Historic Scotland signs cheered us on, sometimes giving the remaining mileage. The broch, visible at the crest of a huge hill full of rabbit warrens, required of us a supreme and breathless effort to struggle up the last bit. We wondered what trick of fate made the biggest hill the last hill! Not being veteran hill walkers, we gave thanks for remembering to bring water along in our daypack. The broch's enormous walls afforded us a good bench.

After resting a bit, we explored the broch and surrounding area. Some excavation took place here in the 1800s, but evidently no modern scientific work has been completed. Historic Scotland interpretive signs explain theories about the broch's origins and structure. The broch could never have been very tall, because it was just too large for any great height. Otherwise, it had normal broch features such as stairs and small chambers inside the massive 15-foot-thick walls and guard cells on either side of the entrance. The walls now stand only about five feet high but may have once reached two or three stories.

The surrounding fort with its double ramparts (now hard to discern) was built before the broch, probably before the Romans arrived. No one knows for sure who built the fort or broch. Some authorities speculate that the broch was home to a powerful Votadini Chieftain. Certainly it was used during the two Roman occupations, indicated by unfortified huts of a later date that surround the broch; during the peace imposed by the Romans, fortifications weren't necessary. Another fort sits just above Edin's Hall on top of Cockburn Law.

To get there: *Directions to Edin's Hall Broch are well*

*signposted from the A6112. Locate the village of Preston,
north of the town of Duns on the A6112. The junction of
the B6365 and the B6355 is a little less than two miles
west of Preston. At the junction, take the minor road north
a short distance to the beginning of a farm track where
cars must be parked and the walk begins. The walk from
the car park to the broch seemed to us about 2½ miles,
requiring approximately 40 minutes to reach the site.*

Hermitage Castle

This castle rises stark, bare and forbidding out of
the surrounding pastoral countryside. No adornment
breaks up the enormous walls. Hermitage clearly represents a war machine, built to withstand armies. The idyllic setting contrasts sharply with this castle's violent
history.

Similar to other Scottish castles, Hermitage probably
started its life as a motte and bailey castle in about 1240
AD, built by Sir Nicholas de Soules. Nothing survives of
this early fortification other than the earth mounds under and around the castle. Hermitage may derive from
the name of a long forgotten Celtic saint's retreat upon
which the castle was built.

The structure now consists of two castles. A remnant of a castle built by Lord Dacre in 1360 sits in the
heart of the central tower. Sometime after 1371, Dacre
was booted out, and Earl William Douglas took over.
Douglas converted the first castle into a huge tower block.
By about 1400, the northwest tower or prison tower and
the well tower were built. Finally in the early 15th century, the kitchen tower on the southwest corner was
added. Window-like openings that stud the castle near
the top of the walls actually form doorways that once
led to wooden fighting platforms. From these platforms,
defenders fired down on attacking soldiers. Holes in the
wall for inserting these wood beams are visible all around
the castle.

Local legends abound about Hermitage, perhaps fueled by the real-life drama and bloody history that played out there. People were tortured and imprisoned. Treasonous activities incriminated various owners who colluded with the English. Depending on the fortunes of the times, control of the castle alternated between English and Scots. During the time the Douglasses controlled the castle, Sir William Douglas, also known as Knight of Liddesdale and the Flower of Chivalry, starved the gallant Sir Alexander Ramsay to death in the prison tower. He had not been pleased that Sir Alexander had been made Sheriff of Teviotdale.

One particularly gruesome legend tells us of a de Soules boiled alive by vassals fed up with his cruelty. This act supposedly occurred on Nine Stane Rig (a hill with nine stones of a stone circle just east of the castle). Another legend describes a giant, Cout O' Kielder, who drowned in the Hermitage Water. The giant was more likely Sir Richart Knout of Kielder, an enemy of de Soules, who was killed when de Soules's men chased him into the river and held him under water with their spears until he drowned.

Mary Queen of Scots also had connections with Hermitage Castle at the time it was owned by James Hepburn, Earl of Bothwell. Wounded by a border bandit, James lay sick at the castle. When Mary, who had been administering justice at Jedburgh, heard of this she rode nearly 30 miles to Hermitage. She comforted James for about two hours before riding back to Jedburgh in miserable weather over rough, wild terrain, rivers and bogs. Afterward, she became so ill she nearly died. Later, when imprisoned in England, Mary lamented that she had not died in Jedburgh.

To get there: *Follow the B6399 for 12 miles south out of Hawick toward Newcastleton. The castle is located on a secondary road that heads west from the B6399.*

Galloway and Dumfries

Galloway and Dumfries lie to the west of the Borders. Little traveled by tourists, the topography ranges from wooded mountains and glens to pastoral farmland and sandy beaches. The strategic yet treacherous estuary of the Solway Firth defines Dumfries to the south, while Galloway, oriented toward Ireland, edges both the Solway Firth and the Firth of Clyde. Most visitors to this relaxed region seek monuments of Robert Burns and birdwatching opportunities on the vast coastal beaches. Others pass through on their way to Ayr, Glasgow or to the Ireland ferry at Stranraer. Unkown to many, castles, abbeys, stone circles, early Christian crosses, prehistoric cairns and both ancient and later Roman fortifications dot this landscape.

Caerlaverock Castle ★★★

The only triangular castle in Britain lies seven miles south of Dumfries. Caerlaverock is like no other castle we've seen. We enjoyed Caerlaverock so much we took our castle-loving sons to visit it in the middle of winter.

Twin drum towers that give a feeling of great strength guard the castle entrance located at the peak of the triangle. The rock used to build the castle is red, striking against a green grassy backdrop. Two moats still surround the castle. Water filling the inner moat laps at the castle walls. A large earth mound 70 feet wide separates the two moats, and a modern bridge affords access to the castle. Most of the original drawbridge, dating from 1277 to 1330, was found in the moat during excavation. Some pieces are displayed in the castle.

The tops of the wall over the entrance remain intact enough to show the machicolations that allowed defenders to shoot down on attackers. The gatehouse, between the twin towers in the north point of the triangle, reveals two periods of construction. The outermost entry with its portcullis slot dates to the 15th century. Just inside, the 13th century entry has a slot where the portcullis would have been lowered. The arrow slot used by defenders is right above the 13th century gate.

Inside, the newer east range was built in the 17th century, while the older west range dates from the 15th and 16th centuries. Most of these two living ranges are well preserved, but the wall that forms the base of the triangle (the south wall) was destroyed during the last siege of the castle in 1640. Not much remains of the southeast tower for the same reason, but the southwest tower, called Murdoch's Tower (named for a man imprisoned there in 1425), survives basically untouched.

Signs make self-guided tours easy to take. An excellent interpretive display board on the remaining south wall depicts life in the castle's heyday.

Caerlaverock is more than 400 years old, owned by the Maxwell family for most of that time. Even before the Maxwells, the Romans built a way station here, and remains of their other camps are not far from Caerlaverock. Most visitors don't realize that an earlier castle had been built just a short way south of the present one. Constructed on unstable ground, it had to be abandoned after only about 50 years of use.

In 1300, Caerlaverock suffered what is probably one of the most famous sieges in medieval times. King Edward I of England attacked with an army of 87 knights and 3,000 soldiers. This siege was well publicized because one of the attackers wrote a detailed account of actual events. The siege itself didn't last long because Edward brought in siege machines forcing the 60-man garrison to surrender. Edward hung some of the defenders, but uncharacteristically let most of them walk away.

The last siege of the castle took place in 1640 during the Covenanting Wars, when religion again divided the Scots and put them at odds with King Charles I. The Earl of Nithsdale, with 200 soldiers held out for 13 weeks against the Covenanting army. The south wall, demolished during this time, doomed the castle.

The castle lay ruinous until 1946, when it was given into state care. However, in the intervening time, many people still visited. One of these visitors was Robert Burns who carved his initials and the date on the south wall of the gatehouse—18th century graffiti!

To get there: *We first visited Caerlaverock after a Burns pilgrimage to Dumfries. Travel south along the B725, heading toward the Solway Firth, a bird-watcher haven. The entrance road to the castle appears out of nowhere in unlikely flat, peaceful countryside along the estuary.*

Dundrennan Abbey

Dundrennan Abbey, famous for its association with Mary Queen of Scots, is situated in a quiet wooded spot with few tourists. The peaceful surroundings of many of Scotland's abbey ruins add to their attraction. Dundrennan Abbey also represents an architectural transition from Romanesque to Gothic.

Dundrennan began as a Cistercian abbey like Sweetheart and Melrose abbeys. King David I may have founded the abbey in 1142, although some believe David's friend, Fergus, Lord of Galloway, was responsible. The monks most likely came from Rievaulx Abbey in Yorkshire. Two monks from Dundrennan became abbots of Rievaulx. Dundrennan eventually became the motherhouse of both Glenluce and Sweetheart abbeys.

The white-robed Cistercian monks worked and lived here for 400 years. Their rule required them to lead austere lives, a reaction to excesses of religious orders on the Continent. They denied themselves comforts, ate no meat and worked part of the day at hard manual labor. Strict rules governed their everyday lives. Nearer Reformation times, these restrictions eased, and some of the abbeys became wealthy by renting farms they owned.

Dundrennan Abbey exported large amounts of wool to the Continent.

Dundrennan Abbey appears much more complete than its daughter abbey, Glenluce. The church's north transept survives almost whole, although only one wall of the south transept stands. A tomb recess contains the badly damaged grave effigy of a knight, thought to have been Alan, Lord of Galloway. The easternmost part of the church, or presbytery, where the high altar stood, remains in fair shape. Very little, however, is left of the cloister area. Like the nave of the church, most of the walls are reduced to their foundations. Several parts of the abbey, including the floor of the chapter house, were restored in the 19th century.

Dundrennan has its own murder story. An effigy of an abbot with a dagger at his throat and a wounded figure at his feet is set into the church's west wall. This depiction suggests that the abbot was assassinated and the assassin captured. Nothing else is known about the event.

Queen Mary spent her last night on Scottish soil in the bishop's residence here, located in the former lay brethren's quarters in the west range of the cloister. The next day, Mary crossed the Solway Firth in a fishing boat to what she thought was freedom in England. We stood in what may have been her room.

To get there: *These ruins lie just 3½ miles southeast from the pleasant artist's town of Kirkcudbright (kirk coo' bree) on a minor road off the A711. You can also get there by driving southwest on the A711 from Dumfries.*

Cairnholy Chambered Cairns ★★

A public television broadcast featured these magnificent 5,000-year-old burial cairns. Despite their notoriety, we found them nearly deserted when we visited in early September. Only a farmer with a wagonload of sheep encroached upon our solitude.

The name Cairnholy may have been derived from *Carn Ulaidh*, meaning treasure cairn. We think the word, holy, in the religious sense, applies here as well. Tradition tells us that this spot was one of the many burial places of both the mythical king, Galdus, and the bishop of Whithorn, killed in a 14th century battle.

A mound of rocks long since taken to construct farm field walls once covered the two cairns, both similar in design. Both tombs have inner and outer chambers, with the inner chambers curiously built like closed boxes and topped with massive capstones or lids. Cairnholy II shows how Cairnholy I probably appeared when it had its capstone in place. While the outer chambers were entered through tall portal stones, the inner chambers could only be reached by lifting these massive capstones.

The more publicized Cairnholy I stands just a few steps from a small car park. A magnificent forecourt contains six tall stone pillars that form a concave arc at the tomb entrance. Drystone walling between the pillars would have created a large curved wall. These pillars probably served as a dramatic background for religious ceremonies held in the forecourt. Excavations documented that six fires had been ignited here at different times. Finds included pottery fragments, burnt bone, a stone with cup and ring marks, a flint knife, beaker pottery shards and a piece of a ceremonial axe of beautiful jadeite stone from the Alps.

Cairnholy II, just north of Cairnholy I, shows more deterioration. No forecourt exists, and the large entry portal stones lean toward each other. One stone has broken, while another points like a finger toward the sky. However decrepit, Cairnholy II still supports the huge impressive slab over the inner tomb.

Both Cairnholy tombs provide tangible evidence of the power of faith or belief that drove people to create such magnificent structures. Even after some 5,000 years these places demand reverence and reflection. We thought the Solway Firth in the distance, visible through the trees, added even more magic to the setting.

To get there: *Cairnholy I and II are located 6½ miles southeast of Creetown. Take the A75 either southeast from Creetown or southwest from Gatehouse of Fleet. Watch carefully for the small sign at a bend in the A75. The one-lane road leads north. At a fork, take the left track up along a farm road. Shortly you arrive at the top of a hill where a small car park has been created.*

Mote of Mark

The Mote of Mark intrigued us because it's supposed to exemplify a Celtic vitrified fort, once a very important native British stronghold of the kingdom of Rheged. We looked and looked for the vitrified rock and still aren't sure if what we saw was truly vitrified! The views from the top of the hill down toward the Solway Firth are superb and make for some good photos, weather permitting.

The earliest fort was Iron Age but later reused as a Dark Age fortress with a massive stone rampart fired to create the vitrified rock. When excavated, metal working tools were discovered as well as fragments of Roman pottery, a rotary quern and clay hearths. The interpretive sign explains that the fort was probably destroyed during an attack by the Angles.

To get there: *This site is located off the A710, on a minor road leading to the village of Rockcliffe on an inlet off the Solway Firth. Leave your car at the car park in the village and walk to the park at the end of the road. It is a lovely area with a lot of walking trails. Although there are signs, they didn't help us much in locating the Mote of Mark. We took the wrong fork and ended up with a longer hike. Actually, we were a bit lost, but we knew the site had to be on top of a very high hill, so we kept the highest hill in sight as our target and ended up walking all the way around it until we came to the entrance path. Because the site is under the care of the National Trust for Scotland, a good interpretive sign can be found at the base, but not much else.*

Sweetheart Abbey ★

Sweetheart Abbey is famous for its red sandstone and, as its name suggests, its association with love. Also one of the more complete Scottish abbey structures, it escaped the ravages of the Reformation. This abbey and Glenluce Abbey were both daughter houses of Dundrennan Abbey.

Lady Devorgilla of Galloway founded Sweetheart, a Cistercian abbey, in 1273, in memory of her husband, John Balliol. When Lady Devorgilla died, she was buried before the high altar along with her husband's embalmed heart. She called his heart her "sweet, silent companion." In those days, people embalmed hearts of loved ones and kept them. Lady Devorgilla and John Balliol were known for their devotion to each other. In her memory, the monks named the abbey *Dulce Cor*, or Sweetheart. Her grave and effigy with her husband's heart in her hands can be seen in the south transept of the church. These same Balliols founded Balliol College in Oxford. Their son John, chosen King of Scots by Edward I of England in 1292 and forced to pay homage, reigned weakly in the face of Edward's power until 1296.

Archibald Douglas, good friend of King David II, also was associated with the abbey, but not romantically. The king made him Lord of Galloway in 1369, and he lived in his island stronghold of Threave Castle. He usually was called Black Archibald or Archibald the Grim, names he earned fighting the English and for his treatment of the local people. In 1381, Archibald controlled Sweetheart Abbey as a liberal benefactor and supporter.

In 1513, after James IV died at Flodden, the monks

of Sweetheart Abbey sought the protection of Lord Maxwell, a powerful Catholic. In 1560, during the Reformation, Maxwell refused to destroy the abbey buildings. Thanks to the Maxwells, the last abbot, Abbot Gilbert Broun, stayed on until 1587 when he was forced to move to France. But, being a stubborn cleric, he returned two years later, only to be arrested in 1603 and imprisoned in Blackness Castle. Again he was released into exile, and again, in 1608, he returned in defiance of King James VI. During another arrest attempt, an armed crowd chased the guard away. Abbot Broun eventually was arrested, but the Privy Council took pity on him and allowed him to stay at the abbey where he continued to practice Catholicism. Ultimately, he was exiled to France where he died in 1612.

The final act to save the abbey occurred in 1779 when some local gentlemen bought the church to prevent theft of its stone. Much of the village contains stone taken from abbey buildings. In 1928, Sweetheart Abbey was given to the state. Thanks to these efforts, the church, although roofless, survives nearly intact. The nave, presbytery, transepts and cross tower all still stand. The abbey also has the most complete precinct walls in Scotland. These walls consist of massive boulders squared on one side.

Our visit to Sweetheart Abbey contained one jarring and somewhat humorous note. We noticed some people trying to get into the abbey without paying admission. They first went to the entry gate to look at the price of admission. After talking together for a few minutes, they left. Later in the car park in back of the abbey behind the church, the two men tried to climb over the spiked wrought iron fence surrounding the area. They weren't successful because one heavy man just couldn't get over and nearly tore his trousers. Apparently, people who want something for nothing can be found everywhere in the world.

<u>To get there:</u> *Sweetheart Abbey is located directly off the A710, about seven miles south of Dumfries and just west of where the River Nith widens out into the Solway Firth. You can't miss it from the A710 because of the majestic red stone.*

<u>Glenluce Abbey</u> ✳

The Rhinns of Galloway constitute an area rich in prehistoric and historic sites, and the sandhills around Luce Bay are full of archaeological remains of all periods. Glenluce Abbey is one of these and, although it lies in ruins, its peaceful setting and nearly intact chapter house make it worth a visit.

Roland, Lord of Galloway, founded the abbey in 1192, recruiting the white-robed, austere Cistercian monks, probably from Dundrennan Abbey or even perhaps from Melrose. Little is known about the history of the people who lived here, except that the monks had a land dispute in 1560 and temporarily went into exile in Ayrshire. Because this was also the time of the Reformation, they adopted the new religion when they returned from exile and were permitted to remain. In 1560, 15 monks lived at the abbey, although probably only about 12 monks lived there most other times. The last monk died in 1602. Glenluce Abbey continued to be used for religious purposes by the Diocese of Galloway until 1933, when the state took over the ruins.

Only the south transept of the church remains at nearly its original height. The layout is typical with a cruciform church and the cloister off the south wall, the east range containing the dormitory and chapter house, the west range providing supplies, and the south range housing the kitchens and refectory.

The east range is the most complete section with its amazingly intact chapter house. Some of the original tiles remain on the floor around the central pillar. The chapter house acoustics are particularly impressive.

The Cistercians were talented builders and engineers and, at Glenluce, some of their clay water pipes have survived undamaged. The museum near the entry to the grounds displays some of the finds. Excavations also unearthed a large hospital where the monks regularly went to be bled by leeches. The wizard, Michael Scot, purportedly lured the plague to the abbey after a 13th century outbreak and locked it in a vault.

The abbey honored its obligation to provide charity and, because it stood along the pilgrim's way from Ayrshire to St. Ninian's shrine at Whithorn, many pilgrims probably stopped here. Robert the Bruce, while on pilgrimage, may have rested at the abbey around the time of his death. Also, James IV supposedly stopped here twice.

We learned a lot from the custodian. He spent time chatting with us, sharing abbey lore and pointing out special features like the fine acoustics in the chapter house.

To get there: *Glenluce Abbey is situated north off the A75 on a minor road, near the village of Glenluce, about 11 miles east of Stranraer. The abbey sits in the tranquil, tree-covered valley of Luce Water.*

Ruthwell Cross ★★

This elaborately carved cross soars more than 15 feet high and may well be one of the most important surviving crosses in Scotland. A specially built recess in the parish church floor contains the cross.

Most probably of Northumbrian origin, the cross consists of carved figures and Latin and Runic text. The Runic text is an early version of a later Anglo Saxon religious poem, while the Latin relates the power and divinity of Christ. On one side, its intricate carvings depict Christ, John the Baptist, Paul and Anthony, Mary and the infant Jesus. On the other side, they portray

Mary Magdalene washing Christ's feet, the healing of the blind man and the Annunciation.

The cross was not always treated with care. In 1640, when considered an idolatrous monument, it was broken up, defaced and buried on order of the established church. In the 1800s, the cross was re-erected and patched. Unfortunately, the restorers put the head of the cross on backwards.

To get there: *Drive to the village of Ruthwell off the B724. Ruthwell lies about 5½ miles east of Annan, southeast of Dumfries. Just off the B road to the north, a sign points toward the cross's location. Another sign directs you to a modern house on the left where the key to the church is kept. After obtaining the key, proceed to the church.*

Burnswark Hill, Fort and Roman Camps

A 17½-acre Iron Age hill fort that may once have held as many as 150 homes crowns the top of the double summit of Burnswark Hill. This large hill visible for miles around affords spectacular views of the surrounding area.

Typical of many of Britain's hill forts, the site hosted various peoples in succession. While the fort's main rampart dates from about 600 BC, Bronze Age people used it as well, leaving a cairn and cist burial at the top. The Romans followed. Roman camps have been found on the north and south flanks of the hill, close to the fort entrances. Three Roman artillery platforms face the native fort in one of the camps. Some historians speculate that the Romans besieged the fort. However, excavation has shown that the fort's walls were reduced before the Romans launched iron and stone missiles at it. In addition, no written Roman records document a battle here. Perhaps, the Romans used this site for training.

To get there: *The hill is located just north of the village of*

Ecclefechan, which is south of the A74 (M). Take the un-
marked road north from the B725 east of Ecclefechan.
Eventually, this road comes into a forest plantation. Park
in a wide spot where the forest roads meet and follow a
cleared path through the trees, over a fence gate and up
the side of the hill. The climb up is very strenuous. Watch
out for stinging nettles.

Wigtown Peninsula

Not promoted widely in most Scottish tourist guides,
remote Wigtown Peninsula sees few international tourists. But the area has important archaeological and historical connections and is particularly associated with
early Christianity.

Whithorn Priory

Celtic Christianity, the first major Christian movement in Scotland, began in Whithorn when St. Ninian
built the first Christian church here in the 5th century.
Ninian was one of several Celtic Christian men and
women who did much to change Scotland's history. Other
important Celtic saints included Patrick, Bridget and
Columba.

After the Romans left Britain, Christianity almost
disappeared. Then, gradually through the efforts of the
Celtic saints, it re-established a foothold and rapidly
expanded into areas where it had never been during
Roman times.

Three sources shaped the Celtic saints. First, native
Druid beliefs affected them. The saints, who deeply re-
spected the old religion, continued these beliefs, including those related to morality. Second, the teachings of
the desert fathers of Egypt appealed to their love of nature and strong individualism. Third, the Celtic Briton,
Pelagius, helped to form the foundations of the Celtic
church. He didn't like the idea of original sin and he

taught people to think of Jesus as a personal friend and helper rather than a divine being. These three sources resulted in a church and people who loved nature, supported individualism, and regarded men and women as equals.

The original structure built by Ninian is thought to have been the first church made of stone in all of Britain. This building was later called the White House or *Candida Casa*, probably because the walls were painted white. The word "Whithorn" is a slight mangling of two Saxon words (*Whit Aerne*) for white house. The name however may have been used even before Ninian. Greek geographer, Ptolemy, recorded the existence of a place in southwest Scotland called *Leukophibia* or Shining Place. This holy spot became a place of pilgrimage for many centuries drawing both famous and common folk. Patrick, patron saint of Ireland, may have spent time here.

Our first impression of the town of Whithorn wasn't positive, as it appeared a bit dingy and run-down. First impressions, however, can be misleading. The town consists basically of one street laid out on a medieval plan, wide where the market was held and narrow on either end where gates could be closed at night. We parked on this street near one of the storefronts with a sign, "Whithorn, Cradle of Christianity Centre." A 500-year-old gatehouse controlling the entrance to the church and monastery stands a short distance from the Centre.

After paying our admission fee at the Centre, we watched an informative audiovisual show on St. Ninian and Celtic Christianity. The Centre contains exhibits displaying artifacts from the site with explanations about how people lived at Whithorn during its 1,500 years of Christian influence. Another museum located in the monastery precinct has some very remarkable early Christian carved stones and crosses, including the renowned 5th century Latinus stone, Scotland's earliest Christian artifact.

The remains of the priory are located just beyond the museum. A large medieval cathedral was built in 1170 by Premonstratensian canons, but the remaining small church is all that's left of the original nave. It also includes portions built in the 12th, 13th and 15th centuries. The central tower and choir once stood to the east, but only the crypts survive today.

Archaeological excavations have been conducted here since the 1980s. Discoveries document an active and varied history. Earliest remains date from the 400s, the soil level where the Latinus stone was found. Then, between 550 and 600, a number of shrines were built. Goods from the eastern Mediterranean, northern Africa, and France also were unearthed. Discovery of the Northumbrian monastery built in the 7th century provided evidence of the Northumbrian conquest. Finally, in the top or most recent soil levels, artifacts of the Vikings and the Scots of Dalriada were found.

We didn't spend enough time at Whithorn and plan to return for another more comprehensive visit. We also want to hike to St. Ninian's Cave, see the Isle of Whithorn and St. Ninian's Chapel.

To get there: *The small town of Whithorn with its famous priory and archaeological dig is located on the southern end of the Wigtown Peninsula on the A746.*

Rispain Fort ★

We had a bit of a surprise on our way to Whithorn. We saw the sign to Rispain Fort and decided to stop. Because there's very little publicity about it, we didn't expect to find this huge fort on the outskirts of Whithorn. Rispain was a Celtic fortified homestead, dating to 60 BC.

A huge earthwork with a deep ditch in front protects the rectangular site. It must be 15 feet or more from the bottom of the ditch to the top of the earthwork, requir-

ing quite a climb. At the top, the immense size of the
fort, about two acres, is evident. The camp has only one
entry, a sort of grassy causeway. An interpretive sign at
the entry explains that for many years archaeologists
thought the Romans built this well-preserved fort.

To get there: *This ancient fort sits on a hill overlooking
the surrounding area a half mile to the west of Whithorn.
A small sign marks the turnoff off the A746.   Most surprising is the paved farm road all the way to the farm—
likely paid for by Historic Scotland. Drive into Rispain farm
and park in the farmyard. Be sure to park out of the way
of other vehicles and watch out for animals.   The path to
the fort is signposted, taking you through a couple of farm
gates and up the hill.*

Torhouse Stone Circle

Not far from the cradle of Scottish Christianity on
the Wigtown Peninsula, prehistoric monuments provide
tangible evidence that ancient religious practices also
occurred in the area. History and prehistory exist almost side by side in Scotland.

Torhouse, sometimes called Torhousekie, is a Bronze
Age stone circle. Its 19 stones form an ellipse on a raised
platform of earth and small stones. The stones in the
circle are graded by height with the tallest rising to the
southeast. Torhouse represents a variation of the recumbent type of circle, where a recumbent stone and two
flanking stones form a line. A true recumbent monument consists of a long stone lying on its side with a tall
standing stone at either end, kind of like a couch. Here,
the stones are really large boulders.

Across the road to the east of Torhouse stands a line
of three stones, graded in height. The stones are aligned
on the winter solstice sunset.

Torhouse is an unmonitored Historic Scotland site.
When we visited, we noticed that someone had removed

some of the small stones on the platform. This kind of vandalism is disheartening. Such "souvenirs" are worthless outside of their context.

A story about a nearby cairn documents some early vandalism. According to local legend, this was a burial place of the mythical King Galdus. In the 19th century, someone took the slab covering the cist. Afterward, people reported seeing a light at night moving from the cairn along the route the slab was carried.

To get there: *Torhouse Stone Circle is located about three miles west of Wigtown on the B733. The circle is easy to find. If you're visiting the peninsula, it's not far out of the way.*

1	Castle Sween	14	Achnabreck Rock Carvings
2	Escart Standing Stones	15	Torbhlaran Standing Stone
3	Balegreggan Standing Stone	16	Carnasserie Castle
4	Campbeltown Cross	17	Kintraw Cairn, Standing Stone
5	Kildonan Dun	18	Dunstaffnage
6	Southend: Dunaverty Castle,	19	Ardchattan Priory
	Keil Cave, St. Columba's	20	Kilchurn Castle
	Church, Columba's Footprints	21	Castle Stalker
7	Saddell Abbey	22	Aros Castle
8	Skipness Castle	23	Lochbuie Stone Circle
9	Tarbert Castle	24	Moy Castle
10	Kilmartin Church, Linear	25	Iona: Nunnery, Maclean's Cross,
	Cemetery		Reilig Oran, Crosses, Abbey
11	Temple Wood	26	Castle Tioram
12	Dunadd	27	Machrie Moor
13	Kilmichael Glassery	28	Carrick Castle

Chapter 6
Argyll and the Islands

Argyll

This western portion of Scotland has rich associations with the first Scots, called Scotti, who migrated from Ireland; with St. Columba, the famous Celtic Christian missionary; and with the lords of the Isles, who ruled it as a separate nation. Molded by their proximity to the sea, inhabitants of the area's jagged coastline and islands relied for thousands of years upon a vast network of waterways for communication and transit. Never far from water, Argyll and its neighboring islands abound with cairns, standing stones, duns and castles.

Knapdale

Getting to the Kintyre peninsula requires driving along the eastern edge of Knapdale on the western shore of Loch Fyne, just southwest of the Kilmartin Valley. Too often Knapdale is simply a thoroughfare to the southern region when Knapdale itself warrants further exploration.

Castle Sween ★★

Castle Sween, the oldest castle still standing in Scotland, may have been the first Norman castle. Although located well off the main highway, the one-lane road to Sween can be crowded, because it is a holiday destination. We were surprised to find a huge caravan or trailer park practically barricading the castle, even though we visited in December when the grounds were deserted. With our backs to the caravan park, we could almost forget this unsettling intrusion of contemporary life. The loch with its wild and picturesque opposite shore, the three Paps of Jura in the distance and the clear blue sky formed a superb backdrop to the castle. Something about the winter light accentuated the colors that afternoon, deepening the brilliant blue of the loch.

The castle stands majestic on a rocky knoll on the edge of Loch Sween. Massive, formidable-looking walls measure more than six feet thick in some places.

Suibhne, the patriarch of the powerful MacSween family, probably began building the main part of the castle in the late 12th century, while Dugald MacSween, a prominent lord, continued the early work.

The 1300s and beyond were turbulent years. The castle frequently changed ownership due to intrigues and support of the wrong side. Sween was even attacked by one of Scotland's great heroes, Robert the Bruce. A Gaelic poem describes an attack against the castle by a fleet of galleys. Castle Sween was garrisoned until 1647 when it was captured and burned by Colkitto Macdonald and his royalist forces.

An arch on the south side gives entry to the main and oldest section of the castle completed about 1200. The large grassy courtyard of today is misleading. At one time, structures built against the walls would have filled the available space. The northeast section of the open area contains the well, and beyond that lies the kitchen range built in the 15th century. Remains of the latrine tower are located in the northwest and west ranges, some built in 1300 by the Menteith Stewarts. Here's a dose of reality in this otherwise romantic place— a chute in the latrine tower dumped sewage and other waste right onto the ground outside the castle!

To get there: *Take the A816 north out of Lochgilphead until you reach the B841 at Cairnbaan. Then follow the B841 along the Crinan canal for about 2½ miles and turn left at the B8025. This road takes you south for about 1.2 miles where a minor road forks to the left leading to Achnamara and the B8025 continues on. (A decision here*

to go left or right resulted in one of our failures to locate a
stone circle. We went left and later learned that the stone
circle is off the B8025.) A copy of the Kildalton Cross sits
at this junction. To get to Castle Sween, go left at the fork
and take the one-lane Achnamara road for about five miles.
Drive into the caravan park, keep to the right, go around
some utility buildings, and follow the track to the castle
where you can park off the road next to it.

Kintyre

Off the main tourist route, Kintyre is more difficult
to reach than other places in Scotland. The Kintyre peninsula is 40 miles long and eight miles wide, so the ocean
is always close. From its southernmost point, Ireland is
visible. The golf course at Machrihanish is supposed to
have the finest first hole in the world. Nearby lie the
islands of Islay, Jura and Gigha. Islay is famous for its
peaty single malt Scotch, and even sparsely populated
Jura has its own single malt.

Kintyre is a land of legend, visited and inhabited by
Bronze Age people, Celts, Somerled, Celtic saints, Robert the Bruce, and many others. Ancient sites such as
castles, churches, duns, forts, standing stones, cairns,
abbeys, and even previously inhabited caves dot the
peninsula. Unfortunately, at the time we visited Kintyre,
many places were poorly marked or not marked at all
due to lack of funds.

We saw only a few monuments and didn't get to Islay,
Jura or Gigha. Islay was for years the seat of the descendants of Somerled, the powerful Lords of the Isles.

Escart Standing Stones

Imagine having prehistoric stones as yard decora-
tions! The first stones we encountered on Kintyre stood
right next to the farmhouse.

Probably once consisting of more stones, the existing five Escart Stones form an alignment directed toward West Loch Tarbert. Trees now obscure any specific point to which they may have been oriented. A high stone wall separates the two stones closest to the barn. The flat stones near the barn measure around 9 to 12 feet tall. The other stones stand between 6 and 9 feet, while the smallest is only about 3½ feet high.

To get there: *Take the A83 1.2 miles south of Tarbert. The farmhouse drive is on the left, clearly marked as a B&B. We asked permission to examine the stones. They stand about 10 feet from the farmhouse.*

Balegreggan Standing Stone

The massive Balegreggan Standing Stone rises high on a hillside like an ancient sentry watching over Campbeltown Loch and Campbeltown to the southwest.

The Balegreggan stone resembles a venerable old thumb sticking out of the field, with a height of about 12 feet. It has a tilt to it and the surface appears smooth. The cows have rubbed against the base. The stone is supposed to have cup and ring marks on it. We couldn't find any, but moss may have obscured them.

When we hiked out to the stone, we greeted a farmer who talked with us about the American military at nearby Machrihanish. We followed his cows, carefully picking our way through the pasture to the stone.

To get there: *Getting to this stone can be a bit of a challenge. Heading south on the A83 close to Campbeltown, watch for 30 mph signs. Immediately after the signs two narrow roads appear on the left. Take the second road and drive through a small housing area. The road continues into the middle of a farm. Drive through the farm and alongside the barn. Go slowly and watch for cows and other animals. After a short distance, look for the Balegreggan Country House, a two-story guesthouse. At this point you may have to open the bar gate. If so, be sure to close it. If the guesthouse is not busy, ask if it's possible to park there briefly to visit the stone, visible from the guesthouse.*

Campbeltown Cross

This cross, the finest medieval carving in Kintyre, stands in Campbeltown, located in the center of a roundabout next to the tourist information center and waterfront. Created in 1390, it was moved to Campbeltown in 1609 to be used as the market cross when the town became a royal burgh.

Kildonan Dun

Kildonan Dun occupies a picturesque rocky coastal spot with outstanding views east across the Kilbrannan Sound to the island of Arran. As duns go, this one is well preserved. The walls once protected several houses, so the interior looks fairly large compared to "single family" duns. In some places the thick dun walls span 12 feet or more, so it is possible to walk around on the top of them. The wide main entrance on the west has a bar hole and socket. One of the walls contains a small cell. Stairs on the west side are easy to climb. South of the stairs, a short stretch of galleried (double) walls forms a space inside the walls. Archaeologists speculate that double- or hollow-wall construction helped reduce the weight on the base caused by tall upper walls.

This dun was built some time between 100 BC and 200 AD, likely Iron Age and probably used until the 9th century before being abandoned. The dun was reused for a time in about the 13th century. When we visited, vegetation obscured some of the area around the walls.

To get there: *This eastern coastline of Kintyre has many ancient monuments, but unfortunately, they are not well* *marked and very difficult to find. The Kildonan Dun is just off the B842 near Peninver. It is about four miles north and east of Campbeltown. Going north on the B842, look for the dun on the right or water side. At our visit, some folks were camping in the large car park on the left.*

Southend and its Sites ★

Southend, on the very tip of Kintyre south of Campbeltown, contains several sites of historical significance. Because of its proximity to Ireland, it may have been one of the first places in *Alba* inhabited by the Scotti from northern Ireland. The area retains strong associations with St. Columba, the Celtic saint who established the community at Iona and converted the Picts to Christianity.

At the end of the golf course at Southend, all that remains of *Dunaverty Castle* occupies a rock jutting out into the sea. Somerled, first legendary Lord of the Isles, may have founded Dunaverty Castle. In medieval days, Dunaverty could only be reached by a swaying bridge over the water. Robert the Bruce supposedly sheltered here in the dark days of his flight from Edward I. In 1647, the castle witnessed one of Scotland's most terrible massacres (said to be worse than Glencoe). The Covenanters slaughtered 300 Irish mercenaries fighting for Charles I, after the Irish surrendered due to thirst.

On a clear day, the coast of Ireland is visible to the southwest from Keil Point, the location of several important caves. In *Keil Cave*, the largest, artifacts documented occupation from the 3rd century. One discovery included 4th century Roman pottery, rare in Scotland. During this time, Kintyre served as home to the Celtic Epidi, who likely used the caves for shelter.

St. Columba's Church stands east of the caves, a narrow rectangular building with the entryway sunken into the ground. Only the walls of the church remain. The oldest part or east end of the church dates to the 13th century. Some carved medieval (and later) grave stones can be seen inside the church and in the surrounding cemetery. The water of St. Columba's well, located on the site, is still used for christenings. West of the church, up on a rocky knoll, _Columba's Footprints_ are embedded in the rock. These include one complete footprint and a partial one. The full print is thought to be ancient, the partial one a modern copy. According to legend, the footprint was burned into the rock when Columba first arrived in 561 and turned his back on Ireland. St. Columba was born into royalty in Ireland on December 7, 521. As a headstrong young man, Columba showed his anger easily. After gathering his clansmen together for a battle where thousands died, his remorse resulted in self-exile to Scotland. Today, Columba is considered the "dove of the Celtic church" because he brought peace and stability to Scotland.

To get there: _Follow the B842 west and south from Campbeltown being sure to take the fork to the left, not the B843 to Machrihanish._

Saddell Abbey *

Hidden away in a quiet glen, Saddell Abbey may be the burial place of Somerled, the great warrior who defeated the Vikings and established the Lords of the Isles dynasty in the 1100s. As Kintyre's most important historical site, Saddell Abbey is in desperate need of assistance. The abbey's few remaining walls just barely stand and a rickety fence surrounding them warns visitors to keep away from the dangerous masonry. A special shelter on the grounds protects a fine collection of medieval graveslabs, carved in Argyll between 1300 and 1560.

Somerled founded Saddell Abbey around 1160, shortly before his death, and his son, Ranald (Reginald), completed it in 1207. It flourished as a Cistercian monastery until the early 16th century when the power of the

Medieval graveslabs, Saddell Abbey

Lords of the Isles declined.

From what we could tell, only small parts of the north transept, presbytery and refectory/undercroft survive, choked by vegetation. These structures may date from the 12th or 13th centuries.

The eleven elaborately carved graveslabs and the shaft of a Celtic cross may have been carved at Saddell Abbey. The abbey, supported by the Lords of the Isles, was considered one of the premier stone-carving schools of the west Highlands. Three slabs show medieval armor, fashionable in the 14th and 15th centuries, while others incorporate swords, galleys, Celtic interlacings and scenes. One graveslab depicts a priest and another a monk.

To get there: *Follow the one-lane Carradale road, the B842, that hugs the east side of Kintyre, until you come to Saddell. A very small sign points toward Saddell Abbey. Turn up the drive about 50 feet or so, park at a wide spot by one of the houses and follow the farm track on the left to a gate into the cemetery and abbey.*

Skipness Castle *

We first spotted Skipness Castle on a sunny clear morning from the Claonaig ferry on our way to Lochranza on the Isle of Arran. We later learned that most of this well-preserved castle dates to late 13th and early 14th centuries with some of the early 13th century wall still standing. Skipness Castle is located on open land away from the water. The castle walls stand at least 35 feet high making it noticeable from a distance.

A castle has occupied this spot since at least 1261 when it belonged to the MacSweens as part of the lordship of Knapdale. In fact, Dugald MacSween probably built this castle in addition to working on Castle Sween. Two freestanding stone structures, protected by a wooden palisade, comprised the initial castle. Beginning in the late 1200s, the palisade was replaced with stone walls and the two ranges expanded.

The northeast corner of the west curtain wall protects an impressive tower house in good condition. When we visited, the tower house was closed for construction. Defenses at Skipness were well used. Arrow-slit embrasures (or arched recesses) stud the courtyard's west wall. These protected archers who could reload in safety. Like most castles in this area, Skipness changed hands as political fortunes waxed and waned. The castle was besieged in 1645 and then abandoned from the late 1600s to 1706 when it became a farm.

The ancient castle chapel, built when the castle was reconstructed in 1300, occupies an open space to the southeast of the castle. Dedicated to the Celtic St. Brendan and called the Chapel of Kilbrannan, it keeps silent watch over the Kilbrannan Sound. We didn't trek out to the chapel because of time constraints and very windy, rainy weather, but from a distance it appeared in good condition. The chapel is known for its fine stonework. It also contains medieval tombstones.

To get there: *Skipness Castle is situated on the east coast of Kintyre very close to the Claonaig ferry landing. Take the Carradale Road (B842) north from Campbeltown or the A83 south from Tarbert, turning east at Kennacraig on the B8001 to Claonaig. Then take the B8001 northeast from Claonaig along Skipness Bay. You drive right to the car park. Castle visitors are supposed to leave their cars at the car park some distance from the castle and walk a tree-lined road to the castle gate.*

Tarbert Castle

Tarbert Castle was one of Robert the Bruce's important castles occupying a strategic location above the picturesque village of Tarbert. Tarbert wraps around East Loch Tarbert at the point where the Kintyre peninsula meets Knapdale.

The word "tarbert" means narrow isthmus. Indeed, Tarbert is the narrowest point on the whole peninsula. According to legend, Viking King Magnus Barelegs claimed all of Kintyre as his own after his men pulled him in his long boat across this narrow isthmus. The Scottish king, Malcolm Canmore, had promised Barelegs any western land he could sail around with his rudder down. In his struggle to maintain his crown against a Scottish chieftain allied with the English, Robert the Bruce duplicated this feat by towing a whole fleet of long boats across the isthmus.

Of very early origin, Tarbert Castle was remodeled extensively and expanded by Bruce in 1325. Tarbert Castle features prominently in the history of Bruce and the Lords of the Isles. Bruce apparently kept the castle in royal hands rather than returning it to his friend and supporter, Angus Og, a Lord of the Isles. Bruce wanted to maintain a royal presence and secure a position of strength in this critical location. It also served as a tangible reminder to the islesmen that he was king.

Unfortunately, little remains of this vital stronghold.

A small keep is the only major structure still standing. James IV supposedly built the keep in 1494, but some people believe Bruce built it. The remains of the keep consist of parts of two walls, still fairly high. Trees and vegetation cover all the flat surfaces and many of the vertical surfaces. The keep is fenced off because of the danger. Other than the keep, only the outline of walls and some structures can be identified in the surrounding area. The interpretive sign suggests how it might have appeared in its prime.

To get there: *The castle is located on the southeast side of town on a rocky knoll. We couldn't see it from town at all; in fact, we had to ask directions to find it. To get there, you first have to find the concrete stairs leading up from the main street on the south side of the harbor. A small sign points to the castle, but it is easy to overlook. If you can't find it, do what we did and ask directions in one of the little shops lining the street. The stairs run alongside a building for a ways at first, and the climb is rather steep. We climbed up and up, at times almost through a jungle of vegetation. At the top, you'll find an interpretive sign and an open, flat area with a great view of the harbor.*

Kilmartin Valley

The accessible and unique Kilmartin Glen is packed with ancient treasures. The area is so special that the Kilmartin House Centre has been created to help visitors learn about it. Situated in the town of Kilmartin in the Kilmartin Church's old manse and outbuildings, the center includes a bookstore, a tearoom, lavatories with artwork not to be missed, and a museum. Exhibits describe the people who created the valley's ancient monuments and provide an overview of valley attractions. More information about the Centre, the area, and the monuments can be obtained from their outstanding web site (www.kht.org.uk).

According to Kilmartin House, the valley has been a special, sacred place for perhaps 9,000 years. It may hold the densest grouping of ancient prehistoric and early historic sites in mainland Scotland, more than 150 within six miles around Kilmartin village. We suspect that only Orkney surpasses Kilmartin in this regard.

We have stopped at many Kilmartin monuments, including cairns, a stone circle, standing stones, the Iron Age and early Scottish stronghold of Dunadd, and Carnasserie Castle. We examined cup and ring marked stones, early carved graveslabs, and old Celtic crosses. Most of the main sites are well interpreted, marked and easy to find.

Because so much is written about the Kilmartin area, it would be possible to spend many enjoyable weeks, even months, learning about the area. In this guide, we won't try to cover the entire valley. We will share our impressions about several sites and describe some that are not as well known.

To get there: *The valley runs north of Knapdale along the A816, a main road leading to Oban from Kintyre and the Loch Fyne area. Recent improvements include large car parks, new signage and paths to the sites closest to Kilmartin and Dunadd. To see the linear cemetery, Nether Largie Stones and Temple Wood, park at the Lady Glassary car park and follow the well-marked paths. The tiny car park at Temple Wood is now marked "handicapped."*

Ri Cruin Cairn stands about a quarter mile south of the secondary road that loops around Nether Largie South and the Nether Largie Stones, passing Temple Wood. We parked well off the road at a wide spot that doubles as a very small car park. The tiny, old sign for Ri Cruin is easy to miss. A rock stile crosses the fence, and the path leads to a wooded area.

For the huge Ballymeanoch Stones, henge and prehistoric art, park at the Dunchraigaig car park just off the

A816 and follow the paths across the road.

Kilmartin Church and Linear Cemetery ★★

The linear cemetery or line of burial cairns is the most prominent feature in the valley. This ancient cemetery comprises a line of five Neolithic and Bronze Age cairns running SSW to NNE. The cemetery was used and altered for more than 1,000 years, beginning about 5,000 years ago.

On our first visit to the valley, we were driving south from Oban and came upon the northernmost cairn first. Unfortunately, this cairn was the most disappointing, because we found only a low pile of rocks. Most of the rocks had been hauled away early in the century to build roads. The cairn wasn't marked with a sign, so we went back to the car and drove on to the Kilmartin Church.

The Kilmartin Church is known for its Celtic crosses and its fine medieval graveslabs. Three Celtic Christian crosses are housed in the church. One of the crosses is considered to be an early British representation of Christ on the cross, possibly dating to the 10th century. The church cemetery shelters a large number of carved medieval graveslabs from the 14th and 15th centuries.

On our first visit, the museum hadn't opened yet and preparation work was in progress, so the complex was a bit muddy and cluttered. A young woman associated with the Centre told us how to find the most interesting sites in the valley. In a small way, we had a preview of what was yet to come once the museum opened.

The four most spectacular cemetery cairns bear the unique names Ri Cruin, Nether Largie Mid, Nether Largie South and Nether Largie North. Glebe Cairn was the one we had chanced upon. We thought Nether Largie South, the oldest, to be the most interesting. In the middle of the line of cairns, it has a protective fence around it and a walkway. Nether Largie South contains a four-compartment chamber. Nether Largie Mid and

Nether Largie North also have interior chambers. Cup and axe carvings decorate some of the interior slabs in Nether Largie North. Ri Cruin contains two cists where the slabs fit together like a wooden box. Axe heads are carved into one of the slabs. Axes were woodworking tools, and the axe carvings symbolize the axes used to make wooden boxes.

A line of cist graves destroyed by gravel mining was discovered west and parallel to the linear cemetery. Only two remain, but several had previously been excavated. Two of the graves contained female bodies with rich burial goods dating to about 1700 to 1600 BC.

Temple Wood ★★

A famous stone circle frequently cited in archaeological writings, Temple Wood consists of two stone circles. The main stone circle surrounds two small burial cists. According to Aubrey Burl in _A Guide to the Stone Circles of Britain, Ireland and Brittany_, Temple Wood dates from about 3075 BC (plus or minus 190 years). This date suggests that the circles could be two of the oldest stone circles in Britain. Be sure to look for the double spirals on one of the northern stones in the main circle. One spiral goes clockwise while the other, on the adjoining face, is counterclockwise. Excellent reader boards describe the development of the circles.

Nether Largie Standing Stones ★

Five standing stones are grouped just across the road, almost opposite Temple Wood. Cup marks cover the surface of one stone.

Some scholars speculate that this group of stones formed a lunar observatory. Two stones at the south end of the arrangement point northwest to a notch in the hills. This notch lines up with the northernmost position of the moon. The southwest view toward

Bellanoch Hill lines up with the southernmost position of the moon.

On one of our visits, we chanced to be in Kilmartin Valley on the winter solstice right at noon! We looked in vain for a solar relationship. Only later we learned that the stones are oriented toward the moon.

Dunadd ★★★

The fortress of Dunadd, one of Scotland's most important ancient historical sites, stands about 3½ miles south of Kilmartin. After 500 AD, Dunadd served as the capital of ancient Dalriada. Before that, it had been an Iron Age fort and, before that, a Bronze Age site.

We love Dunadd. Beside its beauty, Dunadd is steeped in history, occupied for several thousand years. Bronze Age people probably used the site. On the vertical face of a rock outcropping, we found cup marks. Excavations have documented Iron Age occupation. In the years after 500 AD, the Scotti kings of Dalriada were anointed here. Signs of daily life materialized in the 50 small milling stones used for grinding grain into flour found by archaeologists. Artifacts from as far away as France have been discovered. The citadel had its share of violence, too, with a number of documented attacks and sieges.

To get to the fort, visitors must walk next to the farmhouse at the base of the hill, through an entry gate leading up to the path. Although the climb up is not arduous, good traction shoes are needed to scramble over rocks. The path winds up and around the farmhouse garden and above the house. The rocky path eventually comes to a natural large cleft in the southeast wall of the hill, the entrance to the first terrace of the fort. On either side of the entrance, remains of massive stone walls rise up. A walk or tower may have once guarded wooden gates here.

Through the cleft, the climb continues up across a

grassy terrace to the second terrace and some important artifacts. The first and probably most noticeable is
the imprint of a foot carved into the rock on an upper
flat rocky surface. Nearby on the same rock, and requiring a close look (we missed it the first time), an outline of a boar and some ogham script can be faintly detected. The boar and the ogham are thought to be Pictish.

Also nearby, in the surface of another rock, a basin
has been shaped. In the Dalriada king-making ritual,
the chosen one would have been anointed from this basin and placed his foot into the footprint to demonstrate
his intent to follow in the footsteps of his predecessors.
The basin is original, but the rock with the footprint and
boar is not. Unknown to most visitors, the top of the
rock is an exact replica of the original, protected underneath. We were amazed at how perfect the reproduction
looks. Try as we might, we could not find any indication
that it was not real rock. The only clue might be that the
stone appears less weathered when compared to the basin.

The fort crowns the very top, on the west side of the
hill. Here, archaeologists discovered remains of an Iron
Age dun. This area was probably equivalent to the much
later castle keeps with their great halls. The west and
north sides drop off abruptly and dangerously. A 360-
degree magnificent view overlooks the Kilmartin Valley,
the River Add and the moors stretching off into the distance.

Dunadd is so special to us that we made a trip just
to take our grown sons. We've heard that in the summer, Dunadd can be rather crowded. We've visited several times during off-season, to experience its magic and
beauty alone and seemingly distant from the 20th century.

To get there: *Dunadd lies just to the west of the A816 and
is clearly visible from the road. Its large, rocky hill looms
up out of the surrounding flat moorland. A gravel farm*

Cup and ring carvings,
Kilmichael Glassery

road leads to a newly paved road and car park across
from the base of the hill. We visited twice in early Sep-
tember when one group left as we arrived and others came
as we left; another visit took place on the winter solstice
when not another soul was in sight, not even at the farm!
Look for the standing stone under the clothesline at the
farmhouse.

Kilmichael Glassery ★

The Kilmartin Valley boasts a fine collection of Bronze
Age art. Some carvings are located near the road, while
others require short hikes.

One extraordinary set with cups and rings, cups, and
keyhole carvings covers an outcrop of rock in the village
of Kilmichael Glassery. We visited on a rainy day, so
water filled the hollows, emphasizing the designs.

Imagine sitting for hours tapping the hard flat surface with a stone hammer to make a single cup. We

counted a hundred carvings before we got tired and gave up. Many sites like this exist in Scotland, all with numerous carvings. What could they possibly mean? We will probably never know for sure.

To get there: *Follow the A816 north from Cairnbaan or Lochgilphead until you cross the bridge over the River Add. To the right or east, signs on a minor road give directions to the town of Kilmichael Glassery and to the carvings. They are on an upper street behind the school. An iron fence surrounds the site, and wooden steps that straddle the fence allow entry to the enclosure.*

Achnabreck Rock Carvings ★★★

A virtual prehistoric art gallery, Achnabreck displays Scotland's most extensive group of rock carvings. Pecked out with a stone hammer 5,000 years ago, these carvings show the creativity of many different artists and a style unique to Achnabreck.

Carvings cover the surfaces of three sets of rock outcroppings high on a slope overlooking the lowlands around Lochgilphead and Kilmartin. These remarkably diverse carvings feature patterns with cups, cups surrounded by rings, spirals, lines and gutters. Over time, additional artists reworked the designs, pecking out rings to enclose or touch earlier designs, even to erase work.

This particular location, situated strategically on a path leading to the uplands with expansive views below, probably held some special significance to the early people. It may have been a sacred place where they shared their mythology and their past. Certainly, the existence of nearby standing stones and a burial cairn on higher ground reinforced the area's importance.

We visited just after the rain had cleared. Muddy in places, the path was in good condition for the walk to the carvings. In really wet weather, waterproof footwear would be advisable, especially because the path steepens at the top. Both the Forestry Commission and Historic Scotland manage the site and provide excellent signage. Picnic tables and a new car park built in 1996 make Achnabreck especially tourist-friendly.

To get there: Achnabreck is well signposted, east of the A816 just north of Lochgilphead near Cairnbaan. The walk to the carving is about one-third mile.

Torbhlaran Standing Stone

The Torbhlaran Standing Stone (pronounced "torv laran") stands near Kilmichael Glassery, just a short way east of the village. Torbhlaran's flat surfaces face east and west. The base is wide and tapers to the top. We estimated it to be about seven feet tall.

A group of noticeable cup marks decorate the base of the stone's west surface side. Perhaps they represented prehistoric graffiti. The cup marks were large and easy to identify from the fence despite the gentle rain. Cup marks may embellish the east side as well, but we couldn't tell for sure from the road. We have seldom seen so many cup marks on a standing stone. If the stone is Neolithic in origin, then Bronze Age stone carvers probably came along hundreds of years later to decorate the convenient surface!

To get there: *Take the unmarked road east through Kilmichael Glassery for about a mile or less. You can't miss the stone, standing prominently in the middle of a field to the left of the road. There's no place to pull off along the road, so we just parked to the side as much as we dared (the ground was soft), and walked along the fence until we got close to the stone.*

Carnasserie Castle ★★

John Carswell, a bishop of Argyll and the Islands, built Carnasserie Castle between 1565 and 1572. He translated a religious liturgical book into Gaelic, the first book ever printed in Scots Gaelic. In fact, a panel inscribed in Gaelic graces the outside entrance doorway.

Driving down the Kilmartin Valley, we couldn't miss Carnasserie Castle perched high in the hills. Large deciduous trees, some almost as tall as the castle itself, surround the castle, enhancing its park-like atmosphere.

Carnasserie is well preserved despite being captured and partly blown up in 1685. The castle is not large as castles go, but its four stories make it seem so. A climb to the very top provides commanding views of the Kilmartin Valley to the south and the surrounding hills.

Most castles we've visited appeared dark, dank, cold, drafty places evoking the misery of castle life. However, Carnasserie, could be the exception. In this airy hilltop perch, we imagined sunlight streaming through the windows as Carswell sat in his study working on his translation.

Carnasserie Castle represents a key building of its time, combining the medieval tower and great hall as a single unit. Previous castles separated the hall and tower. The fine castle decoration reflects early Renaissance style. The corbelling of the turrets is almost seamless. Finely carved details grace doorways, chimneys, and fireplaces. On the top levels, most of the parapets survive, allowing visitors to walk around on them.

To get there: *The castle is visible from the road just off the A816 a little more than a mile north of Kilmartin village. A large car park is located on the west side of the road below the castle. A path leads to the castle. Although not far, it's a bit of an uphill trek, especially the last hill below the castle.*

Kintraw Cairn and Standing Stone ⭑

The Kintraw stone, 12 feet high, stands like a sentinel over Loch Craignish just north of the Kilmartin Valley. Studies suggest that this stone may have been used for astronomical purposes. The stone and other nearby structures may be related to the winter solstice, possibly functioning as an ancient observatory.

Another large stone, really a boulder, can be seen just to the northeast of a cairn, near the ravine. Farther to the northeast, on the other side of a stream and ravine, an artificial platform is built into the hill. We couldn't see it.

The artificial platform is supposed to be related to the winter solstice. Standing on the platform, an ancient astronomer could see along the stone, cairn and boulder to a spot between two peaks of the three Paps of Jura (*Beinn Shiantaidh* and *Beinn An Oir*) in the distance. At the winter solstice, the observer watched the edge of the setting sun reappear momentarily between the two peaks just after it disappeared behind *Beinn Shiantaidh*. If this was truly a midwinter observatory, the accuracy of the positions must have been very precise.

We did not know about the relationship of the stone to the solstice at the time we visited. Later we realized we were actually there on the winter solstice!

<u>To get there:</u> *The site is just a little more than four miles north of Kilmartin village on the A816. Driving north it can be easily seen off to the right. In fact, it will be straight ahead for a short time. However, the first time we drove to the Kilmartin Valley from Oban we totally missed it, only hearing about it later when we got to Kilmartin village. The second time, again driving south from Oban, we watched for it with our Ordnance Survey map in hand. One of our sons spotted it in the early morning shadows. On the stone side of the road, there's enough room to pull*

*a car completely off the road. Enter through a gate to the
field where the stone and cairn are located, being sure to
close the gate behind you.*

Dunstaffnage ★★

Massive Dunstaffnage Castle served as a significant
stronghold of the Lords of the Isles at one of the most
vital sea-lane junctions of western Scotland. It has associations with Robert the Bruce, the Stone of Destiny
and Flora MacDonald. The castle and its chapel exemplify medieval Scottish construction, said to equal the
great buildings of Europe at the time.

The castle rises out of solid rock. Its mostly intact
walls seem to soar to incredible height, about 60 feet
from the bottom of the rock. In some places the curtain
walls reach 10 feet thick, intensifying the castle's formidable appearance. Dunstaffnage supposedly looks even
more immense when approached from the sea.

Nowadays, visitors enter the castle by a stair and
small bridge, but in earlier times they entered by drawbridge. The shape of the rock platform determined the
position of the towers and the walls, so the plan of the
castle is an odd-shaped quadrangle. Only two of the three
towers remain. The west tower housed a prison and the
damaged north tower probably served as the main private residence. What used to be the east tower became
the gate or entry house.

Signs around the courtyard describe the various
structures once part of the castle interior. Displays in
the gatehouse exhibit some of the castle's history and
describe the imprisonment here of Flora MacDonald, who
helped Bonnie Prince Charlie escape from Scotland by
disguising him as her maid.

While the present castle was probably built by
Duncan or Ewan MacDougall around 1275, Pictish kings
held court at this strategic location beginning about 300
AD. The famous Stone of Destiny was believed kept here

until Kenneth MacAlpin took it to Scone in 843. The castle changed hands according to the fortunes of war. Even the Vikings held it for a time, and, in 1308, Robert the Bruce besieged and won the castle from his enemies. In 1746, Hanoverian troops used Dunstaffnage as a temporary prison for Flora MacDonald.

The lovely chapel ruin lies in the woods just a short walk from the castle to the southwest. Restrictions imposed by the castle rock likely necessitated the chapel's construction outside the castle walls. It's not hard to picture medieval lords and ladies filing down the woodland path in their finery to worship in this serene and secluded grove. While only the chapel walls remain, the windows show evidence of superb construction and intricate stonework.

To get there: *Driving to Oban on the A85, Dunstaffnage is just off the road to the north on a small peninsula, about four miles east of Oban. The turnoff to the castle is clearly marked. A Historic Scotland custodian staffs it, manages the small gift shop and collects the small entrance fee.*

Ardchatten Priory

Historic Ardchatten Priory is located not far from Dunstaffnage Castle and Oban. In 1308, Robert the Bruce convened the last Scottish parliament here to be held all in Gaelic.

Duncan MacDougall built the priory in about 1230 for the Valliscaulian order of monks (an offshoot of the Cistercian order). Cromwell's troops burned and destroyed it in 1654.

Ardchattan Priory is under the care of Historic Scotland but not staffed by a custodian, a sure indication that it is not a major tourist destination. It was not well signposted—or if it was, we didn't see any signs. So, we had some trouble finding it. After driving up and down the road a couple of times, we stopped at the Ardchatten

House Gardens, located right where our map showed the priory. No one was around to give us directions, and some fierce-looking dogs made exploration particularly uninviting. Nevertheless, we discovered the ruins of the priory around the back of the house. We would have avoided all this had we turned into the drive next to a wall just past the house going east. Later, we learned that Ardchatten House is the second oldest inhabited house in Scotland. The gardens are open to the public.

The priory itself is joined to the house; in fact, parts of the cloister buildings and the church nave are really part of the house. Signs clearly describe various building periods. Some of the structure contains original architecture, dating to about the 13th century.

The carved stones and graveslabs were some of the more interesting features, many in excellent condition. The cover of one of the stone coffins displayed an intricate carving, a skeleton beside a monk, likely symbolizing death.

To get there: *Take the A828 north from Connel off the A85. Just after crossing the bridge at Connel, turn on the first unmarked road to the right or east, and drive about five miles. Loch Etive will be on the right or south. Instead of looking for the priory, watch for Ardchatten House Gardens. Park in the small car park right at the priory.*

Kilchurn Castle ★

Jutting out into the northeastern part of Loch Awe on its own little peninsula, the ruins of Kilchurn Castle loom majestic against a backdrop of mountains. Frequently pictured on postcards and calendars, Kilchurn Castle projects a haunting beauty. Not only is this striking castle great for photos, views from the fifth level of the tower house afford a unique perspective of the loch and surrounding hills.

Kilchurn, home to a branch of the Campbell family,

was constructed in two phases. Sir Colin Campbell, first lord of Glenorchy, built the five-storied tower house in the mid 1400s. Today, with the help of Historic Scotland improvements, it's still possible to climb to the top. The second phase involved the addition of a barracks wing, built in the late 1600s to house about 200 soldiers. It served as a garrison for government forces during the Jacobite uprisings. After being struck by lightning in the 1760s, the castle fell into disrepair

To get there: *There are two ways to get to the castle, the "official" and the "unofficial" method. Historic Scotland cares for the monument and specifies access via boat across the loch from the town of Lochawe. We took the unofficial route, a path down the peninsula to the castle that is not marked or signposted from the road (A85). The walk is about half a mile and very pleasant if the weather is good. To take the unofficial route, watch closely for a white post on the south side of the A85 less than one-quarter of a mile after the A85 and A819 intersection, on the way to Oban. If you reach the Stronmilchan road, you've gone too far. Park in the makeshift car park, and follow the path across the railroad tracks to the castle. The tracks are dangerous and, therefore, gated on both sides. This was the first place we saw a sign to the castle.*

Castle Stalker

Scottish calendars and postcards regularly depict Castle Stalker rising out of the water on its own little island, with loch, hills and maybe a sunset to frame it. In fact, along with Eilean Donan and Kilchurn, it is probably one of the most photographed castles in Scotland. We spotted it as we were driving toward Port Appin on the secondary road. We always find it thrilling to see these picture postcard castles in real life. We had erroneously assumed Castle Stalker was in ruins and were surprised to find it roofed. In Port Appin village we learned that Stalker serves as a holiday retreat for an English family, who own and maintain it. The family opens the castle once a year to the local people.

The Stewarts of Appin built the mid 16th century tower house as a residence. Like most castles in the area, it changed hands many times.

The ruins of another castle stand close by on the island of Shuna—the 16th century Castle Shuna, another tower house castle once also belonging to the Stewarts of Appin. It's supposed to be easily seen from Port Appin, but we didn't know about it at the time of our visit.

To get there: *Due to private ownership Castle Stalker can be viewed only from a distance. With a height of about four stories, it's visible from almost any point overlooking Appin Bay off Loch Linnhe. It stands in the middle of the bay, on a rocky outcrop. At high tide, water completely surrounds the castle, while at low tide mud flats surround it. We had some good views from the road leading to Port Appin, but we read that there is an even better view from a hill above Portnacroish off the A828.*

Moidart

An out-the-way area in the very north of Argyll with one-lane roads, secluded Moidart attracts few international tourists. Rich in history and intrigue from the days of the Lords of the Isles and the Vikings, Moidart borders the scenic Ardnamurchan peninsula located to the southwest. If only to experience the beauty of this region, we suggest a visit.

Castle Tioram ★★★

In our minds, Castle Tioram (pronounced "cheerum") is synonymous with Robert the Bruce, Christiana MacRuari, the early 1300s and romance. We'd wanted to visit this isolated spot ever since we'd read of it in

Castle Tioram

Nigel Tranter's trilogy on Robert the Bruce. We count Tioram as one of our favorite castles.

Castle Tioram is located in an isolated area of tree-covered hills cut by sea lochs. The few small villages connect to each other by narrow one-lane roads, and vegetation abounds in a mild climate.

Tioram rises out of a rocky island in the middle of a tidal flat near the mouth of Loch Moidart. A causeway at the end of the beach provides access. Very high tides cover the causeway, and a sign on the shore warns of this danger.

Maybe it was the warmth of the sunshine, the shifting clouds or the soft breeze. Whatever the reason, the ambience was magical. A few people, who seemed more interested in the views of the loch than the castle itself, wandered around the island. At first, we weren't sure how to get inside the castle, and we walked around to the southwest. Cliffs soared high above, making the castle appear to grow out of the rock cliffs. We backtracked around the base and up the northeast side, finding an easy path to the top and the north-facing entrance.

Tradition suggests that Amie NicRuairi built the castle, but archaeological work places the first structure in the mid 13th century, long before Amie NicRuairi was born. (Note: in Gaelic, *nic* means "daughter of" while *mac* designates a son; in English, *mac* refers to both.) In 1337, Amie NicRuairi married John MacDonald, son of Angus Og; their son became the first chief of Clanranald.

Some sources have romantically linked Christiana MacRuairi, a generation prior to Amie, with Robert the Bruce. The only lawful child of Alan MacRuairi, great grandson of Somerled, she may have protected Bruce during the days he was in hiding. However, any intimate relationship is only romantic conjecture. Nonetheless, having read Nigel Tranter's book, we could *feel* their presence in the castle. Perhaps they looked out the same windows 700 years ago. We could even visualize longships rowing up the loch.

The castle hasn't changed much since 1715 when Alan Dearg, the 14th Clanranald chief, set fire to its interior to keep it from enemy hands. He walked out the door to sadly watch it burn from a nearby hill. He never returned, dying later that year in the battle of Sherriffmir, fighting for the Jacobite cause.

Alan Dearg's father committed so many evil deeds that a legend tells of a giant black frog haunting him. No matter what he tried, he couldn't get away from this great frog. Even sailing away didn't help, because the frog always waited for him at his destination. When near death, he saw something frightful and desperately tried to escape it.

Despite two artillery sieges and the 1715 fire, the castle remains in good condition. The fire demolished its interior, but walls of the keep and hall still stand. Any wood has been destroyed and the higher levels of the castle cannot be reached. Bases of a couple of turnpike stairs lead nowhere. On the west wall the remnants of the stair lead toward the parapet. The kitchen is located in the southeast corner.

In 1984, the castle hosted a major gathering of Clanranald. Members came from all over the world to celebrate and rededicate the clan's banner, which survived the 1746 Jacobite defeat at Culloden.

To get there: *We followed the A861 east from the Corran ferry. The road follows the north shore of Loch Sunart until it turns north at the village of Salen. About a mile north of Acharacle, two secondary roads turn off to the left. The second road left, Blain Road, leads to the castle. There's supposed to be a sign at the beginning of the road but we didn't see it. The correct road is the one on the northeast side of the river Shiel. It is a very narrow one-track road with few pullouts and leads to a large car park and pleasant picnic area. About nine cars were parked there when we visited, mostly picnickers.*

Cowal

The major thoroughfare from Glasgow into Argyll, the A83, crosses the northern edge of Cowal. Tourists sometimes travel through the Cowal peninsula on their way to the island of Bute or to see the picturesque Kyles of Bute, said to be one of the most beautiful drives in Scotland. Because Cowal is close to Scotland's urban areas, it attracts its share of holiday-seekers.

Carrick Castle

A guidebook described Carrick Castle's location as isolated but easily reached by car. With that description, we envisioned the castle to be in the boondocks. We found otherwise. Nevertheless, the surrounding area is indeed rugged and beautiful, which is probably why the locale serves as a holiday destination. The area right around Lochgoilhead is given over to a huge holiday and caravan park.

Our guidebook described the loch as "fjord-like," but maybe only in a small way, even though the loch was beautiful. The castle, a very large, late 14th century rectangular keep, disappointed us. All of our sources described it as a large or massive tower. The existing walls appeared intact. Although not destroyed, the east-facing wall looked worse for wear with shrubs growing out the side. Scaffolding climbed the north and south walls with renovation in progress. A new roof had been installed, in marked contrast to the ancient walls. The castle was locked, so we could view only the exterior.

Carrick Castle served as a 14th century Argyll stronghold. Supposedly, the clan kept prisoners in this isolated spot. James IV also used it as a hunting lodge.

To get there: *We took the B828 that leads off the A83 as it climbs up over the mountain pass, called "The Rest and Be Thankful." At the turnoff, a large car park provides an excellent place to savor the grand view. The hills around here are called the Arrochar Alps. The B828 starts just at the car park. This one-lane track twists and turns going deeper and deeper toward Loch Goil. In fact, it drops 1,000 feet in three miles. The B839 joins the B828 after a couple of miles and they apparently run together the remainder of the distance to Lochgoilhead. We took Loch Goil's west shore route. About four miles from Lochgoilhead, we arrived at Carrick. The castle sits on a bit of promontory jutting into the loch.*

Mull

We recently read a book that described Mull in dismal terms—e.g., barren and "the wastes." We couldn't disagree more. The book's author, also seeking ancient monuments, couldn't find anything of value on Mull. Unfortunately, in his haste to get to Iona, he missed much of the island. Mull contains duns, standing stones, ancient castles, cairns, brochs, Celtic crosses, hill forts, crannogs, a Celtic church and stone circles. It would take weeks to see them all.

Most people take the Cal-Mac ferry from Oban. We crossed from Lochaline. Another ferry crosses to Tobermory during spring and summer from Kilchoan on the Ardnamurchan peninsula. Other ferry destinations include Fishnish via Lochaline, or Craignure, the main ferry stop from Oban. Excursions from Mull can be arranged for trips from Fionnphort, Iona and Ulva for the uninhabited island of Staffa, famous for the cave that inspired Mendelssohn.

On the map, Mull looks small, as though one could drive around the island in one day. Not so! Getting around Mull is not easy, and the twisting one-lane roads make speed difficult. Also, the configuration of Mull lends itself to going either northwest from the Oban ferry toward Tobermory or southwest toward Iona. It takes about two hours to drive from Tobermory to the Iona ferry at Fionnphort (pronounced "fin-i-fort"). To be fair to the island and all it has to offer, a minimal visit should consist of at least a day for each route.

Aros Castle

Aros Castle was once the most important castle on Mull, a vital and vibrant fortress of the Lords of the Isles. Sadly, today a few remaining walls of Aros teeter on the hillside. This gaunt crumbling shell barely resembles a castle.

The castle was built by one of the MacDougalls of Lorn in the 13th century, its ownership changing with fortunes of the clan in control. It eventually became the administrative center of Mull and retained its importance until the early 1800s. In 1608, Aros featured in a famous story of treachery when Lord Ochiltree convened the Chieftains of the Isles on board his ship docked at the castle. After they dined, Ochiltree informed them they were prisoners of King James VI and had them hauled off to castle prisons in the Lowlands.

We easily viewed the castle from the side road but had difficulty getting to it. Weeds choked the path. We weren't dressed for bushwhacking, so we did not attempt to explore it. We could see rubble inside the castle, and the south wall of the keep stood fairly high. The remains of some outbuildings jutted up through the weeds.

To get there: *Aros Castle is just off the A849, about 1½ miles northwest of Salen. To get closer to it, we turned off at Aros Mains, drove the one-half mile to a cottage named "Castle Steadings." We parked the car there, walked down the driveway alongside the cottage and looked for a trail to the castle.*

Lochbuie Stone Circle

We haven't found this stone circle yet, but we haven't given up. Apparently in excellent condition, it contains nine stones arranged in a perfect circle and three others outside the circle. We visited in winter when the soggy ground hampered exploration. The circle stands on private land and getting to it requires hiking across a marshy cow pasture.

However, our short side trip to Lochbuie was worth the extra effort and time. A one-lane road winds in and out of a hilly, wooded area quite different from the barren moorland on the road to Iona. In dead of winter, we thought the scenery haunting. Bare, gnarled and twisted trees lined the road the first few miles, eventually giving way to fertile fields, a few houses and finally the broad bay of Loch Buie. The Lochbuie postmistress provided us general directions to the stone circle. We retraced our way back to a small bridge just the other side of Lochbuie village, parked off the road, entered a gate into the cow pasture, and aimed for a grove of trees to the south. A tiny, almost unreadable sign at the gate said to follow the path to the stone circle, but we couldn't find a path— probably because the soggy ground had been trampled by cows. From there, we hopped, skipped, jumped over the muddy field, sometimes sinking into watery grass up to our ankles. We had waterproof walking shoes but the pasture consisted of pools of standing water and muck. At one point, we crossed a wide ditch, where someone had kindly built a plank bridge. Just a little beyond this point, we admitted defeat.

To get there: *Travel the A849 as though you are on the way to Iona. Turn at Strathcoil, about two miles after the Duart Castle road. This road ends at Lochbuie village. Since our visit, someone has marked a trail to the circle from the bridge (see above) with white-painted stones. This should help immensely.*

Moy Castle

Moy Castle, the ancestral seat of the Lochbuie MacLaines, a rival branch of the MacLean clan (Duart Castle), stands not far from Lochbuie Stone Circle. Moy Castle is a late 15th century ruined tower house, now closed to the public. Kilchurn, Skipness, Tarbert, Dunollie, Breachacha, and Saddell are other classic tower castles of about the same era.

To get there: *Walk east along the shoreline footpath from the village.*

Iona

The tiny island of Iona just off the southwest coast of Mull, one of the most important religious sites in Scotland, is famous for its association with St. Columba. St. Columba built the first monastery here and converted thousands of 6th century pagans to Christianity. Iona has been variously called the "holy island," the "cradle of Christianity," the "sacred island," the "spiritual oasis," and the "jewel in the ocean." Most of Iona, 1,800 acres, is owned and protected by Scotland's National Trust. The abbey, a few sacred buildings and historic sites belong to the Iona Cathedral Trustees. Historic Scotland cares for MacLean's Cross.

Diminutive Iona draws about 100,000 pilgrims a year, most in the high summer season. In the deep winter on a cold, windy day, we were the *only* tourists! We discovered this was a mixed blessing. Even the tearoom was closed.

To get there: *Take the A849 to Fionnphort and the Iona ferry. Cars must be left at Fionnphort because only service vehicles and those of longtime residents can be brought onto the island. Allow plenty of time to reach Fionnphort, because the busy A849 is one-lane most of the way.*

Watch closely for standing stones as you near Fionnphort. Three separate stones, marked on the ordnance map, line the road within seven miles of the Iona ferry. Two stand north of the road, one next to a house and one in a field behind a stone fence, making it difficult to glimpse. The other is south of the road, northeast of Bunessan, just under a slight hill and best seen when driving west.

Nunnery ★

After leaving the ferry, like most pilgrims, we headed

toward Iona Abbey, visible all the way from Fionnphort. We came first to the Nunnery, founded in 1203 by Somerled's son Ranald (Reginald) MacDonald. (Note: it is correctly called the Nunnery, not convent.) Somerled's daughter, Beatrix served as the first abbess of this small, medieval Augustinian community. We wondered if she knew about a pagan fertility symbol, called a s*heela-na-gig*, just above a window on an outside wall. The Nunnery is shaped like a quadrangle with the church on the north, the refectory on the south and the chapter house on the east. The center formed the cloister.

St. Ronan's Chapel, now the Nunnery's museum, just north of the Nunnery, was closed when we visited. St. Ronan's, built about 1200, functioned as Iona's medieval parish church. Excavations beneath two walls of the existing chapel unearthed a chapel with clay walls. Some believe this may have been part of Columba's monastery. An older cemetery belonging to the early Christian monastery was also discovered beneath the present chapel.

MacLean's Cross ★

This tall stone cross stands near the present parish church and manse. Created in the 15th century, it depicts Christ on its west surface, now weatherworn, and elaborate Celtic designs on its other side.

Reilig Oran ★★

Reilig Oran, situated just south of the Abbey, is one of the most sacred places on the island. As the graveyard of Oran, it became the resting-place for about 60 kings, all buried before the Norman Conquest of 1066. Forty-eight Scottish, four Irish, eight Norse kings, and one English king, Ecgfird of Northumbria, are interred here. The Scottish kings included Shakespeare's Duncan and Macbeth, as well as Kenneth MacAlpin, the

Dalriadan king who united the Picts and Scots to become the first king of a united Scotland. Recent archaeological evidence indicates that Columba's monastery may lie under the Reilig Oran, not under the exisitng medieval monastery.

St. Oran's Chapel stands in the middle of the graveyard. Built by Somerled in the middle of the 12th century, it is the oldest building to survive intact on Iona. Unfortunately, it was locked when we visited. Its only door is beautifully carved in the "Irish syle." Until the 16th century, Lords of the Isles were buried inside the chapel. Kenneth MacAlpin may have built a chapel here prior to this one.

Iona's Crosses ★

Two important crosses, dating from the 8th century, stand as timeless sentries for Iona Abbey. St. John's Cross, on the left facing the abbey in front of St. Columba's Shrine, is a replica of an 8th century cross. Its original pieces are protected in the abbey museum, located behind the abbey on the north side. St. Martin's Cross, a complete 9th century original, stands to the right of St. John's Cross. Before the Reformation, more than 300 crosses stood on Iona. Unfortunately, pieces of these amazing works of art now lie in the water off Iona's shore.

Iona Abbey ★

Even before its restoration in 1938, the abbey church's walls stood intact. Only the roof was gone. Abbot Dominic, whose effigy lies in the church, built most of this medieval structure between 1421 and 1465. However, the original abbey constructed by Somerled's son, Ranald, in 1203, had largely disappeared.

Today, visitors enter the abbey through an office area of the Iona Community. In tourist season, the church door may also be open. An ecumenical Christian organization, the Iona Community sponsors events and programs throughout the year at the abbey. It also offers spartan accommodations for approximately 50 guests who share in community worship, chores and meals. The abbey cloister, opening off the office area, resembles all other cloisters except for one variation. It was built on the north side of the church rather than the south because of the availability of running water to flush the sewage. Except for two medieval arches on the west side, the entire cloister was rebuilt in 1938.

On the incredibly cold day we visited, the church seemed surprisingly warm, even cozy. We didn't notice any heat ducts. Alone in very still and serene surroundings, we wandered around the church admiring the fine carvings on the arches and doorways. A small chapel or place of worship had been created on the south aisle, just off the sanctuary. Pillows covered the floor and candles had been recently snuffed. Standing quietly, we listened to the wind blowing outside, buffeting the ancient walls, first strong, dying down and then swelling again. We felt touched by the peacefulness of that sacred place; we were safe and warm, yet so close to the rawness of nature.

The abbey tearoom and museum had closed for two hours over lunch, so we walked back to the village to find shelter. Unfortunately, nothing in the village was open either. With an hour to wait for the ferry, we huddled in the lee of some buildings, braving the unbelievably bitter wind. One of these buildings stands on the shore of Martyrs' Bay where the Vikings killed 68 monks in 806. The monks and other ancient inhabitants of the island must have been very hardy because their lives could not have been easy. We thawed out a bit when both a grocery store and gift shop opened after the noon "siesta." In warmer weather, we would have explored the island.

Had we been prepared for the cold, Iona in its winter mode, bereft of visitors and wreathed in solitude, would have made for great hikes. A woman we met in Oban told us winter is the best time to visit Iona; she takes her dogs on long walks on the deserted beaches on the western shore. However, even in high season, we believe it's possible to experience the Iona's peace. The island is only 3½ miles long and less than a mile wide, with good walking potential. From up in the hills above the abbey the outline of the ancient vallum or ditch below that defined the boundaries of the abbey is visible. Excavations of this ditch turned up artifacts like leather shoes worn by the monks, wooden bowls, pottery and glass.

Arran

We took the ferry (summer only) from Claonaig to Lochranza and drove down the west side of Arran on the A841. Other than late spring, summer or early fall, the year-round ferry from Ardrossan, north of Ayr, provides the only access to Arran. We visited on a clear morning and could easily see Kintyre across the Kilbrannan Sound from Arran. The climate of this coast is mild enough for palm trees to grow!

The island of Arran contains some spectacular archaeological remains. Not only does the archaeology make a trip worthwhile, the varied geography of the tiny island provides outstanding scenery. Many consider Arran to be Scotland in miniature. The north consists of rugged mountains, while the south is flat and gentle. The southern half of the island has the most prehistoric remains.

Machrie Moor ★★★

Machrie Moor is a superb place to see numerous stone circles consisting of varying types of stones. Grouped in six circles, the stones are so architecturally varied that no other site in Europe can match it. The Machrie Moor monument actually comprises two sites: Moss Farm Road Stone Circle and Machrie Moor proper.

We walked about a mile or so to reach the Moss Farm Road Stone Circle, off to the right and very easy to spot. The Moss Farm Stone Circle is not a stone circle at all, but a burial cairn, bereft of its cairn. Over the years, local people robbed the cairn stones to build field walls, so the massive kerb stones that once marked the edge of the cairn resemble a stone circle.

After about another quarter of a mile we passed a stone cist on the right (south side) on the fence line. We could also see small standing stones off in the fields on both sides.

Just a short distance farther, the Machrie Moor circles stand in an open field with hills in the distance and moorland all around. We believe Machrie Moor to be one of the most mystical and beautiful sites we have encountered in our Scottish travels. Somewhat akin to the standing stones at Callanish, it radiated mystery, maybe even holiness. We visited when the heather bloomed, cloaking the surrounding hills in purple. The bright blue sky, the warmth of the sun and a soft breeze all made the day especially memorable. The only other people at the circles were a man and a woman seriously photographing one of the stones.

Fortunately, we had brought a map that detailed each stone circle. This map helped us locate all of the circles. (For more complete descriptions of each circle, see Burl's book, *A Guide to the Stone Circles of Britain, Ireland and Brittany*.)

Circles, ellipses, standing stones, cists and cairns ranged everywhere. We even found a double circle. The contrasts make these early Bronze Age circles especially remarkable. Several consist of small boulders. One circle contains stones so small we nearly overlooked it. Some circles have tall reddish stones while others consist of gray, squat granite boulders. In one circle, the stones alternate between granite and limestone with different textures and shapes. Another artistic circle displays large, squat boulders that alternate with very small stones. Some of the most beautiful we have ever seen, large flat sandstone megaliths in one circle towered far above us. The tallest at 17.5 feet high had grooves at the top, probably caused by the thousands of years of erosion. Another looked like a triangle. Hauled here by ancient people for mysterious and unknown reasons, these fabulous stones are all pieces of art in their own right.

All around we felt the mystique of a hidden landscape with all sorts of ancient structures poking up through the peat. Recently, archaeologists discovered a new stone circle as well as traces of wooden fences outlining parcels of land before the stone circles were built. Radiocarbon dating of these fences yielded a date of 3900 BC, while the circles have a median date of 2900 BC.

"Machrie" probably means a place of good soil. However, other areas of good soil exist on the moor, so why were stone circles only built here and concentrated in such a small area? Perhaps it's because four of the circles line up with a notch in hills to the northeast. On the summer solstice, the sun, the notch and the circles exactly align.

To get there: *Machrie Moor is located just south of Machrie Bay, off the A841, on the west side of the island. Going south on the A841, watch for the car park just south of Tormore on the west side of the road. The car park can hold as many as six cars if everyone is careful parking. The entrance to the site is marked with a small sign; we had no trouble finding it, but only because we were watching for it. A turnstile on the east side of the road begins the 1¼ mile walk to the stones. The walk itself is easy, but the initial farm road consists of rough gravel. On our way back, we came upon two couples trying to push baby strollers. We wondered if they ever made it.*

Stone circle, Machrie Moor

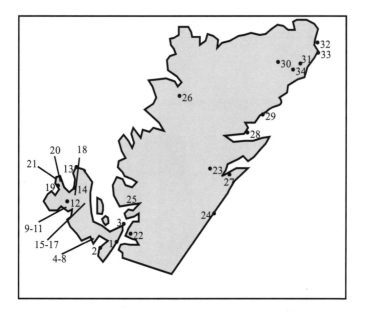

1	Knock Castle	18	Dun Suledale
2	Dun Sgathaich Castle	19	Dun Fiadhairt
3	Castle Maol	20	Dun Hallin
4	Kilchrist Church	21	Trumpan Church
5	Clach na h'Annait Standing Stone	22	Glenelg Brochs
6	Dun Ringill	23	The Eagle Stone
7	Na Clachan Bhreige Stone Circle	24	Urquhart Castle
8	Dun Grugaig	25	Strome Castle
9	Dun Beag	26	Ardvreck Castle
10	Cnoc Ullinish Souterrain	27	Beauly Priory
11	Cnoc Ullinish Chambered Cairn	28	Nigg Stone, Church
12	Vatten Chambered Cairns	29	Carn Liath
13	Duntulm Castle	30	Grey Cairns of Camster
14	Uig Standing Stone	31	Hill O'Many Stanes
15	Dun Gerashader	32	Sinclair and Girnigoe Castles
16	Clachan Erisco Standing Stones	33	Old Wick Castle
17	St. Columba's Island	34	Cairn O'Get

Chapter 7
Skye and the Northwest Highlands

Skye

Skye is filled with prehistoric monuments, many not mentioned in most tourist literature.we found them because we had an excellent resource, *In Search of Prehistoric Skye* by Ian Donaldson-Blyth. This little book fully describes 45 prehistoric sites. Best of all, it provides extremely complete directions to each site. It would take weeks to see all the sites he's covered. We selected ones that looked interesting, remained fairly intact and provided variety. Another very helpful pamphlet had just been printed but was not yet available at the tourist information centers. Our B&B hostess happily loaned us an early copy she'd received. This pamphlet, "In the Footsteps of Early Man: An Introduction to the Archaeology of Skye and Lochalsh," is small but full of useful information. We highly recommend both, the latter for casual visitors with limited time, the former for those who are seriously interested in seeing the archaeology of Skye.

To do Skye justice, we recommend a minimum of two days/three nights on the island. The southern end of Skye is entirely different from the north, and it isn't simple to zip from one end of the island to the other. On the second trip to Skye, we spent two nights in the south and two nights in the north and still wished for more time.

Knock Castle

Our maps of Skye showed Knock Castle not far from Armadale. We didn't know much about Knock Castle, but because it was on our way, we decided to stop. We later learned that this late medieval castle was a MacDonald fortress called *Caisteal Chamuis* in Gaelic.

The MacDonalds held it on the condition that they would host the monarch or his representative at any time. A female sprite or *glaisrig* who can be pacified by offerings of milk is thought to haunt the site.

To reach the castle, we had to follow a path through a pasture strewn with sheep and sheep manure. While trekking down this path, taking care to sidestep the manure, we experienced something for which all our years of raising sheep did not prepare us. We startled two ewes who darted into the bay and swam across to the other side. We never knew sheep could swim!

Not much remains of Knock Castle. It consists of parts of two walls, neither very high. The east wall is the best preserved with one keyhole-shaped opening. It rests on the edge of a cliff, requiring great caution to explore. The south wall can scarcely be called a wall. Only a few piles of stone mark its location. The rest of the castle was mined in 1825 for material to build Knock Farm, and much of it fell into the sea. Weeds, especially stinging nettles, covered everything.

To get there: *We had some trouble getting to Knock Castle. Our ordnance map clearly indicated its location, and we could see it from the road, but we couldn't find the road to it from the A851. Finally after driving back and forth a couple of times, we decided to drive into a farm that appeared to be near the site. We followed the drive in and knocked on the door of a home just past the farm to ask directions and permission. No one answered, so we drove a little farther to where a gravel road bent to the left and followed it to a closed gate. At this point we could see castle ruins off on a little knoll in the sheep pasture. A wooden gate just to the right of the main gate looked well used. This led to the path we followed.*

Dun Sgathaich Castle

This place is worth visiting if for no other reason than

its beautiful surroundings. The scanty remains of Dun Sgathaich sit on a rocky headland on the west coast of the Sleat Peninsula. This headland may have been the earliest fortified site in the Hebrides. The MacDonalds called this home until the late 1500s. The site also traditionally has been the home of Queen Skiach of Celtic lore. Here, she supposedly taught the great Ulster hero Cuchulainn the art of war and peace. He left his sobbing wife Bragela at the castle as he went off to try his new war skills in some far-off place.

We didn't walk out to the headland, although it's not far off the road. Very little of the structure remains, but we could see where a castle once stood.

To get there: *A lovely, winding one-lane road leads to the west coast of Sleat. The south entrance to the unnamed road begins at Kilbeg, northeast of Armadale. The other end of the loop or north entrance is about a mile northeast of Teangue on the north side of Knock Bay/Castle off the A851.*

Castle Maol

The ruins of Castle Maol greeted countless travelers taking the Kyle of Lochalsh ferry before the controversial bridge to Skye was opened. The jumble of stone looks nothing like a castle when seen from the ferry, but it had enough structure to cause us to wonder about it on our first trip. The stones occupy a rocky outcrop in the Kyle of Akin, in the community of Kyleakin. This often-photographed late medieval castle sometimes appears on postcards. The new bridge bypasses the area so, to see it, visitors must go into Kyleakin.

For hundreds of years, Castle Maol belonged to the MacKinnons, vassals of the MacDonalds. Local legend tells us that Saucy Mary, the daughter of a Norwegian king, originally built the castle. The saucy part of her name derives from a tale that she stretched a chain across the Kyles to levy tolls on ships passing through.

To get there: *Walk a few hundred yards to the castle from the ferry slipway at Kyleakin.*

Kilchrist Church

This pre-Reformation church ruin occupies a mound just off the Elgol road on its northwest side. Only the walls of this rectangular, gaunt old ruin stand. It is worth a stop simply because it is so very accessible. The Gaelic name is *Cill Chroisd.* Built sometime between the 12th and 16th centuries, it is considered late medieval.

Kilchrist was a church of a MacKinnon clan, so their graves are scattered in and around the building. The church is very plain. The altar was likely located in the northeast end, unusual because most altars are situated due east. A recess, possibly once a window, occupies the east end.

To get there: *Take the Elgol Road southwest about two miles or so out of Broadford. A small parking area is provided on the southeast side of the road.*

Clach na h'Annait Standing Stone

We think this stone has a unique personality. It's square instead of round with an artistic bend in it. On the way to Elgol, about two miles past the Kilchrist Church, it's worth a stop.

The stone stands about seven feet, with its unique square shape and a curve about halfway up. What appears to be a stone platform is noticeable at the base. A stone circle may have once existed beyond the house, but today no trace remains. The name, *Clach Na h'Annait,* means stone of the chief church. This site is also supposed to be associated with the pagan goddess *Annaitis.* The sacred well of *Tobar an h'Annait* is purportedly nearby.

To get there: *Finding the stone is a little tricky. About four miles out of Broadford, just as the Elgol road bends to the right, a sign points left to Kilbride. Go left onto this rather bumpy one-lane track for about 600 yards to an asphalt drive on the right leading to a handsome, white, two-story house. We parked on the road and walked down the drive until we saw the stone in the field to the right. It is an easy, short walk through the gate to the stone. Because it is located on private land, ask for permission if possible.*

Dun Ringill ★★

A great way to experience the countryside of this beautiful region is to search out the many duns that line its jagged shoreline. One of our more interesting adventures turned out to be our quest for Dun Ringill. On a warm June afternoon, we set out with Ian Donaldson-Blyth's book in hand, indispensable because of his clear directions. We probably wouldn't have found the dun without the book. Dun Ringill is a true dun (not a broch), a structure supposedly built before brochs and sometimes called a semi-broch or a proto-broch (pre-broch).

The dun is D-shaped with its flat side on the edge of the eastern sea cliff. On this cliff side, the wall is totally gone, so extreme care must be taken. Dun Ringill is particularly dangerous, because its promontory is so high. Both the north and south sides of the dun also drop off precipitously to the sea, but substantial walls still remain on these sides.

It was Dun Ringill that taught us about a different type of danger, Scotland's ubiquitous stinging nettles. Those who experience stinging nettles don't easily forget them, because the pain lasts for several hours. Even contact with a small amount of exposed skin can cause pain. In fact, it was surprising we hadn't wandered into them before, as they grow prolifically at neglected ruins.

Dun Ringill began as an Iron Age structure and was used into late medieval times by the Mackinnons. The Mackinnons probably laid the mortared stone just inside the entryway. The entrance contains an unusual ramp that slopes upward, emerging in the center of the dun interior. The entryway also has door checks and holes for the wooden bolt. The roof of the entrance remains in good condition.

Archaeologically, Dun Ringill is an impressive structure. Furthermore, the walk provides some spectacular views of cliffs and sea. We encountered no other people on our hike to the dun. We felt alone, yet peaceful, in a landscape that might have been very similar to that of the dun's builders.

To get there: *Drive along the Elgol road to Kilmarie, about three miles from Elgol. Just after the Abhainn Cille Mhaire River bridge, an unmarked road turns off left to Kilmarie House. Take this road about a quarter of a mile to the house. Right before we got to the house, we parked in a wide place on the left.*

Now the walk begins. Donaldson-Blyth recommends two ways. We suggest the route we chose, because his alternate route requires hopping over stepping stones, possibly slippery, to cross the river. Go through the wooden gate near the parking spot on the left side of the road, and follow the well-defined path to a picturesque bridge, crossing over to the other side of the river. This area is tree covered (unusual for Skye). When we visited, sunlight filtered through the leaves, causing the water to sparkle as it bubbled over moss-covered rock. It was a pleasant beginning for our hike. The woods disappear as the path approaches the sea. Follow the path along the fence. When the fence turns inland at a corner, cut across the corner, and continue to walk along the coastal side until you reach a stile over the fence. Climb over the fence

*and follow the path on the land side for quite a way until
you see the dun.*

*We seemed to walk forever. We thought we might have
missed the dun, being fooled by some rock formations
along the way. However, once the dun comes into view, it
looks unmistakably like a tumbledown fort. A faint path
leads to it from the hill, and the doorway is obvious.*

Na Clachan Bhreige Stone Circle

Just a short way out of Kilmarie on the road to Elgol,
if visibility is good, it's possible to see remnants of this
circle, Skye's only remaining stone circle. Without bin-
oculars, we could just barely identify three stones.

This circle is the only one left on Skye complete
enough to be able to say with certainty that it was a
stone circle. Even then it is hard to tell what the circle
looked like. Some speculate that it was a four-poster,
while others think that these three stones are all that
are left of a circle of least ten or more stones.

To get there: *Just past Kilmarie, stop at the car park near
a cemetery. A gravel road on the west side of the main
road starts the footpath to Camasunary. From here, face
west toward the footpath to look for the stones. You should
just be able to see three stones on a mound some distance away on the south side of the footpath. It looks easy
to reach them, but Ian Donaldson-Blyth warns that the
site is now almost an island surrounded by water and
marshy ground. We elected not to go.*

Dun Grugaig ★

Our visit to Dun Grugaig was probably one of the
more perilous and possibly one of the most spectacular.
Both its location (except for those afraid of heights), condition and unique architectural features make it worthy
of a visit if time allows. The existing wall is massive,

and the entry passage has an intact roof with a huge triangular lintel stone.

Dun Grugaig is a promontory fort, clinging to a very narrow projection of cliff that soars high above the water. Extreme care is absolutely required because one false move could send the unwary visitor tumbling down cliffs to certain injury or even death. Needless to say, children and/or pets should not go. On our visit, we double-checked our directions with a resident of one of the cottages, who sternly cautioned us about the dangers of the site. He specifically warned us about the crevices covered with vegetation.

Getting to the dun entrance requires crossing a narrow neck of land onto a promontory that's just large enough for the dun. This impressive location high on the cliffs makes it dangerous. The interior of the dun is filled with vegetation, so we couldn't see where to step or where the cliff gave way to the sea. The only remaining visible wall stands at the entrance. All other walls or even the remnants of them are either gone or covered with vegetation. It was scary and perhaps even thrilling to look down the steep cliffs into the sea. The calm pools of water at their base reflecting various shades of green and blue in the afternoon sunlight seemed to mock the danger. We could only imagine the terror of a storm here.

The wall of the dun stands 15 feet thick and still about 12 feet at its highest point. A huge lintel, two feet high in the shape of a trapezoid, spanning the opening by three feet, crowns the entryway. The roof of the entry passage extends about 12 feet. A flashlight is handy for exploring the stonework. Both ends of the front wall have fallen into the sea.

Our friend at the top who cautioned us about the danger of this place also told us that dun is pronounced "doon" as in "sand dune." However, in other cases, the "done" pronunciation is correct as in Dunvegan.

To get there: *From Elgol, an unmarked road leads to*

Glasnakille, just past the newly constructed set of cement block toilets near the new community center. A sign points the way to Glasnakille. The road winds up and over the Strathaird peninsula to the other side. Turn right at Glasnakille and drive for about a half mile through a small valley to a white cottage on the right. Both sides of the road will be fenced at this point. Park off the road and follow the seaward side fence back the direction you came until it ends at a stile. Here, the fence turns down toward the sea. Don't cross the stile, but very carefully make your way down the steep slope, following the fence and keeping it to your right. In June it was even more hazardous because the ground was slippery. Eventually a stile at the bottom corner of the fence appears. However, keep walking straight ahead and slightly to the left, through a small clump of silver birch trees. Soon, the cliff and dun will come into view.

Dun Beag ★★

Dun Beag occupies a special place in our hearts as it was our first Scottish broch. This broch is also one of four or five best preserved in western Scotland, out of about 500 brochs in the country. But, at first, we couldn't find it! We didn't know where to look and must have driven by several times before we finally spotted it high up a steep hill. We had overlooked both the car park and a small sign. On our first trip, this experience underscored the value of good maps.

As an unmonitored Historic Scotland site open all the time, Dun Beag is one of the easier Skye brochs to explore. About 2,000 years old, Dun Beag's walls, once rising to 40 or 50 feet, have been reduced to approximately 10 feet at the highest and 9 to 12 feet thick. The galleried walls are constructed as hollow and double drystone (without mortar). The inner court forms an exact circle entered via only one door (on the east). Door checks, still visible, locked the door with a wooden bar.

A guard chamber opening to the interior leads off to the right of the doorway. Very well-preserved stairs climb inside the galleried walls.

Standing on the walls we could easily see the double-wall construction, now filled with rubble. We could also faintly detect remains of outbuildings around the outside of the walls. According to Historic Scotland, people lived at Dun Beag until the 18th century, a 2,000-year occupation!

On both visits, March and June, we were the only visitors. We experienced the dun and its surroundings in the early morning light on one trip and the late mid-summer sun on another. Both times the majesty of the countryside awed us. From the top of the broch walls looking toward the sea loch and its headlands, the view rivaled travel posters of Scotland.

To get there: *The broch is off the A863, a half mile to a mile west of Bracadale. Bracadale is near the single track B885. Or, alternatively, it's about eight miles southeast of Dunvegan very close to Struan. The broch is on the north side of the road, the car park is on the south side. Watch for it. At the car park going west, the broch is behind your right shoulder, high up on a rocky knoll, appearing quite a distance away. However, once you have spotted it, it's quite obvious. It looks like a bit of a castle on top of its hill. And it isn't that far, but it is uphill and good walking shoes are useful. The wet grass can be very slippery.*

Cnoc Ullinish Souterrain

This was our first opportunity to see a souterrain, an ancient structure we'd only read about. Souterrains are tunnels or subterranean passages lined with stone. Some archaeologists think they were places of refuge, while others believe they were used to store food and supplies. Perhaps they had a ritual use. No one knows for

Entrance to Cnoc Ullinish

Souterrain interior

sure.

In 1773, Dr. Samuel Johnson visited Cnoc Ullinish during his famous highland journey. He described the place as "a specimen of the houses of the aborigines."

When we visited in June, the ground was still quite damp, making an inspection of the souterrain more difficult. The very low lintel of the dark entry required us to squat and duckwalk with flashlights. After about seven feet into the structure, the 20-foot passage became filled with mud, halting any forward progress unless we wanted to crawl on our stomachs in the mud. A chamber was visible at the end of the tunnel. The entire passage was lined with stones including a well-constructed stone roof.

To get there: Cnoc Ullinish is very close to Dun Beag broch. In fact, our guidebook recommended we park our car at the Dun Beag car park. The souterrain is about ½ mile down the road to Ullinish. Look for a gate leading into the field on the right on the way to Ullinish. Because no one was around, we parked off the road next to this gate. The space is only big enough for one car. At this gate a small sign points to the souterrain; it's easy to miss. Go through the gate and walk ahead toward the rocky knoll. Upon reaching the knoll, keep to the right and follow along the base of it. Walk for about a hundred yards until the side of the knoll becomes a cliff with a rocky face. The entrance to the souterrain is about 12 feet downhill from the face of the cliff. Look for a shallow depression or hollow in the ground. A plaque is located near the depression. The depression slopes down to the souterrain entrance. The souterrain was a bit tricky to find because vegetation partly filled the slope and entryway. Once we spotted it, however, we recognized it immediately—unmistakably the opening to a man-made underground tunnel.

Cnoc Ullinish Chambered Cairn

This cairn is near both Dun Beag and the Cnoc Ullinish Souterrain. Its entire stone covering has disappeared leaving the interior exposed. Cnoc Ullinish belongs to the round Hebridean group of cairns and probably would have been about 80 feet in diameter and as much as 10 or 12 feet high. Vegetation obscured most of cairn rubble and its perimeter.

Six large boulders about waist high and some smaller stones arranged in a "pear" shape outlined the cairn. The doorway would have been located in the southeast section. Because of the large chamber, we could get a feel for the immensity of these cairns. The location, as in most coastal areas of Skye, provides outstanding vistas of the sea and small nearby islands.

To get there: *From the A863, take the Ullinish road, near the Dun Beag car park toward the Ullinish Lodge Hotel. The road makes a sharp bend to the right at the entrance to the hotel and then heads in a northwesterly direction. Watch the mileage carefully, looking for a mound on the left after a quarter mile. The cairn is hard to see from the road due to the vegetation. It is off the road about 30 feet or so and necessitates climbing a barbed wire fence.*

Vatten Chambered Cairns

From the road, the two Vatten cairns look like huge piles of rocks. Although these cairns have been used over the centuries to supply rock to the surrounding crofts, they are still enormous. It is hard to believe that ancient people carried all the stones by hand to build them. Some of the large kerb stones remain, but most stones are fairly round and small. The southern cairn has been robbed substantially, verified by the large center depression. Despite this, the cairn soars well over six feet.

To get there: *The cairns lie off the A863 north of Dun Beag. As you follow the A863 north, go through Caroy. The cairns stand on the left or west, on the side of a hill just after the Feorlig road turns left. You can park just beyond the cairns at a gate leading into the field. In June, the ground around the cairns was marshy.*

Duntulm ✷

Duntulm Castle, or rather what's left of it, clings precariously to a cliff at the very top of the Trotternish peninsula. Parts of the cliff along with the castle have eroded away into the sea. Duntulm means "the fort on the green grassy headland." This ruin was once a stronghold of the MacDonalds of Sleat. James VI authorized the clan to build their castle here on the site of an earlier fort or dun, so they could help keep the Hebridean chiefs in line. A memorial cairn on the site commemorates this location as the home of bagpiping.

Not much remains of the castle except some walls. One section that looked as if it might have been a gable contains a large hole, possibly a window. Views through this opening down the cliff to the sea and to a small island just offshore are dramatic. A storm would be terrifying! Fencing runs all around the outer edges of the ruin to prevent mishaps on this unstable headland. We visited on a cloudy, windy day, and everything looked rather desolate. Stretching the imagination, it might be possible to visualize this castle as it once was, a palatial building visited by royalty.

Like most castles in Scotland, Duntulm Castle also has its stories and its tragedies. In the 1700s, a nursemaid accidentally dropped the laird's infant son out of a window to his death below. To punish her, she was set adrift at sea in an open boat full of holes. The family left the castle for good after 1730.

To get there: *Follow the A855 north of Staffin and around the tip to the west side. The coastal vistas are lovely, and the castle can't be missed, easily seen from the main road as it rises grimly out of its rock pinnacle. It is well signposted.*

Uig Standing Stone

Also called the Uig (pronounced "oo-ig") High Stone, this Bronze Age monument was not very impressive except for superb views across the sea to the Western Isles. The one remaining standing stone is not tall, about five feet high and square in shape. A stump of another can be seen a few feet away. The current standing stone has been re-erected in its socket.

To get there: *Take the A856, or the Portree to Uig road. Approaching Uig from the south, about a mile before the road heads down toward the village, a house sits next to a school on the right near a 40 mph speed sign. Just south of the house, uphill from it, is an old dock once used to load animals on trucks. Park next to the dock and go through the iron gate to its right. Head right and up the rather steep hill, about 100 yards, aiming toward the power pole on top. Once at the top, you'll see the stones on a raised mound.*

Dun Gerashader

This Iron Age dun resembles a promontory fort, with some key differences. First, it does not stand on an ocean promontory and, second, it is huge, measuring about 90 by 100 feet. Access is easy, but the hilly ground can be wet and muddy, depending on the time of year.

Approaching Dun Gerashader, we could see remnants of a massive wall about 14 feet high and 14 to 15 feet thick. The main wall contains some enormous stones. Rows of large boulders run parallel with the wall just in front of it. The rocks possibly formed obstacles to protect the fort against attackers. On an upper terrace, rock formed a rectangular enclosure, perhaps a hall. Due to the jumble of stone, we had difficulty finding the two entrances on the east and west. The easiest way into the fort is from the east. Once inside, we could detect parts of a light wall along the cliff edge.

To get there: *Dun Gerashader is located about a mile north of Portree off the A855 up on a ridge to the east just before a minor road toward Torvaig. We pulled onto the Torvaig road and parked at a wide spot off the road near the intersection of the A855. The fort is clearly visible on its high ridge just south of the Torviag road. To get to the fort, you may have to jump across a stream or two, depending on the time of year and your route up. The ground was marshy even in June. Cliffs protect the west, north and south sides of the fort, so it must be approached from the east. Follow the base of the ridge in a southeasterly direction until it's possible to climb the hill. It isn't easy, but it is manageable.*

Clachan Erisco Standing Stones ✱

Clachan Erisco should be called the lazy person's monument. We could examine these standing stones without leaving the car.

Three stones form a curve running parallel with the road. Two of them reached about 4 ½ feet and the third about a foot shorter. They may have once formed part of a large circle, because large monoliths that might have come from a circle have been found in a nearby wall.

To get there: *These stones stand in the little community of Borve, southeast of where River Snizort enters Loch Snizort Beag. An unmarked road on the east leads to Borve off the A856, just northwest of the A850 intersection. Follow this road until you reach a T. Turn right and follow the road for a short distance until the stones appear on the right just off the pavement. It is nearly impossible to miss them.*

St. Columba's Island ✱

St. Columba's Island, near Skeabost, was a holy place from the Dark Ages at least until late medieval times. This secluded site affords an opportunity to experience Skye's medieval past in contrast to its abundant prehistory.

The legendary St. Columba may well have founded this ancient Christian settlement that bears his name. From 1079 through the 1499, the Bishops of the Southern and Western Isles maintained a small cathedral here. Its cruciform outline can still be traced. In 1499, the Lords of the Isles, patrons of the cathedral, lost their power. The seat of the bishops moved to Iona, and this site lost its importance. The island also contains the ruin of a small 16th century chapel. Pre-medieval and medieval graveslabs are scattered in the grounds. One particularly excellent carved gravestone depicts a warrior with sword. Interpretive signs provide additional information.

To get there: *Take the A850 to the minor road south to Skeabost that leads to the village of Skeabost. Just a short way east of this intersection, a road on the north side of the A850 leads to the village hall, just west of the River Snizort. Getting to the Skeabost House is easy, but we got confused finding the island and drove through Skeabost House property a couple of times before we figured it out. We finally parked across the highway from the entrance to the Skeabost House Hotel drive, and walked. Trees framed the drive entrance and the vegetation grew thick. Just to the right of the hotel drive, a gated road leads to an old stone bridge across the river. Go through the gates, cross the bridge, and follow the path to a new bridge that crosses to the island.*

Dun Suledale

We enjoyed our trek across empty moorland to get to Dun Suledale. This dun is one of Skye's better preserved brochs, crowning the hill of a remote area where tourists rarely venture.

Dun Suledale's outside walls rise more than seven feet high, but fallen stones and weeds clutter the inside. Fairly well-preserved stairs ascend to a height of about four feet. We found the remains of a guard cell and a few places where the hollow walls were not completely filled in with rubble. Standing on the walls of the broch we could see for miles around. Only a few crofts dotted the empty landscape.

<u>To get there:</u> *Follow the A850 on its way from Portree to Dunvegan. About seven miles out of Portree, the road bends to the left and away from Loch Snizort. A road to the left leads to the village of Suledale (on the Ordnance Survey map it was spelled Suladale). About a mile beyond Suledale, a track marked on the OS map heads off to the left or south. Park on the old road that runs parallel to the modern A850, walk across the A850 to the gate and go through (we climbed over). Follow this track south for about a mile when the broch should come into view. The track is a fairly level, easy walk following a fence on the left for much of the way. After about a mile, ahead and to the left, the broch appeared on top of a knoll. When we were roughly alongside the broch, the fence ended. Leaving the track, we made our way as best we could up and down hills, across rough moorland, over a small stream, trying to keep the broch in sight. We probably crossed two gullies in very marshy terrain where we wished we had worn good waterproof boots. It took us about two hours for the whole excursion.*

Dun Fiadhairt ★★

We remember the hike to Dun Fiadhairt as one of our most pleasant. The dun survives in excellent condition and provides outstanding views of Loch Dunvegen and the opposite peninsula. Galleys of Norse and Islesmen plied these waters centuries ago. They might have monitored traffic on the loch from Dun Fiadhairt. To think that the dun stood as a silent watchman over such events (old even in those times) gives one a sense of the extensive history of this area. Dun Fiadhairt is an Iron Age broch. One of its unusual features is the rare double entry similar to the one at Clickhimin in Shetland.

We were disappointed at our first glimpse of the broch, because it looked like a pile of rocks with no structure. But once inside, we found that first impression to be misleading. Its double-wall construction is conspicuous, and we could walk around in the cavity between the walls, although fighting ferns all the way. A few years ago, the broch was cleared of vegetation, which sadly has grown back with a vengeance. The broch's two entrances are usable, and the guard cells on either side of the main entrance remain in good condition. The center of the broch contains foundation remnants of a structure built after the broch. Six stairs lead to an upper level. We are consistently amazed at the excellent condition of stairs in these ancient brochs. It is possible to walk around on the top of the broch, but care is required because of loose stones

To get there: *Take the A850 north out of Dunvegan. Drive past Dunvegan Castle, its huge car park complete with attendants, teashop and gift shop. Later you may want to stop for tea or lunch as we did. You may even want to visit the castle, the ancient home of the MacLeods, although much modified over the years. Today, the castle swarms with tourists. If coaches come this far north on Skye, Dunvegen Castle is a requisite visit for them.*

One and ½ miles beyond the castle, cross the bridge spanning the tiny Loch Suarda. Just after the bridge, look to the left for a large area to park. We climbed over the locked gate at the west side of the parking area and followed the path. It's a 20- to 30-minute walk out, but the terrain is not rugged. The path soon disappears and becomes ruts created by a tractor. At the stone fence or enclosure, take the track to the right and proceed up and over the hill. Going out, we mistakenly took the left fork and went around the other way, making the walk a bit longer. Our Ordnance Survey map provided a good deal of security. To get to the broch, it is necessary to cross a small isthmus with two little bays on either side. At this

*point, we could see the broch ahead on the other side.
After crossing the isthmus, walk up the track for a couple
hundred yards and then veer to the right, going over the
small hill. At the top, Dun Fiadhairt reappears. Marshy
ground could be a problem here, but in June we found
the terrain fairly dry. As happens so frequently in Scotland, we didn't encounter anyone else.*

Dun Hallin

Our tour of Dun Hallin was more invigorating than
we bargained for due to wind and Skye's continual mist
as well as a substantial uphill climb. Dun Hallin on its
rocky hill commands a superlative view of Loch Bay and
Dunvegen Head across Loch Dunvegen. That day, mist
shrouded Dunvegen Head, offering a dark contrast to
the green hills below us. Off in the distance we could
just barely detect the Uists of the Western Isles.

Besides the scenic beauty all around, this broch has
a charm all its own. Dun Hallin is the best-preserved
broch on the peninsula. Only Dun Beag has the distinction of being better preserved on the whole of Skye.

Dun Hallin's entrance is in the southeast. The interior is filled with rubble from the broch walls that unfortunately also obscures the broch's guard cells, wall cavi-
ties and steps. However, the condition of the outer walls
made the uphill trek worth the trouble. They tower more
than 12 feet on some sides. The stones are all purposely
shaped into squares and rectangles. The lower courses
are very large, and progressively become smaller the
higher the wall goes. It is also easy to see the inward
taper of the outer walls. Early people took a lot of care in
constructing Dun Hallin, yet another example of Iron
Age craftsmanship. Outside the broch, walls of an outer
defense can be detected.

To get there: *Take the B886 north from the A850, about
three miles east of Dunvegan. Watch for the signs to Stein*

and Geary. Turn onto the B886, and pass the Fairy Bridge where three rivers and three roads meet, and, according to legend, a MacLeod chief parted forever from his fairy wife. Drive for about four miles until reaching a T-junction with the left going to the little town of Stein. Turn right and drive to the village of Hallin. The broch is clearly visible from the village off to the right (east) at the top of a hill. Drive through Hallin and continue on for about half a mile. When you reach a long white house on the left and a long asphalt drive on the right (house numbers 16 and 17), turn up the drive and park at the end of it.

After parking, walk straight ahead, past the home on the right and across the field ahead. Go through the gate in the corner. Cross a steam and keep it more or less to your left with the fence on your right. Follow the fence up the hill. The broch remains in view most of the hike up. Go through the rusty gate at the top of the field and continue on up to the broch's mound. Once you reach the hilltop, because of the steepness, climbing up to the broch itself is a bit challenging, especially if the ground is wet.

Trumpan Church ✶

Trumpan Church, a late medieval church, sadly bears witness to the tragedy of real highland life. It occupies a position high above the Little Minch not far from Waternish Point, the northernmost point on the peninsula. In fact, when our ferry passed Waternish on its way from Uig, Skye, to Lochmaddy on North Uist, we could just barely distinguish Trumpan Church in the distance.

The church stands as a shell, roofless with most of the south wall gone. Walls that remain are about a yard thick. The fenced-off east end or altar end contains graves. The only windows include a narrow window in the east wall and another in the easternmost part of the north wall. The door is in the north wall.

Two unusual features made Trumpan particularly

memorable. Coins filled a hollowed-out stone in the northwest corner of the church. Most were British, apparently there for years. And, on the outside southwest corner, an old, illegible information plaque contained a faint outline of a bishop. We had no idea what either of these objects represented.

At the time of our visit, we knew nothing of the church's history. Nevertheless, we had a sense of sadness and gloom. We later learned the tragic story of Trumpan Church. In the late 1500s, the MacDonalds of South Uist attacked worshipping Macleods, burning the congregation to death inside the church. One woman cut off a breast to escape through one of the tiny windows. She warned the rest of the Macleods who slaughtered the MacDonalds before they got away. So much for the romance of highland life!

<u>To get there:</u> *After Dun Hallin, continue on the same road past Hallin north. A little over a mile, the road bends sharply to the right, giving a superb view of Ardmore Bay and its small peninsula below. After the right bend, drive a little farther and at the top of a hill on the right stand the Trumpan Church ruins.*

The Northwest Highlands

The majestic unpopulated Northwest Highlands of Scotland lure Scots when they want to get away from it all. The scenic beauty of the rugged coastline, mountains, lochs, glens and rivers, as well as more urbane attractions like the Inverewe Gardens, provide superb recreation. Not only Scots find this area appealing. While driving near the Atlantic coast, we encountered our first tourists from the Continent who didn't know how to drive the one-lane roads!

Glenelg Brochs: Dun Troddan and Dun Telve ★★★

Anyone interested in the brochs of Iron Age Scotland should make the effort to visit the two Glenelg brochs, Dun Troddan and Dun Telve, located in Lochalsh, east across the kyles from Skye. While their location is not convenient to the main routes, the countryside makes for a scenic side trip. Other than Mousa and Dun Carloway, few other Scottish brochs remain in such excellent condition. The brochs' setting, state of preservation and workmanship all combine to give the visitor a taste of Iron Age life.

Located in a narrow, wooded glen, the brochs are so huge they are impossible to miss. There's something really awesome when such structures suddenly loom up. Just imagine how the primitive people must have felt, especially when the brochs reached their original size!

Less than half of both brochs still stand but enough for visitors to visualize the complete brochs. We drove first to the farthest broch, Dun Troddan, a short distance down the road from the Dun Telve. Historic Scot-

Dun Telve

Double-wall construction, Dun Telve

land cares for both sites, so they are well maintained with fences and excellent interpretive signs.

Dun Troddan is not complete as Dun Telve, but still impressive. We estimated the remaining wall to be about 30 feet high. Going around to the back of Dun Troddan and looking up at the outer wall gives a better sense of its height. Dun Telve's wall must be about 40 feet high. The outside surface walls of both brochs are remarkably smooth and symmetrical. This is especially amazing when no mortar was used to hold the stones together.

Stairs and galleries fit snugly inside the hollow walls. The fact that people trod these very same stones 2,000 years ago never ceases to thrill us. Although Historic Scotland has done some work to ensure that the brochs don't topple, most stones look original.

To get there: *We approached Glenelg by way of the Kylerhea ferry, because we were staying in Broadford on Skye. We drove to Kylerhea via the spectacular and mountainous Glen Arroch road. The Kylerhea ferry, incidentally, is the only turntable ferry in Scotland. It holds about six cars or so and operates only in the summer months. While we waited at the ferry landing, we watched the small ferryboat fight its way across the strong current of Kyle Rhea. The trip takes about 15 minutes. An alternative and more direct route is to take the road west out of Shiel Bridge off the A87 to Glenelg.*

We drove through Glenelg village past the old gutted 18th century Glenelg Hanovarian barracks, built to keep the rebellious highlanders under control. The road forks at Eilenreach, and the brochs lie straight ahead off the left fork a short way up the tree-covered Glen Beg. Because there are no car parks, we had to park in turnouts off the road as much as possible. The road ends a couple of miles farther on, so most people who drive it are visiting the brochs.

The Eagle Stone ★

Strathpeffer is filled with large Victorian homes and hotels dating from the days when Victorians came here to take the waters. Once a bustling spa town, it now looks a bit like an elegant lady the morning after the ball. Besides a very pronounced Victorian flavor, Strathpeffer is home to the Eagle Stone, a 7th century Pictish symbol stone. The accessibility of this Class I stone (created by the Picts before they were converted to Christianity) with clear carvings makes it a "must see" for travelers in the area. Class of stone refers to the method by which art historians categorize these stones.

The stone stands just a few feet tall in a field near Eaglestone House. One of its faces pictures an eagle and a horseshoe, two of about 45 possible Pictish symbols.

This particular site is not the original location of the Eagle Stone. And, it is no haphazard occurrence that its base is embedded in concrete. The stone came to Strathpeffer from lower in the valley where, according to local tradition, it marked the graves of Munro clansmen killed in a battle. The most widespread legend relates to the famous 17ᵗʰ century Brachan seer who prophesied that if the stone fell three times, boats could sail to Strathpeffer and anchor at the stone. The stone has fallen twice so far.

To get there: *Take the A835 to the A834 and drive to the village of Strathpeffer. It is opposite the Ben Wyvis Hotel and well signposted.*

Urquhart Castle ★★★

Urquhart Castle (pronounced "urk urt"), one of Scotland's most visited tourist attractions, stands on a promontory overlooking famed Loch Ness. Urquhart's condition, its place in Scottish history and its commanding location on cliffs above Loch Ness place it in a class with Edinburgh and Stirling castles.

We couldn't have asked for a better day for our first visit. The cloudless blue sky and warm sun provided a splendid backdrop for the green hills and the loch's peat-blackened water. We heard bagpipe music as we approached Urquhart's sprawling remains, after our long walk down a steep hill from the entrance to the grounds. A piper had positioned himself in the second story of what had once been the gatehouse, giving a stirring, if touristy, welcome!

We were fortunate. Not only were we blessed with good weather, we had the castle mostly to ourselves. Tour groups had gone on to hotels and dinner.

A stone causeway and a modern bridge where a drawbridge once stood give access over a deep, wide defensive ditch. The entryway leads into a passageway between the bases of the two towers of the gatehouse. The north lodge in the gatehouse contained a prison cell. This cramped little cell must have been miserable, particularly with the constable's latrines just above.

The upper bailey is the oldest part of the castle lo-

Urquhart Castle

cated to the right on the highest hill. Only the wall stubs of this section remain, but the position provides an excellent view of the entire castle precinct. Vitrified rock from an Iron Age fort found around the summit proves that this site was used for defense for at least 2,000 years.

Between the upper bailey on the south end and the lower or nether bailey in the north, the grounds narrow in the center so that the castle walls form a shape like the letter B with the straight side against the landward ditch. The east wall contains the water gate. That gate leads downward to a beach where ships unloaded supplies in safety. Before the Caledonian Canal was built, the water was six feet lower than today. This would have made the castle appear even higher above the water.

Remaining foundations of the chapel occupy a prominent low hill in the nether bailey, while closer to the loch, low walls are all that are left of buildings once the center of castle life. Only the basement of the great hall remains where food and drink were stored for the banquets.

The private residence of the lord survives as the best preserved and most familiar structure of the complex. Most of this tower was built in the 16th century and parts of the parapet in the 17th century. The tower house rises over four stories high in the northeastern section of the nether bailey. The massive north and east curtain walls butted into the west and south walls of the tower house so that the thick base of the tower formed part of the outside defense. Even inside the castle walls, the tower house was planned with defense in mind. A deep ditch surrounds it and stone corbels jut out above from the walls. These corbels likely held a platform to allow defenders to fire down on invaders.

The tower entryway opens into the lord's dining and reception hall. From the hall, a turnpike stair leads down to the basement and a postern gate. Another stair leads upward to the rest of the tower. It is possible to climb all the way to the top passing what were once the private chambers of the lord and others. At the very top, we enjoyed the fine view of Loch Ness and surrounding hills, much like lords and ladies of the past. The strains from the great highland bagpipes provided a fitting backdrop.

A castle likely existed here during the time of King William the Lion in the 12th century. The style would have been motte and bailey, consisting of two baileys with the rock as its motte or high part. The current castle was begun in 1229 by Alan Durward, Justiciar of Scotland, one of the most powerful men in the country at the time. Unfortunately, he ruthlessly exploited his lands.

Urquhart has many associations with Scotland's Wars of Independence. Edward I took the castle in 1296 and although some believe he built the gatehouse, it was probably erected at a later date. Edward captured the castle with more difficulty a second time in 1303, and, five years later, Robert the Bruce's forces recovered it.

Even Edward III tried to capture Urquhart. In the late 1300s, the castle served as a royal stronghold to keep the Lords of the Isles and the MacDonald clan from becoming too powerful. Nevertheless, the MacDonalds managed to seize the castle four times, pillaging the surrounding countryside. Covenanters inflicted considerable damage on Urquhart in 1644, so badly damaging it that Cromwell did not even try to garrison it when he conquered Scotland. The last fighting at Urquhart took place in 1689 when a Hanoverian garrison beat off a small Jacobite force. Highland troops of Protestant monarchs, William and Mary, blew up the gatehouse in 1692 before finally abandoning the castle.

To get there: *Urquhart Castle lies 17 miles southwest of Inverness on the west side of Loch Ness. It is reached from the A82, at the village of Strone, southeast of Drumnadrochit. Just follow the crowds!*

Strome Castle

We visited Strome Castle, standing atop a picturesque, rocky outcrop jutting into Loch Carron, because we had read about excavations sponsored by the National Trust for Scotland in 1994. Not many artifacts were recovered, although archaeologists discovered that the castle had been modified many times. The fact that the National Trust owns it is also unusual, because the Trust normally owns tracts of land or rebuilt castles and manor houses, not ruins like Strome.

No one knows much about the early history of Strome Castle, except that it belonged to the Lords of the Isles, one of their strongholds from at least 1472. In 1602, Kenneth Mackenzie, Lord of Kintail, laid siege and then blew the castle to pieces. Other than normal wear and tear due to time and weather, it hasn't changed since then. Large pieces of toppled wall project from the surrounding water.

Strome Castle probably once included a hall and a tower. Today, the only major structures are parts of the north and west walls. The base of the keep can be identified under an enormous pile of rubble. The grass is kept short by grazing sheep, so everything is visible. We found a good interpretive sign on the path up to the castle. We visited on a sunny, warm day and could see across Loch Carron to the Isle of Skye.

To get there: *Follow the A896 to the village of Lochcarron. A minor road heads southwest, following the north shoreline of Loch Carron. This road leads through the village of Slumbay and eventually past the castle. The castle is signposted.*

Ardvreck Castle

Ardvreck Castle, built in 1597, is one of the few ancient monuments in this remote portion of the Northwest Highlands. It also has associations with Montrose, gallant supporter of Charles I in 1643. Montrose may have been betrayed to the government by Ardvreck's Macleod laird. Whatever the truth, he was imprisoned here before being taken to Edinburgh for execution.

The castle occupies a small peninsula in Loch Assynt. Only a fraction of the castle remains. Its gaunt and dangerous crumbling stone walls stand about three stories high. The stubs of wall are badly ravaged, making it difficult to identify the castle's layout. An undercroft appeared to be the best-preserved section.

To get there: *This castle is one of the most accessible. It lies just off the A894 north of Ullapool. There is plenty of space to park on the west side of the road where the loch and castle are located.*

Beauly Priory

Along with both Ardchatten and Pluscarden abbeys, Beauly Priory shares the distinction of once belonging to the French Valliscaulian order, an order that existed nowhere else in Britain. Sir John Bisset, the lord of Aird, founded Beauly in 1230. Beauly means "beautiful place," a designation endorsed by Mary Queen of Scots, who visited in 1564. Beauly is known for its elegant stonework. Robert Reid, who served as prior during the middle 1500s, rebuilt the tall lancet windows in the west wall of the nave. Most of the church's windows show evidence of fine carving even though the stone tracery has been lost to time and elements. At our visit, stonemasons were repairing the building's red stone structure smoothed by centuries of wind and rain.

Over the years several important families like the Frasers of Lovat maintained Beauly, so the priory incurred relatively little damage, especially during the Reformation. Even so, only the nearly intact shell of the roofless church still stands.

Priory buildings occupied the space south of the church, a clue to their whereabouts being the door to the monks' night stair in the south wall of the south transept. The church plan consists of the usual cross with nave, choir and transepts. However, its original plan may have been a rectangle, because the transepts are accessible only through a door in the wall of the church. The north transept may have served as a separate chapel and the south transept might originally have been part of the cloister buildings. Both transepts are considered chapels.

Graves now fill the nave, choir, and presbytery. The north transept is blocked off to the public. A second story and a stair were added to the north transept in the 15th century so it appears more complex than the rest of the church. It serves as a burial place for the Mackenzie family. Sir Kenneth Mackenzie of Kintail (d.1491) is buried in the tomb next to the door leading into the transept. Prior Mackenzie was interred in a tomb near the door to the south transept.

Two interesting and important features of the church have been preserved. In the east wall, behind the spot for the high altar, remains of a twin aumbry (cupboard recess), where the consecrated bread was kept, still exist. A double piscina, or wash basin, survives in the south wall.

To get there: *The priory is located in the heart of Beauly just off the A862. We parked in the car park for shoppers at the west end of the church.*

The Nigg Stone and Church ★

We visited remote little Nigg Church looking for a carved Pictish stone. To our delight, the church itself and adjacent graveyard provided treasures we hadn't expected.

No one knows for sure when Nigg Church was built. However, reference was made to it when its parson, John of Dunbretan, swore allegiance to King Edward of England in 1296.

An important religious movement started here in 1739 that eventually influenced all of northern Scotland. Lay preachers known as "the men" characterized this movement. Some of these were reputed to have supernatural powers.

The graveyard contains a fascinating collection of stones. A 1679 box tomb of Marie Urquhart and John Grant displays some intricate carving. A table stone carved by the legendary Hugh Millar is easy to find by looking for the scalloped edge on top. A stone with Gaelic verses is located in the north end. The parish spoke Gaelic until the 20th century. A sign marks the spot of the "Cholera Stone," a legend dating to the cholera epidemic of 1832 when an elder saw a cloud of vapor hovering just above the ground. He believed this to be cholera and immediately threw a blanket over it, later erecting the stone to keep the cholera from getting out. The famous Nigg stone stood for centuries in a small porch at the east end of the church until a gale blew it over and split it. Now it's kept inside at the west end of the church in its own separate room. The reddish Class II stone (carved after the Picts converted to Christianity) stands about six feet high and three feet wide. The cross side portrays figures of St. Anthony and St. Paul in the desert. Although the carving is somewhat worn, we could easily differentiate the figures. The other side of the stone has Pictish symbols, a horseman, an eagle, a harp and a sheep.

Interesting features inside the church include communion tables, the precantor's desk and the pulpit. An illegal still was reportedly kept under the pulpit!

To get there: The little village of Nigg hardly seems like a village at all with few homes or other structures. It sits on the east side of Nigg bay in the very eastern part of Easter Ross. We took the B9175 off the A9 and headed south toward the Cromarty ferry. Just past the village of Pitcalnie, we took the first unmarked road to the left. Approaching Nigg going south, the church is located on the right side of the road at a little turn off just past a building (possibly a school) that looks like a church. The small space at the gate can hold only two or three cars. Nestled in amongst the trees behind its moss-covered wall, the church is hard to see. We drove right past the entrance the first time.

Carn Liath ★

Anyone driving along the Dornoch Firth on the A9 can explore this typical Sutherland broch. Not only is it in excellent condition, Carn Liath stands right off the road. We explored it on our way north to Wick.

Like other brochs, Carn Liath dates to about the 1st

*Cairn Liath entrance and
lintel stone*

century BC or AD and was occupied for at least four or
five centuries. Today, the 20- to 30-feet thick walls reach
what was once the second floor. Around it cluster the
remains of a settlement. Some restoration occurred, evident in the reddish brown color of upper courses of rock
wall. White lichen covering earlier rocks has not yet taken
hold on the restored parts. The stairway inside the wall
remains intact to the second floor. The entrance to it on
the first floor still retains its rock ceiling. A great lintel
rests above the doorway and much of the entry passage
is covered.

Because the broch occupies a knoll, views of the sea
are superb. The hills to the west of the broch had patches
of brown in June, probably heather that will turn the
hills a vivid purple in fall. Green grass and yellow gorse
intermixed with the brown contributed additional color.

From the broch, looking south, we could see Dunrobin
Castle as well as the statue of the wretched Earl of
Sutherland, infamous for his role in Highland clearances.
He became one of the wealthiest landowners in the Brit-
ish Isles. Controversy rages about whether or not to re-
move the statue or keep it as a reminder of the area's

history.

To get there: *The broch is located on the seaward side of the A9, just three miles northeast of Golspie. The car park is on the opposite side of the highway, and slightly south from the broch. It seems a little confusing because a sign gives directions to the car park on one side of the road when the broch is clearly visible on the other side. Park at the south end of the car park. Signs direct you to a crossing over the A9 and to a path leading to the broch. It is just a short hike.*

The Grey Cairns of Camster ★★★

The color grey could not be more descriptive of the day we visited this remarkable monument. The rain fell lightly on the vast grey moors, and a cold breeze whipped against us. From the car park, the grey cairns against a grey horizon rose out of the landscape as great piles of grey rock. One of them, the long cairn, resembled an alligator or other reptile with its humps. We could see tiny dark doors leading into the cairns. Well-kept boardwalks marched across the soggy moor to each monument.

A sign erected by Historic Scotland explains that these cairns are the best-preserved chamber tombs in Britain. They were recently excavated and restored to show visitors what they actually looked like 5000 years ago when the climate and soil supported farming and raising of stock. In the distance, behind the cairns, trees planted by the forestry commission demarcate the moorland. Trees were common in Neolithic times, providing nutrients and stability for the soil, but the increasing cold and rain destroyed them, causing erosion and loss of soil.

We first toured the nearest cairn, the round one and older of the two. This nearly intact cairn stands more than 36 feet high and 54 feet in diameter. A grated iron

Camster Long Cairn

Entrance to passage

door keeps livestock and other creatures out, and a long, narrow, low entry passage required us to stoop and duckwalk. A flashlight (torch in Britain) helped, especially because we didn't know what was ahead. The first chamber we entered formed a small antechamber marked by two standing stones. The main burial chamber itself surprised us with light instead of inky blackness. Historic Scotland installed a skylight when repairing damage caused by 1865 antiquarians.

A massive stone slab about four feet wide and five

Forecourt, Camster Long Cairn

feet tall, forms part of the back wall of the main chamber. The dry stone walls rise to standing height at which point each layer overlaps inward to form the roof. This technique is called *corbelling*. The ancient people did not know how to make arches, so corbels were used instead. At the very top of the cairn, before the layers of corbelling meet, the roof was capped by a huge capstone. Standing stones guard both sides of the chamber entrance and form part of the walls. A large lintel stone tops the doorway.

The long cairn, although not as old as the round cairn, incorporates two earlier round cairns visible as humps along the top. Therefore, it has two entrances and two passageways. The entrance and passage to the left when facing the cairn is somewhat larger and shorter, so, it's a little easier to explore. A hat helps protect against bumps and scrapes when ducking through the low passageway roof. These are not places for people with claustrophobia!

The building techniques inside the long cairn's two chambers are similar to the round cairn. The chamber on the right was built first. A bend in the passage of this chamber marks the end of the original round cairn exterior. Both chambers contain skylights.

The forecourts on either end of the long cairn were probably used for ceremonies honoring the dead. Ancient priests might have stood on one of these platforms, chanting incantations toward the heavens, trying to understand the mysteries of life and death.

<u>To get there:</u> *Just a short way east of Lybster south of Wick, a sign on the A99 marks the road to the cairns. Take this unmarked one-lane road for five miles. The car park for the cairns is just off the road. A sign, probably erected by a local farmer, cautions drivers to watch for lambs. When we visited in June, ewes and lambs ranged freely, crossing and even lying in the road.*

Hill O' Many Stanes ★

This mysterious 4,000-year-old Bronze Age site consists of at least 200 stones (stanes) in 22 fan-shaped rows on the slope of a small hill. The stones run north to south, although the hill is oriented to the east and overlooks the North Sea. About 50 stones have been lost over the past 100 years. At one time, 600 of these knee-high stones may have completed the pattern. Driving to or from Wick, the site is easy to reach and one that has no parallel in all of Scotland.

Other sites similar to this one have been discovered only in Caithness and Sutherland where about 20 have been documented. No one knows why the stones were placed this way. One theory suggests that this hill served as a solar or lunar observatory. Evidence found at other locations implies burial or religious purposes. Whatever the purpose, building this site obviously took a lot of time and work.

<u>To get there:</u> *Take the first road northwest out of Lybster on the A99. Follow this small one-lane road for about a quarter of a mile. The monument is signposted. Once there,*

park in the car park, possibly big enough for two cars, and walk up the hill to the stones.

Sinclair and Girnigoe Castles ✶

The dangerous but spectacular site of the twin castles of Sinclair and Girnigoe made a deep impression on us. Thanks to directions from the local people, we finally found the castles on a part of the windswept coast near the Noss Head lighthouse. Their dramatic setting clearly sets them apart.

We followed some hand-scrawled signs over two stiles and across a field and will never forget our approach to these castles. As we drew nearer the sea, the building tops became visible, looming larger until we reached the crevasses where the castles cling precariously to their pinnacles of rock rising out of the sea. The flat shale rock stacks of the cliffs seem to merge with the stones of the castles. In fact, the castle stones came from the site, especially from the deep moat just in front of the castles that cuts the castles off from the mainland.

Remaining parts of the castles still stand about four or five stories high but the devastation and constant erosion is obvious. We didn't realize just how high and precipitous the cliffs rose until we reached the site.

Construction of Girnigoe, the older of the two castles, began in 1470, most likely occupying the site of an older Viking stronghold that was possibly preceded by a Pictish fort. Little remains of Girnigoe other than a tall chimneystack of rock and a few smaller wall fragments. Once we knew they were two separate castles, we could easily distinguish Sinclair Castle from Girnigoe. Sinclair (pronounced "sync-lar" with emphasis on the first syllable as a contraction of St. Clair) Castle, begun in 1600, is far more complete and characterized by its distinctive reddish sandstone trim at the corners and around the windows. Cannon fire from a 1680 battle destroyed much of the two castles, after which they further decayed.

This site is extremely dangerous. The cliffs fall a long way down to the rocks and sea below. In many places, the sea has eroded the rock, resulting in increasing erosion of the castle walls causing them to collapse into the sea. Attempts are underway to save the remaining structures but all visitors currently tour at their own risk. For example, anyone running full tilt through the front entrance of Sinclair Castle would fall directly onto the rocks below where the floor slopes sharply through a large opening right over the cliff. In addition to dangerous cliffs and falling debris, stinging nettles choke the grounds.

For about 600 years the earls of Caithness, chiefs of the Clan Sinclair held these two castles. The clan originated in 1057 with a William St. Clair, an escort of the Saxon Princess Margaret who came to Scotland to marry King Malcom Canmore. The long succession of Sinclairs included one who fought with King Robert the Bruce and another who discovered Greenland and also reached North America in 1398. Some Sinclairs earned unsavory places in history, such as the earl who imprisoned and tortured his own son to death in this very castle, and still another who was known as the Wicked Earl or Ogre of the North.

The Wick Heritage Centre displays a large model of the castles and provides additional history. Visitors can obtain clear directions and a map to the site.

To get there: *We drove to the castles by a roundabout route. The most direct route would have crossed the airport runway, but that was closed for safety reasons. We eventually took a route through the outskirts of Wick heading toward the Noss Head lighthouse. Just before reaching the locked gate to the lighthouse we found a large car park where we left the car. A handwritten sign pointed over a stile toward the castles, about a quarter of a mile walk toward the sea.*

Old Wick Castle ✶

In contrast to Girnigoe and Sinclair Castles, Historic Scotland cares for Old Wick Castle, resulting in improvements like fences, signs and stabilization work. Nevertheless, the setting is almost as dramatic if not as dangerous. The remaining portion of the tower sits high on the cliffs, another rocky promontory that falls away to the sea far below. A red sign on the gate leading to the castle underscores the danger of the site: "Visitors proceeding beyond this point are advised to exercise extreme caution and stay well back from the cliff edges."

The day we visited Old Wick Castle, the weather turned sunny and warm. On a rainy, windy day, the trek to the site could be nasty. The castle was visible from a long way off appearing like a squat, square tower. Just before we got to the castle, we were surprised to find a concrete guard post with a sign indicating this to be a military firing range. The sign warned visitors to stay out if flags flew. Apparently, at times the site is not accessible.

We later learned that the route we took from the south end of town close to our B&B was not the normal approach. This sunny morning, however, we particularly enjoyed the 20-minute walk to the seacliffs through green fields and pastures filled with wild flowers.

The Earl of Caithness, Harald Maddason, probably built the castle sometime in the late 12th century, making it one of the oldest castles in Scotland. Harald was half Norse and half Scot, and he became the earl of Caithness and Orkney in 1159. He most likely built the castle sometime after that as his main stronghold on the mainland. Some years after Harald, a supporter of the English King Edward I held the castle. Eventually, the castle passed into the hands of the earl of Sutherland.

The castle occupies a peninsula that juts out into the North Sea with deep crevasses on either side. A narrow strip of rock joins this peninsula to the mainland where remnants of a gatehouse and outer rampart can be detected. A drawbridge once spanned the ditch. The lord's tower house with parts of three walls survives as the only major structure. It features a few window openings and scarcements, or ledges, to hold floor beams. A fireplace on the second floor is difficult to see. Farther out on the promontory some grass-covered mounds hide the foundations of the kitchen, bake house, brew house, stables, and other such buildings. No fences give protection to unwary visitors in this section.

While we explored, we could hear the waves breaking on the cliffs below. We wondered what this place would be like at night and in a storm. How many people fell to their deaths here?

To get there: *The regular signposted route to the castle goes through Wick and follows the sea on the east side. Specific directions can be obtained from the Wick Heritage Centre. Our B&B hostess gave us directions for the route we took. We approached the castle from the south, walking from town. As we left the houses, we passed an old cemetery and then a new cemetery. Just beyond the new cemetery, we took a path that headed toward the southeast. It looked as if it would end up south of the castle, but eventually it bent east toward the firing range and castle.*

Cairn O'Get

A walk to Cairn O'Get affords a pleasant stroll across moorlands provided the weather is decent. We recommend this site mostly for the expansive views and the hike out, about a mile or so. Not much remains of the cairn itself. Cairn O'Get is somewhere between 4,500 and 6,000 years old, probably the oldest cairn we've seen.

The roof is gone, but at least this makes it easy to see inside. Under Historic Scotland care, the site displays an information board indicating that this distinctive Caithness type of tomb has "horns" on either end. From the air the cairn would look like a rectangle with concave ends. The horns created forecourts where ceremonies took place. The best way to see the horns is to climb on top of the mound. The horn at the rear is the best preserved. Beware the stinging nettles. The cairn was used for a long time. When excavated in the late 1800s, seven or eight entire human skeletons were discovered on top of a layer of burnt human and animal bones mixed with charcoal, pottery, and other artifacts.

To get there: *Drive to Ulbster on the A9 and then follow the signs to the west along the secondary road. Park off the road in a rather small car park about a quarter mile off the A9. Eight black-and-white posts mark the walk, and the path is easy to follow. We crossed several stiles and followed a well-maintained boardwalk across the boggy portion of the moor, always keeping the marker posts in sight.*

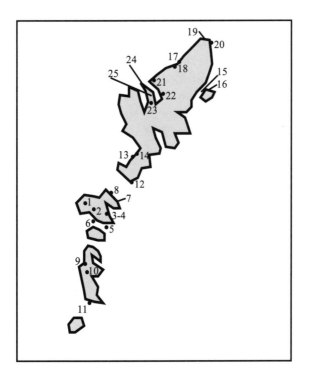

1	Cleitreabhal Stone, Cairn	15	St. Columba's Church
2	Clach Bharnach Bhraodag	16	Dun Bayble
	Standing Stone	17	Clach an Truiseil Standing
3	Pobull Fhinn Stone Circle		Stone
4	Barpa Langass Cairn	18	Steinacleit Cairn, Stone Circle
5	St. Michael's Chapel	19	St. Moluag's Church
6	Trinity Temple	20	Clach Stein Standing Stones
7	Na Fir Bhreige Standing Stones	21	Dun Carolway Broch
8	Dun an Sticir	22	Callanish: Main Site, Cnoc Ceann
9	Howmore		a' Gharraidh, Cnoc Fillibhir
10	Unnamed Dun		Bheag, Ceann Thulabhaig,
11	Pollachar Standing Stone		Stonefield Stone
12	St. Clement's Church	23	Cleiter Standing Stones
13	Borvemore Standing Stone	24	Bernera Iron Age Village
14	Macleod's Stone	25	Dun Bharabhat

Chapter 8
The Western Isles

"Handwoven in the Outer Hebrides" (Dodie's introduction)

For more than 20 years, I'd longed to visit the fabled Outer Hebrides, ever since I'd learned to weave and read about the cottage industry made famous by the Harris tweeds. In fact, long before I knew of the existence of the Uists or Barra, I had heard about Harris and Lewis. To me, these islands were Scotland.

After learning to weave, I took up spinning. Sitting and spinning at my wheel, I would play waulking songs on our old phonograph. Waulking or "chorus" songs are the lively, romantic and perhaps bawdy music sung by women who gathered to finish the Harris tweeds. With this musical introduction it wasn't long until both Jerry and I discovered Scottish Gaelic and Celtic music. This trip to the Western Isles was almost a pilgrimage for me, something for which I had waited many years.

Needless to say, it was with great excitement that I approached the barren rocky island of North Uist on the ferry from Skye. The Uists weren't Harris and Lewis, but they were close enough.

North Uist

We chose to go to the Uists because we were in the vicinity, not necessarily for any archaeological or even nostalgic reason. However, as soon as we made the decision to go, we began to read about numerous prehistoric sites on these islands. We were not prepared for the exquisite and unusual beauty that greeted us. Had we been, we would have allowed more time in this southern portion of the Western Isles.

From the air, the Uist chain resembles a fish skeleton with Barra the tail, the land the bones and the water the in-between spaces. The Uists and Benbecula (the island separating North and South Uist) appear to be more water than land—although in reality, we were surprised at the actual amount of landmass and mountains. Not only numerous sea lochs, but many inland fresh-water lochs dot the surface. The islands are famous in Britain for their sandy beaches. Gazing out over the expanse of North Uist from a hillside, we marveled at how all the water shimmered in the sunlight like so many glittering jewels.

Driving around sparsely populated North Uist is relatively easy even with the one-lane roads. The main road circles the island in a distorted heart shape. The only decision to be made is whether or not to take a major secondary road that cuts off the western third. Either way, some backtracking is necessary due to the location of several of the prehistoric sites.

We took the A865 north and west from Lochmaddy after stopping in the small grocery store there to buy a few lunch fixings. We passed a picturesque white thatched cottage (probably the one featured on our ordnance map and photographed by every tourist) and the sandy Vallay Strand, a large bay, that can be crossed at low tide to get to the island of Vallay. We later learned that the sands can be dangerous and knowing where to cross is essential.

Cleitreabhal ★

The first ancient site we visited happened to be a rather unusual combination of monuments situated on one of North Uist's hills. A standing stone, a Neolithic chambered cairn unique to the isles, and an Iron Age wheelhouse all occupy this one spot. On a clear day, the view south is breathtaking. We were blessed with sunny weather and we could see for miles.

The cairn, a "Clyde" type (like cairns from around the Clyde River), has a well-defined burial chamber and a huge tipped entry stone. Three thousand years after the cairn was built, Iron Age people robbed all of its covering material to build their wheelhouse and farmstead located just west of the cairn. The inner chamber extended about 36 feet long and divided into five smaller chambers. The cairn was supposedly once a magnificent structure more than 90 feet long. An east-facing 75-foot-wide forecourt provided entry with large stones lining the face, similar to the forecourt at Cairnholy I.

Used over long periods of time, the remains of many individuals were often all jumbled up together inside. Sometimes pieces of skeletons were taken from the tombs, perhaps to be used in various rituals. Succeeding generations obviously considered them important.

The standing stone is visible from the cairn about 450 feet down the slope to the southeast. The stone is short, about five feet high, but large in circumference. It may have been taller before the peat buildup.

<u>To get there:</u> *What makes the view so grand is its location on top of a 133-meter hill called Taigh a Ghearraidh. It's easy to get there without an ordnance map although we found it useful to have one. The mountain is located in the western part of North Uist. Driving south on the North Uist's main road, the A865, go past Loch Hosta. Just before Loch Eaval, a minor road heads due east, right up the side of Taigh a Ghearraidh; at the same intersection, the right-hand road goes west to Tigharry. Turn left and follow the road nearly to the top of the hill. A radar installation sits near the summit. To the right and down the slope, look for the cairn stones. As soon as you can see these stones, pull off and park in a wide place. We drove right up to a gate in the fence and parked there. Go through the gate to get to the cairn and wheelhouse. The standing stone is farther down the slope. The walk was fairly easy.*

<u>Clach Bharnach Bhraodag</u> ✶

We saw this stone up on its hill while driving northwest on the secondary road that cuts across the great western loop of the A865. Although easy to see from below, the hike up to the stone can be strenuous. The hill is called *Beinn a' Charra* and provides spectacular views of the island from the top.

If personality can be attributed to a stone, this massive, flat, tall stone has a gentle, yet powerful, one. The flat side must span a distance of 12 feet with a thickness of two to three feet. Even though the stone leaned considerably, it towered more than eight feet.

The base of the stone looked as though someone had dug around it. No visible socket stones indicated where the base began. Perhaps a very thick peat layer obscures the real base.

One visitor noted that when he first saw the stone, two ravens perched on it; when he approached, they flew off in different directions. This might have been an omen for those who believe in them. He explained that the name of the stone is Norse for "the limpet stone of Freya." Norse mythology reveals that Freya taught magic to the god Odin, and Odin learned knowledge of everything from two ravens. A Gaelic saying translates roughly that a person who knows more than is normal has the raven's knowledge.

To get there: *We approached Beinn a' Charra on the cut-off road from the southeast; this made finding the stone simple because we could see it in the distance off to the east as we drove north. At the base of the hill, the stone disappears as the road bends left to skirt the hill. A cattle-loading ramp and gate make a wide spot here where it is possible to park off the road. Go through the gate and climb the hill. Eventually the stone comes back into view.*

Pobull Fhinn Stone Circle ★

Aubrey Burl, in *A Guide to the Stone Circles of Britain, Ireland and Brittany,* almost rhapsodizes about this stone circle. He wrote that its location is "one of the love-liest settings of any stone circle." We agree that the setting is lovely, but we have seen other circles that favorably compare. Nevertheless, we like it and recommend a visit. The pub in nearby Langass Lodge will furnish a welcome pint or cup of tea.

Pobull Fhinn means white or holy people. This spot has been a sacred place for a long time. Even today, people revere it. We were told that modern mystics still assemble here. Indeed, we found the remains of a fire in the center of the ring two days after the summer solstice.

The Neolithic people who built the circle went to an enormous amount of effort to construct it. The entire circle sits on an earthen bench constructed by humans. The ancients dug out the hillside to the north and filled the slope to the south so that a level surface could hold the stones.

The stones don't form a true circular shape but rather a slightly flattened ellipse. The best way to see the circle in its entirety is to climb a short way up the north hillside. The circle is quite complete, even though the stones aren't massive. They vary from "step high" to well over six feet. Clearly defined entrances mark either end of the ellipse.

To get there: *Take the A867 and look for the Langass Lodge turn-off a little less than two miles northeast of the A865 intersection. Drive to the lodge and park out of the way. At the end of the lodge drive, a path with steps, small bridges and walkways leads to the circle, about 750 feet away. This is one of the easiest sites to reach.*

Barpa Langass **

One of the most majestic and extraordinary cairns in Scotland occupies the top of a hill close to Pobull Fhinn and Langass Lodge. This complete cairn has never been robbed of stone and actually looks the way it did when Neolithic people built it.

The entrance is on the southeast, so it's necessary to walk around the massive pile of stones to reach it. An interpretive sign is located off to the right of the entry. The narrow three-foot-wide entry is about 12 feet long. A flashlight helps immensely to inspect the tomb's dark interior. The inner chamber measures about 6 by 12 feet and reaches high enough for a tall person to nearly stand upright. Massive stones with spaces filled in by smaller stones make up the roof and side walls. Unfortunately, graffiti has been carved into one of the huge stones.

After visiting Barpa Langass, we read some material that recommended people not actually enter the cairn. Two reasons were given: first, for safety because of falling stones, and second, many visitors might weaken and destroy the structure. We suspect that due to the cairn's remote location, few people probably visit it.

Barpa Langass was built about 5,000 years ago. It is a puzzle as to how the ancient people hauled thousands of rocks, large and small, to a location so high. And where did the stones come from? We couldn't see any rock outcroppings nearby. Barpa Langass gives yet another example of the industry and ability of the Neolithic people.

One last feature worth noting is the grand view from the cairn. On any high hill in North Uist, it's possible to see moorland, lochs and hills that stretch for miles.

To get there: *Anyone driving to the Langass Lodge and the Pobull Fhinn Circle will see it just to the north of the lodge road. It is possible to walk to the cairn from the lodge, but our waitress there told us the easiest way was from the A867. Just a short way northeast of where the Langass Lodge road meets the A867, a gravel and dirt pull-off looks like the beginning of a drive. An interpretive sign at this spot explains the monument. We parked there and walked a short way northeast along a fence; a stile of rock and boards allows access over the fence. A clearly defined but steep path leads up to the shoulder of Ben Langass.*

St. Michael's Chapel

We did not plan to go to St. Michael's Chapel. In fact, we didn't even know about it until we saw the ruins and talked with our B&B hostess. Just a short walk from our B&B, we enjoyed a pleasant midsummer evening stroll in the unique landscape of these islands. We visited the chapel shortly before dusk. The last rays of the sun illuminated the only remaining stone wall. All around us the water and the unusual, almost supernatural rocky landscape turned a purple tint. While the chapel structure wasn't impressive, its location on a knoll amidst the water and rock was ethereal, an ideal setting for reflection and prayer.

A column of what once must have been the west gable is all that's left of the tiny chapel. We traced its rectangular shape in the grass. Stones from its walls lie in a jumble all around. We could find nothing about this little monument in our literature, but it probably originated in medieval times.

To get there: *This intriguing little chapel ruin sits in the southeastern corner of Grimsay, a small island between North Uist and Benbecula. Take one of the two turnoffs from the A865 that lead to the road circling the small island. Signs on the A865 point to the small community of Kallin. Park at any convenient location in Kallin, or better yet, near the school if school is closed at the time you visit. The ruins are visible on a grassy knoll. A long driveway heads east to the southwest of the school. Go past the drive and enter the second drive to the left on the same side of the road. Turn right toward the house, but before reaching the yard, cut off toward the ruins.*

Trinity Temple (Teampall na Trianaid)

Only piles of rock and ruined building walls mark what was once a major medieval monastery and college renowned throughout Europe. A visit requires little effort other than a short detour off the main road and a pleasant walk. This particular area of Uist experienced a lot of action, including the last major battle in Scotland in 1601 using swords, bows and arrows. The local population kept their cattle and valuables out of harm's way in the church precinct.

According to a 17th century Book of Clan Ranald, Bethag, daughter of Somerled, founded Trinity Temple. She also founded the Nunnery on Iona. Much later, between 1350 and 1390, Amie NicRuairi, first wife of John, Lord of the Isles, enlarged the site. Trinity Temple was reconstructed in the 16th century, only to be destroyed during the Reformation. Finally, some restorative work, typical during Victorian times, occurred in the 1800s. For most of its life, Trinity served as both a monastery and a college for training priests. The Franciscan philosopher, Duns Scotus may have received part of his education here.

The school functioned until the 18th century. Sculptures adorned the interior until the beginning of the 19th century, and a spire graced the east gable. Sadly, little is left of this once imposing monastery. A barrel vault passage connecting a smaller side chapel to the main church still exists. Remaining walls stand remarkably high, maybe due to restoration work. Many of the gravestones are so worn they are illegible.

To get there: *This site, located in the south part of North Uist, requires a little searching. North of the causeway to Benbecula, turn off the A865 to Carinish. Incidentally, before the Carinish turnoff, the A865 goes right through a stone circle; although we saw some stones from the road, a circle is difficult to identify. Drive to Carinish and park in the car park at the two white houses. A gate and a plaque identifying the site are located right between the two houses.* Go through the gate, walk down the farm track to the second gate, and take the path to the monastery.

Na Fir Bhreige Standing Stones

Na Fir Bhreige ("three lying men" or "three false men") gave us more of an adventure than we anticipated. We had seen the three standing stones marked on our ordnance map but knew very little else. When we set out to find them, we had no idea what kind of a trek it would be or how long it would take. We eventually found the stones after a 20-minute walk around the side of a Uist hill. While the stones themselves are not particularly impressive, the walk to the site was invigorating. Extensive views south and west overlooked empty hills and moors shimmering with lochs. That, coupled with a quiet and ever-so-peaceful morning, made it very pleasant.

The three standing stones form an alignment northwest toward a hill in the distance. They are tiny, as standing stones go, just about two feet high and small in girth. They might well be the smallest standing stones we have seen. However, there is no way to calculate depth of the peat down to the original Neolithic base. When we finally reached the stones, we couldn't help but laugh.

Several legends are told about these stones. All generally refer to three men who lied to their wives and were turned into stone by a local witch as they crossed the hill.

To get there: *The stones stand on the northwest side of Blashaval hill, about three miles north of Lochmaddy off the A865. (You really need the Landranger Ordnance Survey map for the Sound of Harris.) We weren't sure of the best route to get to the stones so we chose a southwest approach after driving back and forth along the road*

*a couple of times. A northerly approach might be shorter
but fences there would make it more difficult. Watch for
the Lochmaddy Water Supply Treatment Works. We
parked our car off the road at the entrance to the treatment plant and went through the plant gate, walking uphill to the first terrace. At that point, we crossed over the
moorland and followed a sheep trail southwest around
the hill. The trail and ground could be slippery if wet, but
we were fortunate to have clear, sunny weather. The
stones were probably about a half-mile walk or so. Plan
on allowing at least 45 minutes for the trip out and back.*

Dun an Sticir ✱

This unusual Iron Age dun contains a rectangular
medieval hall and is approached by two causeways. It
occupies an islet in *Loch an Sticir*, right off the road to
the Harris ferry.

Because the dun was used until medieval times, its
condition is excellent. Unfortunately, stinging nettles fill
the interior, preventing much exploration. Walls rise to
a height of about seven feet enclosing a couple of fairly
intact chambers. The square medieval hall inside the
dun is well preserved but also sadly covered with nettles.
Swans glided around the loch the morning we visited.

To get there: *Take the B893 north off the A865. A secondary road to the ferry crossings forks off to the right
and the B893 ends in Newtonferry. We parked off the
road just past the ferry turnoff on the B893, because it
seemed less heavily traveled than the secondary road.
From there we walked back and crossed over the open
ground to the loch. It's easy to see the two causeways
from the edge of the loch. The causeway rocks are slippery and require caution if crossing over. The first causeway ends on a small islet; the second goes from that islet
to the dun's islet.*

Benbecula

Getting to Benbecula is an adventure for drivers not used to one-lane causeways! We certainly weren't prepared for the three-mile causeway that connects Benbecula to North Uist. This one-lane road has very few pullouts and is restricted by stone walls on either side. Although we could see ahead for some distance, we thought we might be stranded forever in pullouts because of the heavy traffic coming from Benbecula. Our other concern was to reach a pullout in time, particularly because the walls on either side tightly hemmed us in. Imagine driving this at night! We were told that this causeway linking the islands was comparatively new. Prior to its construction people had to walk across the dangerous tidal flats, a feat requiring intimate knowledge of the route to avoid quicksand.

Benbecula is dominated by a military reservation with a more commercial and industrial atmosphere than anywhere else in the islands. We didn't spend much time on Benbecula, instead driving through to get to South Uist. However, a few prehistoric sites can be visited there, including standing stones. Near the airport in the northeast of the island stand the ruins of St. Columba's Chapel, or *Teampall Chaluim Chille* in Gaelic, where people came to drink the holy water at the nearby well. Two additional sites can be seen from the B892. The first site, the ruin of a chapel located two miles south of Balivanich at Nunton, once belonged to a nunnery. The nuns were murdered during the Reformation. The second site comprises scant remains of a medieval tower house called Borve Castle, or *Buirgh* in Gaelic; it lies on the east side of the road four miles south of Balivanich. Borve Castle is not supposed to be easy to reach nor does it look particularly remarkable from the road. It once belonged to Clanranald and many a bloody fight occurred here. The crumbling ruins of the castle chapel lie on the other side of the road.

South Uist

Thousands of archaeological sites likely exist on South Uist. Unfortunately, we underestimated its potential and only thoroughly explored two sites. We didn't get to Barra or its smaller surrounding islands either, where archaeologists have classified more than 1,400 new sites in recent years. These islands provide outstanding opportunities for visitors interested in ancient monuments. Everywhere we drove we saw standing stones, duns and other ruins.

South Uist contrasts markedly with Protestant North Uist. Its Catholic religion is instantly recognizable after crossing the short causeway linking it to Benbecula. Small wayside chapels to the Virgin Mary dot the roadway. On a hill farther south overlooking the main road, the statue of Our Lady of the Isles welcomes travelers to South Uist.

Howmore (Tobha Mor) ★

Four different churches and chapels comprise the site called Howmore or Tobha Mor. A fifth structure, a chapel, was torn down in 1866. A mix of mystery, myth and historical fact abounds here along with a mellow sort of beauty. Yellow lichen grows almost everywhere on the exposed rock intermixed with green grass that manages to survive between the stones. Howmore is easy to visit.

The architecture and the grouping of the churches and chapels hint at an early Irish influence, but none of the structures now standing seems to predate the 13th century. Nevertheless, it is known that chapels existed here from the 7th or 8th centuries, and these were probably built on top of a prehistoric broch or chambered tomb. In medieval times, Howmore became the burial center for the Clanranald chiefs.

To explore the four structures, start in the southwest corner at the entrance to the site. The first structure consists of a very small chapel called *Caibeal Dubhghaill*, or Dugall's Chapel (or Chapel of the Kindred of Dugall's son). The four walls of the chapel are nearly complete. Due north of this chapel lies the church called St. Mary's or *Teampall Mor* (the large church), built in the 1200s. Only the east gable is left. Almost due east, but a bit north stands St. Dermot's Chapel, or *Caibeal Dhiarmaid*. In 1659, it was also called St. Columba's. Only the east gable remains, but it was apparently only slightly smaller than St. Mary's. In the nave a stone with a cross on it may have been an early Celtic Christian gravestone, reused for a much later burial. The fourth building occupies the northeasternmost area of the site. Clanranald's Chapel, or *Caibeal Chlann'ic Ailein*, was built in 1574. Both gables and parts of the walls remain. This small but significant building housed the late medieval carved stone bearing the coat of arms of Clanranald.

The Clanranald stone remained in the chapel until 1990, when it disappeared, an event that understandably upset the local people. The police and Historic Scotland were called in to help, but to no avail. In 1995, a young Canadian man died in London. The stone was discovered in his flat along with photos documenting its theft. After a short stay at the British Museum, the stone was returned to South Uist but not before some sensational stories evolved. The stories claimed that a curse on the stone took the young man's life. The stone is now displayed in the museum at Kildonan.

<u>To get there:</u> *The site is just 300 feet north of Howmore (Tobha Mor in Gaelic), a mile west of the A865. We had some difficulty at first finding it. In this case, our ordnance map wasn't very helpful. We eventually parked in the Church of Scotland parking area and got out to explore. We found the site to the right about 100 feet away from the drive to the church. It was hard to see because*

farm buildings, located just to the west of the monuments, obscure the structures. From the church car park, we walked back down the road a bit, skirting to the right of the farm buildings. The site was once an island surrounded by marshes.

Unnamed Dun

Just past the village of Kildonan off the A865, Mill Loch contains the remains of a dun. A rock causeway leads to it, but little of the dun is visible. The Western Isles have numerous duns like this one. In fact, nearly every little loch contains a dun islet and causeway. After a while, we found ourselves looking for their telltale signs.

Pollachar Standing Stone

The Pollachar, or *Pol A Charra*, marks the very southern end of South Uist. This single standing stone overlooks the Sound of Eriskay, and a most beautiful view of the islands of Barra to the south and Eriskay to the east. The view and the fact that the Pollachar Inn is just a dozen feet away, make this a delightful place.

This stone at six feet one inch once fell but has been re-erected. A nearby interpretive sign tells its story. After examining the stone and the views beyond, we walked over to the inn for a pub dinner, a pint and a chance to experience some of the local scene.

To get there: *Just follow the A865 south until it joins with the B888. The A865 turns left (east) to Lochboisdale and the B888 continues straight ahead. Keep on the B888 until it ends in the Pollachar Inn car park. The tall stone stands right in front.*

Harris

While the island of Harris is considered separate from Lewis, in reality both comprise the same landmass. Barren, rocky hills divide Harris from the much more even terrain of Lewis. The unusual topography of Harris enchanted us. In some ways, the mountains resemble a desolate moonscape. However, the vastly different and magnificent white sandy beaches lining the western coast of Harris took our breath away. Blue-green ocean contrasted with long stretches of white shell sand that accentuated the coastline's numerous rocky promontories and craggy inlets. We sat on a bench overlooking one of these incredible beaches, enjoyed a light lunch and gulped in the scenery. Only one other couple and a dog romped and played along the water's edge.

St. Clement's Church at Rodel ★★

After leaving the ferry at Leverburgh, we visited St. Clement's Church at Rodel. Our route first took a short detour south causing us to backtrack to the main road that travels the west coast. St. Clement's, a Norse church, although restored, still appears much as it did when built sometime between 1520 and 1540. The figures on the tower and the finely carved tombs should not be missed.

St. Clement's (*Tur Chliamainn*), is well cared for by Historic Scotland. The church is not in use nor is it staffed, so for details, we recommend obtaining a flyer from the tourist office entitled "St. Clement's Church at Rodel, Isle of Harris." The church is supposed to be open at all times. If the key isn't in or near the door, it can be obtained at the nearby hotel.

St. Clement's name suggests Norse influence because St. Clement was a popular Norse saint in medieval times. Alexander MacLeod (Alasdair Crotach "Humpback") built the current structure. He and his son William are buried in the church in two finely carved wall tombs. The church deteriorated after the Reformation but was rebuilt in 1784 by a Captain Alexander MacLeod of Berneray. A fire in 1787 required additional repair work. The Countess of Dunmore completed the last restoration in 1873.

The tower dominates the building, adorned by unique, carved figures. On the west side, above the doorway, a figure of a bishop supported by a bull's head most likely represents St. Clement. Below the bishop on either side of a window, two human figures are depicted. The figure to the left is considered the earliest known representation of a man in a kilt. The figure on the right shows a man in jerkin and hose displaying his genitalia. Two men in a boat, possibly Peter and Andrew, decorate the east side of the tower above the roof. The north wall features a bull's head, probably a symbol of the MacLeod badge. The south wall reveals a *sheela-na-gig*, a figure of a woman displaying her genitalia. *Sheela-na-gig* carvings originated in ancient Ireland and later became symbols to ward off evil.

The church entry is in the north wall of the nave. We noted the lead rain pipe to the left of the doorway in the corner; the gutter could also be lead. A panel of the Crucifixion and one noting the Countess' restoration are inscribed above the door.

The church layout consists of the usual nave, choir, and north and south transepts. The magnificent tomb of Alexander occupies the south wall of the choir and his son's the south wall of the nave. The superb carvings that surround Alexander's tomb remain in excellent condition. The south transept houses the tomb of John MacLeod of Minginish. Five graveslabs, once set in the floor of the sanctuary, stand fastened to the west wall of the north transept. Four of these date from the early 16th century, while the fifth has a date of 1725.

We climbed to the top of the tower, entered through a doorway inside the nave of the church. A couple of very steep ladders give access to the upper floors.

At St. Clement's, we met Norman. Norman was one of two Historic Scotland staff, high on a scaffold against the south wall of the tower, washing the stones. As we wandered around the church, we had been reading aloud from a Historic Scotland booklet describing St. Clement's. Norman came down from the scaffold, explained he'd overheard us and asked to look at our book. He scanned the section about the church without comment. Then he thumbed through the rest of the book, coming to a description of the Arnol Black House on Lewis. This he read with interest, all the while exclaiming about the roof. We learned that Norman, one of the few roof thatchers still working the craft, had thatched the Arnol Black House. Norman shared with us some of the art and techniques of thatching.

To get there: *Head for Rodel, a village at the very southernmost end of the A859. When we drove off the ferry at Leverburgh, we mistakenly took a secondary road south along the water. Checking the map again, we turned back to Leverburgh and linked up with the A859. So, make sure you're on the right road. Drive around Rodel until you see the unmistakable shape of St. Clement's Church with its square tower.*

Borvemore Standing Stone

The Borvemore (*Burigh Mhor*) stone, the only remaining stone of a stone circle, stands about six feet high making it easily seen from the A859. The sea provides a dramatic backdrop for the stone. Some of the other stones from the circle lie fallen nearby in what is now a fenced sheep pasture.

We didn't walk out to the stone. From a distance, it appeared to be on the edge of a circular mound, perhaps the base for the circle.

While touring Lewis we discovered Finlay J.

Macdonald's books describing his boyhood on Harris. *Cowdie and Cream* and *Crotal and White* charmingly portray his family's life eking out a living on a croft in the 1930s at Scarista. We should have read these books before our visit. We would have appreciated this portion of Harris even more than we did.

<u>To get there</u>: *The stone actually lies to the north of the A859 on a stretch where the road runs east and west for a short way. Look for the stone approximately halfway between Borve and Scaristavore.*

<u>*Macleod's Stone*</u> ★

The magnificent Macleod's Stone (*Clach Mhic Leoid*) overlooks one of the most beautiful beaches we have ever seen. While the walk out to the stone is fairly ardu-

Macleod's Stone, Harris

ous, the grand vistas and the huge stone make it very rewarding.

Massive Macleod's Stone stands over nine feet tall with a "V" shaped notch at the top, almost like ears. Socket stones show around the base. It's possible other nearby scattered stones could be associated with this large standing stone.

Looking to the west out to sea from the stone, the tops of the St. Kilda islands were visible very far off. During the equinoxes, the sun is supposed to set exactly due west over St. Kilda when sighted from the stone.

To get there: *This stone is a short way north of the Borvemore Standing Stone just south of the village of Horgabost on the A859. A car park with a bench overlooks the beautiful Traigh Iar beach, and a sign at the car park points to the stone. The stone can just barely be seen from the car park, high on a hill to the north. Getting to the stone requires a walk either over the beach or over the sandy grassland. We walked along the road for a way and then turned inland across the grass. We couldn't find a well-defined footpath to the stone, so we simply headed overland for it, keeping it in sight as much as possible. We came back by way of the beach, a much easier and more pleasant route. Hiking out to the stone necessitates some caution as the very high sandy cliffs can give way easily underfoot.*

Lewis

Lewis, the larger portion of the island, contrasts considerably with its southern neighbor. On Lewis the roads run straight over flat land for long stretches, many of them two-lane and wide. Ewes with lambs constitute the biggest hazard on Lewis, roaming everywhere, especially on the roads. Lewis offers numerous opportunities to explore a variety of ancient sites from its famous standing stones at Callanish to Iron Age wheelhouses to medieval churches. Lewis has abundant evidence of habitation for thousands of years. Of all the Western Isles, it is probably best known and draws the most tourists. Both Stornoway and Tarbert in Harris serve as arrival points for the ferries from Skye or from Ullapool in the West Highlands.

St. Columba's Church

St. Columba's Church (*Eaglais na h-Aoidhe*), just six miles east of Stornoway, was built in the 14th century and in use until 1828. Its graveyard holds the remains of 19 MacLeod chiefs. According to tradition, the current structure stands on the site of a cell of St. Catan from the 6th and 7th centuries.

The building consists of a well-preserved long rectangle with three gables. The chancel, or altar end, faces to the northeast. Margaret, a daughter of one of the MacLeod chiefs, is buried here. Her graveslab is in the north wall. Another graveslab propped up against the south wall depicts a man in long quilted coat holding a sword. In the nave, a door through the southwest wall leads to a burial aisle. Added later, this was probably intended to hold the remains of some important person.

As we wandered through the church, we tried to imagine what it would have been like to attend services here in the 14th century. The sea has eroded parts of the old graveyard to the north of the church. In time, even the church itself will be at risk.

To get there: *Follow the A866 east out of Stornoway to the strip of land connecting Lewis to the Eye Peninsula (An Rubha). Park at the very east end of this strip next to the wall of the old cemetery of Aignish on the north side of the highway. A sign gives directions to the church, a short walk farther.*

Dun Bayble

Dun Bayble survives as a tall pile of rock tumbled from the walls. Typical of most duns in this area, it occupies its own islet with a causeway leading to it. We didn't cross over to the dun.

We had read a description of this dun by a fairly well-known popular writer. We couldn't tell if he was jesting or serious when he incorrectly stated that the Scottish people piled rocks up like this for no real purpose. He apparently didn't realize that this particular pile of rocks once formed a substantial Iron Age fortress or dun.

To get there: *This dun is situated in the southwest part of the Eye Peninsula in a loch called Loch an Duin, near the village of Pabail Iarach. The ordnance map shows it clearly at coordinates NB 516304. Drive south through Pabail Iarach. You'll come to a farm road to the right, just before crossing the Allt Driseach River. Drive up the farm road. We stopped the car at the gate and walked the rest of the short distance to the edge of the loch. The dun is just a short way from the village and the loch is in the middle of a large farm field.*

Clach an Trushal Standing Stone ★★

At 20 feet high, this massive, very accessible stone, is purported to be the tallest standing stone in Scotland. Leaning slightly to the southwest, it dwarfs the human figure. Thousands of years ago ancient people erected this huge stone with only hand tools, ropes and probably timbers. Lichens cover the stone, giving testimony to its age. From out at sea, the stone can probably be seen for miles.

To get there: *Follow the A857 north out of Stornoway until it passes the A858 junction leading west. Continue north on the A857 for about 3½ miles to the village of Baile an Truiseil. Directions to the stone are posted on signs. The ordnance map can be helpful in keeping you on track here because to get to the stone it is necessary to go into someone's driveway. A small asphalt car park sits at the head of a path to the stone. Turn your back to the ocean and you can't miss it.*

Steinacleit Cairn and Stone Circle

Historic Scotland refers to this site as "the remains of an enigmatic building of early prehistoric date." The site is hard to interpret and not very impressive. Nevertheless, it has generated a lot of controversy. Just what was it? No one knows for sure.

Archaeologists have not yet excavated Steinacleit; perhaps after they do, the mystery will be solved. At any rate, no one doubts that some sort of structure of large boulders, maybe a chambered cairn, once stood here. Remains of a very large oval foundation, possibly a great hall, survive. A boulder wall surrounds the complex. In some places, field walls also exist. Speculative dating puts the site in use from 3000 to 1500 BC.

To get there: *Steinacleit is close to the Trushal stone. Take the A857 to Siadar. As a Historic Scotland site, it is well signposted. Follow the minor road to the southeast for about 2,500 feet. It leads past Loch an Duin with its Iron Age dun and causeway. Park in the large car park; additional signs and a path lead up to the site.*

St. Moluag's Church ★

St. Moluag's Church, also called St. Molau's and *Teampall Mholuaidh*, stands near the northernmost tip of Lewis. An unusual church in design and architecture, it resembles St. Clement's at Rodel in Harris.

St. Moluag's past remains hidden in time. No date

has been assigned to St. Moluag's because restoration of the church in 1912 destroyed any available evidence. However, this church has been here since the 16th century. A Norse church in Greenland, built in the 12th and 13th centuries, consists of the same plan as St. Moluag's, so Norse origin is likely. The church's similarity to the Greenland church, its dedication to St. Molua, a 6th century Irish saint who may have taught Christianity here, and accounts of a "pagan" tradition all suggest a possible 12th century origin.

The current structure has stayed basically the same since the 16th century; photos taken before the 1912 restoration show only the roof missing. The church's Norse plan consists of a rectangle oriented east to west with two small chambers, something like transepts, on the east end. The entire shape resembles a fat "T." The north chamber serves as a small sacristy, its only door opening into the chancel of the church. The corresponding chamber on the south forms a small chapel with its only door leading to the outside. This chapel's connection to the church is through a small squint window that allowed worshippers to view the altar. A note in the church explained that this chapel was set aside for pregnant women!

The building currently belongs to the Episcopal Church of Scotland with services occasionally held here. At our visit, we found ourselves completely alone in St. Moluag's peaceful little sanctuary. Outside a light rain drizzled. This tiny chapel on the very northern tip of the Isle of Lewis seemed quite distant from the chaos of the 20th century.

To get there: *St. Moluag's is situated in Eoropie (pronounced "yorr-op-ee"), the most northerly village on the island. Go into Port Niss and take the road marked B8014 northwest; it will be signposted to St. Moluag's Church. We mistakenly took the first road, the B8013, and had some difficulty finding the church, going toward the Butt*

of Lewis instead. However, the B8014 goes right by the
church. If you drive as far as the road to the Butt of Lewis,
you've gone too far. Look for a small colorful sign on the
right (northeast), "Scottish Episcopal Church Welcomes
You." A 300-foot-long path between two houses leads to
the church. Don't take the drive by the house on the left; it
goes to their garage. The church path is about three feet
from the house on the right. Be sure to close the two gates
plus the gate into the churchyard. St. Moluag's resembles
a little barn in the field, so it's easy to overlook.

Clach Stein

These two standing stones can be spotted from the
road outlined against the horizon on a hill behind a
house. They are marked on the ordnance map off the
B8014 on the way to St. Moluag's Church. Watch for
them between the first and second house on the right.

Dun Carloway Broch ★★★

Although built a couple thousand years after the more
famous Callanish stones, Dun Carloway is a major prehistoric treasure. No other broch, except Mousa in Shetland, is so complete.

Dun Carloway's tallest wall stands nearly 30 feet high,
and the rocky knoll on which the broch sits makes it
appear even higher. Unfortunately, a large part of Dun
Carloway's tower is missing, caused by its walls collaps-
ing internally, rather than stone being pilfered. Local
people must have revered the broch. It may have served
as a dwelling for centuries.

Historic Scotland has constructed a wide path and
steps up the hill to the broch. A huge lintel forces visitors to duck low to enter the broch through a small door
on the northeast. The characteristic guard cell is located
immediately to the right of the entry. Four doorways from
the interior courtyard lead to various compartments,

including one to the stairway that once reached the upper levels. In 1861, four upper galleries and part of a fifth were still intact. These double-walled galleries are still visible on the remaining lower levels. Inside the courtyard, at the first gallery level, look for the ledge (or scarcement) in the wall, which would have supported a floor or edge of a roof. Also, note the incredibly smooth outer wall displaying the extraordinary skill of the builders. The entire broch is built of dry stone, meaning that no mortar holds the stones together.

To get there: *The broch is just a short way southwest of the village of Barhabhagh, off the A858. Good signage directs the way to the side road and the large car park.*

The Standing Stones of Callanish

Sometimes Callanish is referred to as the Scottish Stonehenge, but compared to Stonehenge, the Standing Stones of Callanish remain relatively unknown. We hadn't heard of them until we bought a Celtic music album named after these stones. Yet, in many ways, Callanish rivals Stonehenge. Even more remarkable, the main Callanish site is just one of approximately 20 standing stone groupings as well as numerous cairns and duns in the area. It's even possible that many more ancient monuments await discovery under the peat. A couple of years ago, an unknown cairn was discovered during road-widening operations. In fact, the stones at the main site of Callanish were buried in four feet of peat until the middle of the last century. In 1857 when the peat was removed, a small burial cairn was also discovered inside the circle.

Callanish, the Main Site ★★★

Photographs of Callanish (the Gaelic spelling is *Calanais*, pronounced "kallanish") now frequently appear in books and even travel magazines. In June of 1995, a visitor center was built and parking space provided for large tour groups. Callanish is awesome and world-class.

Historic Scotland cares for the site and no entry fee is required to visit the stones. The locally managed visitor center occupies a discreet spot below the hill on which the stones stand. A small fee is charged to see an audio-visual exhibit.

While the stones are not fenced off, a sign requests visitors to stay on the path around the stones in order to protect the ground close to the stones. Therefore, it's not possible to touch the stones except for a few near the path. Callanish is still a far cry from Stonehenge where everyone views the monoliths from a distance. When we visited in late June, we encountered only a few other people. At one point, we were alone with the stones.

The layout of the main site is unique. A small circle of 13 stones, some reaching almost 11 feet, encloses a single massive stone of almost 15 feet, the famous heel stone. From the circle, an avenue of stones leads off to the north, and stones in several single lines lead off to the east, south and west. The ancient people must have

Callanish, Main Site

selected stones they thought beautiful, producing a variety of textures and colors. Standing close to the circle, we felt the same awe we experienced in the great cathedrals of Britain. Callanish is a spiritual place—both mysterious and powerful.

Scientific dating shows that the stones were erected sometime between 2900 and 2600 BC, about the same time as the active years of Orkney's renowned Neolithic village, Skara Brae. Even more incredible are findings of stone field boundaries under the standing stones. This location was farmed for a long time before the stones were erected.

The possibility exists that a Greek historian, Diodorus Siculus, visited Callanish sometime during the 1st century BC. He wrote of a spherical temple from which the moon danced the whole night. In fact, when viewed from the avenue of stones, every 18.6 years the moon appears to float just above the hills to the south until it sets briefly, then reappears again in a notch between the hills.

To get there: *You can't miss Callanish. Follow the A858 and the signs. Approaching the site, keep looking toward the west. The grouping of stones will be visible for some distance.*

Cnoc Ceann a' Gharraidh ★★

Another name for this stone circle is Callanish II, but the Gaelic, *Cnoc Ceann a' Gharraidh,* seems to prevail. For pronunciation, we rely on Patrick Ashmore's rendition from his book *Calanais: The Standing Stones.* He suggests an approximate pronunciation of "krok kyain a gaa ree." We delighted in touching the stones in this superb little stone circle. Although just a short distance from Callanish, few people seem to visit, instead heading straight for the main site. From this circle, the main site of Callanish looks like jagged teeth rising up from the hill to the northwest.

Five large stones of many varied shapes are left of the original circle. One of them with a pointed top reminded us of a hooded monk. Some of the stones are close enough together that we could stand between them and touch both with outstretched arms. These stones easily match those of Callanish for beauty. Unfortunately, some of the stones have fallen. Although extensively robbed, we could see remains of a cairn in the center of the circle. Archaeologists have discovered evidence here of a wood circle that was later replaced by the stones.

To get there: *The circle is easy to see from the A858. Just take the farm road a short distance southeast from the turnoff to Callanish. About 900 feet from the turnoff, the farm road ends in a car park. Go through the gate provided and walk the 600 feet to the stones.*

Cnoc Fillibhir Bheag ★★

This double stone circle, sometimes called Callanish III, also stands within sight of Callanish. The Gaelic name, *Cnoc Fillibhir Bheag*, is pronounced roughly "krok filliver veg."

The circle consists of an outer ring of eight stones, and an inner one of four stones. The outer circle originally had five more stones, now fallen, for a total of 13. The inner circle with taller stones than the outer ring also once contained more stones. None of the stones appears to have been worked with tools. They all display a natural beauty in their rough shapes. *Cnoc Fillibhir* doesn't seem to have a cairn associated with it.

This circle attracts people with mystical leanings who feel some sort of energy here. Even a couple of rock bands have recorded concerts at the site. Although we don't consider ourselves mystics, we could also sense the power of these circles.

To get there: *Like Cnoc Ceann a' Gharraidh, Cnoc Fillibhir Bheag can be seen from the A858. The two circles are close to each other, and, in fact, a path connects them. We walked from one to the other, although the ground was a bit soggy. Alternatively, take the short unmarked road from the A858 directly to the site.*

Ceann Thulabhaig ★

Part of joy of exploring *Ceann Thulabhaig* ("kyain hoo-la-vig") was the discovery process itself. This small circle, high on a hill, is not signposted or maintained by Historic Scotland. Clearly, it is not a circle that tourists frequent. Other names for this circle are Callanish IV and Hulavig (the Norse style from which its name derived).

Our only comment on reaching the circle at the top of the hill was "Wow!" Views of the surrounding area were grand. Today the circle consists of five stones of what once may have been 13. The tallest stone stands more than eight feet high. All stones are large with regular shapes, although obviously not worked with tools. Lichens cover them giving an old, mysterious feel. The circle retains remnants of a small central cairn.

To get there: *About two miles from Callanish, this circle is not easy to find. An ordnance map is extremely useful for locating circles like this one. From the A858, take the B8011 to the southwest for one mile. At about this point, it's possible to see the tops of the stones on top of a hill to your right. We parked off the road on what seemed to be a side road. We simply headed toward the stones' location, climbing over a barbed wire fence with the help of a rather rickety stile. Once over the fence, we climbed the short distance up the hill to reach the stones at the top.*

The Stonefield Standing Stone

We had some difficulty locating this stone until we realized that it stands in a modern housing complex—another example of the easy, almost taken-for-granted co-existence of contemporary and prehistoric structures. This stone remains in its original position, even though the base is embedded in a concrete and pebble apron, and a fence surrounds it. This single stone also sometimes is called Callanish XII.

To get there: *You can easily see the stone from the A858 at the entrance to the Stonefield Housing Estate in Breasclete.*

Cleiter Standing Stones ★★

Pronounced "kletch-er," and also known as Callanish VIII, this site consists of four standing stones on a purposely leveled area high on a cliff above the sea channel separating Great Bernera from Lewis. This semi-circle of stones on their rocky slope, 40 feet above the water, resembles no other site in Great Britain. The open end of the semi-circle faces the cliff edge, so that if the circle were complete, it would extend out over the water. Three stones, approximately nine feet tall, still stand while the fourth has toppled.

Gerald and Margaret Ponting, writing in *The Stones Around Callanish,* describe a strange phenomenon that occurs here. On a sunny winter day, when the sun is low, a double shadow of a person walking between a stone and the cliff edge appears on the stone. The direct sunlight and the sunlight reflected on the water form this twin shadow.

To get there. *Access is very easy. Almost due west of the main Callanish site, take the B8011 from the A858. Turn north on the B8059 and drive until you reach the bridge*

*that crosses to Great Bernera or Bearnaraigh. The stones
are visible ahead from the middle of the bridge on the cliff
to the left. We parked in a wide spot on the road just after
crossing the bridge. Go through the gate and climb the
hill to the stones. Be very careful. Even though a barbed
wire fence protects the cliff edge, this spot could be dangerous.*

The Bernera Iron Age Village at Bostadh ★

The Bernera Iron Age Village, located on a lovely beach
on Great Bernera, is a unique example of an entire village of Iron Age homes. A series of gales in the spring of
1993 uncovered the village, but it was not excavated
until 1996. Most of the houses date to around the 7th
and 8th centuries. The circular shape is similar to those
of the much earlier neolithic village of Skara Brae in
Orkney. Originally, most of the house structures were
built fairly deep in the ground for wind and gale protection.

During the excavations, the local residents wanted
as much as possible left of the houses, but the archaeologists and Historic Scotland thought the site too diffi-

Wheelhouse, Bernera

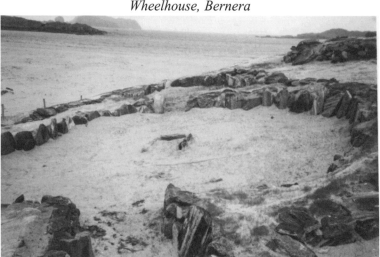

cult to protect from the winds and sea. So, coastal protection was provided, and a few courses of the stone walls were left in place to show the location of the houses. Plans are underway to rebuild one of the houses. Other than stone outlines of the foundations, we couldn't see much at the actual site.

Information about the site can be obtained at the local museum in Breaclete. After the archaeological work is completed, the local people hope to display the artifacts at the museum.

To get there: *Take the B8059 north over to the island of Great Bernera. Continue north to Breaclete. We stopped at the Community Centre to have tea and to visit the local museum. The staff delighted in telling us about the excavation and other sites to explore. Follow the unmarked road north, taking the first turn to the right and then to the left. Drive until you reach the graveyard at Bostadh where there's plenty of parking. Take the path alongside the cemetery walls, following it around to the left. The site has interpretive signs and plastic mesh covering the sand to prevent further erosion.*

Dun Bharabhat of Great Bernera ★★

Our visit to Dun Bharabhat ("var a vat") was memorable not only for the excellent condition of this very complete 2,000-year-old dun but also for the exhilarating walk there and the beauty of this remote and isolated area. The fortress is situated in a loch and approached by a rock causeway 100 feet long. A visit to this dun requires energy and at least an hour to get there and back. For a walk in the wild, this is the place.

Like other Iron Age duns, oval-shaped Dun Bharabhat occupies an entire islet. The tallest remaining wall rises to a height of about nine feet. According to an informative pamphlet from the museum in Breaclete, the inside of the wall shows evidence of three galleries and a stairway that connected them. The interior once supported a wooden floor probably used for a main hall with a basement for storage underneath.

Our trek to Dun Bharabhat was complicated by a brisk wind that pelted us with rain. No specific trail exists; rather, green posts marked the way, requiring us to pick our way across the rocky and marshy moorland. Once we reached the dun, we decided against crossing the causeway because of slippery stones and strong wind. From the shore end of the causeway, Dun Bharabhat appeared massive, mysterious and perhaps a little ominous with its rocky humped outline and darkened entrance. It was covered by moss that gave it a yellowish-green hue. We had a sense of overwhelming loneliness.

To get there: *Park at the cattle grid on the B8059 about three-quarters of a mile south of Breaclete. Look for the green painted posts starting on the west side of the road. At the beginning of the walk, it is necessary to use a stile to cross a fence. The green posts are not always easy to see, but one is always just ahead to provide direction over the moorland. After about 1,800 feet, Loch Bharabhat and the dun come into view. We recommend waterproof boots if you plan to cross over the causeway. A walking stick for balance also would help.*

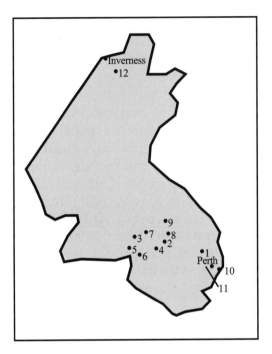

1   Dunkeld Cathedral
2   Croft Moraig Stone Circle
3   Machuinn Stone Circle
4   Oakbank Crannog
5   Finlarig Castle
6   Kinnell Stone Circle
7   Fortingall Yew Tree, Hand Bell, Stone Circles
8   St. Mary's Church
9   Dunfallandy Pictish Stone
10 Elcho Castle
11 Huntingtower Castle
12 Clava Cairns

Chapter 9
The Central Highlands and Perthshire

Prehistoric and historic monuments, including crannogs, stone circles, standing stones, castles, Roman forts and Celtic Christian remains, fill the heart of Scotland. Perthshire is convenient to Scotland's central cities, and most people drive through on the A9 to get to Inverness. Given enough time, many places require just a short detour off the A9.

Dunkeld Cathedral ★★

The peaceful and pleasant town of Dunkeld, located adjacent to the A9, gives little indication of its turbulent past and prominent place in Scotland's religious history. Dunkeld Cathedral, part ruin and part parish kirk, occupies an idyllic park-like setting on the banks of the River Tay, a location graced by some sort of religious structure for more than 1,000 years. In 849, King Kenneth MacAlpin brought the relics of St. Columba to Dunkeld from Iona to save them from the Viking raids, although ironically the Danes attacked Dunkeld shortly afterwards. The first abbot of Dunkeld served as primary bishop of the new kingdom, demonstrating Dunkeld's importance, until church headquarters moved to St. Andrews about the 10th century.

Work began on the current cathedral in the middle of the 13th century and continued for 250 years until completed at the end of the 1400s. Unfortunately, the cathedral was sacked in 1560, during the Scottish Reformation. The local people restored the roof of the choir and sacristy in 1600 for use as their church but left the nave roofless.

Although weather continues to ravage the open nave, much of the structure has survived in remarkably good condition. The western tower, built in the 1400s, looks new and contains wall paintings and carved gravestones

Dunkeld Cathedral

from medieval times. Even the nave's walls still reach their original height with the only obvious damage consisting of missing stone tracery in the huge west window and weathering.

Fortunately, the covered choir suffered little over the centuries, although some restoration work occurred in 1814 and 1908. Special choir features include decorative arcading on the north wall created in the mid-1200s and 14th century sedilia built into the south wall. The priest and his assistants sat on these sedilia, or stone chairs, during parts of the service. The tomb of the Wolf of Badenoch rests behind the screen and altar. The notorious Wolf of Badenoch, otherwise known as Alexander Stewart, Earl of Buchan, died in 1405. He committed many atrocities during his life, but the burning of Elgin Cathedral stands out. Because he repented of his evil ways before he died, he received burial in the cathedral. The headless and legless statue of Bishop Sinclair (died 1337) lies nearby, likely defaced during the Reformation. His effigy must have been quite elaborate as the finely carved folds of his robes suggest.

The sacristy, entered through a door in the north wall near the altar, contains two Pictish stones, a Celtic saint's hand bell and, sometimes, if not put away for protection, the "Great She Bible." One of the stones, called the Apostle's Stone, dates from the 800s and depicts 12 weathered figures. The other reddish stone contains a simple cross and probably hails from the 8th or 9th centuries. On our first visit, by happenstance, we discovered the "Great She Bible" when we lifted a cloth that covered a glass case. This unusual Bible might be considered the first feminist Bible! Printed in 1611, it contained an error making all references to God "She" instead of "He." The saint's hand bell probably dates to around the time of Kenneth MacAlpin in the 8th or 9th centuries. Celtic saints, preaching as they traveled from place to place, carried these hand bells to call people to worship. Church bells later replaced them.

The town of Dunkeld was caught in the crossfire of the 1689 battle of Killiecrankie between government forces and those loyal to the Stewarts (the Jacobites). Most of the old burgh surrounding the cathedral burned to the ground. The town was later rebuilt in its present position, a bit east of the original site. Therefore, most of Dunkeld's buildings are comparatively recent. The famous engineer, Thomas Telford, built Dunkeld's signature bridge over the River Tay in 1809.

On our first visit to Dunkeld Cathedral, a light snow covered the ground and a vivid blue sky framed the ruin. We visited the studio of Scottish musician Dougie MacLean on the street leading to the cathedral. He has since moved to larger quarters near the river.

To get there: *The town of Dunkeld is just off the A9 heading toward Inverness, about 15 miles north of Perth. Park on a side street and go west following the river to the cathedral.*

Croft Moraig Stone Circle

Several stone circles accessible convenient to the road dot the Loch Tay region. The Croft Moraig circle is maintained by the state. In the days of horse-drawn coaches, drivers would point out the "Druid temple" to their passengers.

Work began on the circle in the Late Neolithic Age, about 5,000 years ago, and probably continued for hundreds of years. The monument rests on an earthen platform, surrounded by a bank. Stones in the circle are graded in height. Some are oriented to the southernmost moonset, others to the equinoxes and one to the summer solstice. A recumbent stone with cup marks adds interest to the mix.

To get there: *The circle is located on the A827 about two miles northeast of Kenmore, just a short distance south of the road and to the west of a home and other buildings. It is easy to see from the road, but watch for it. We nearly missed it.*

Machuinn Stone Circle

In contrast to Croft Moraig, this circle is in poor shape. Four huge stones, remnants of a west section of a big elliptical stone circle, are visible. Other overgrown stones lay some distance to the southeast and northeast. A number of smaller stones appear to have been dumped near the base of the four big stones.

To get there: *This stone circle is located off the A827 as it follows the north shore of Loch Tay, just about ½ mile northeast of Lawyers. Look for it on the north side of the road almost directly across from a farmhouse on private land in a pasture. There is really no place to park except to pull as far as possible off the road; take care because we've seen huge tour coaches on this narrow road. We*

*climbed over a stone wall topped by barbed wire to get a
closer look at the stones.*

Oakbank Crannog ★★★

Scotland's lochs contain many crannogs, manmade
island dwellings approached by various sorts of causeways. Eighteen crannogs have been discovered in Loch
Tay's waters. No one knows why crannogs were built,
possibly for defensive purposes. They are thought to date
from the early Iron Age. Loch Tay's Oakbank Crannog
provides a 20th century perspective on how a crannog
might have looked and how ancient people possibly lived.
In tourist season, knowledgeable staff members demonstrate activities of daily life, such as spinning, firemaking
and grain milling using primitive tools.

Dr. Nicholas Dixon of Edinburgh University reconstructed Oakbank Crannog. After research and experi-
mentation by the Scottish Trust for Underwater Archaeology, students and volunteers recreated the crannog to
match the original. The dwelling is distinctive, its coni-
cal thatched roof visible from Kenmore on the southeastern edge of the loch. Admission to the site includes
tours of the crannog itself. Be prepared to tread precariously over the lashed-together creaking hickory sap-
ling floor with the loch visible underfoot. It took a while
to develop "sea legs." The crannog's cozy interior contains a central cooking area and pie-wedged "rooms,"
partitioned to give the inhabitants a degree of privacy.
We wondered if these buildings caught fire on a regular
basis as they are constructed all of wood and grasses.
Our guide had helped build the crannog and shared in-
numerable details about this remarkable structure.

To get there: *The crannog is located at the east end of
Loch Tay on the south shore. To reach it, take the unmarked road that heads southwest out of Kenmore. The
crannog sits in the loch near the Croft-na-Caber Hotel and*

a water sports center.

Finlarig Castle

The ominous ruin of Finlarig Castle stands at the west end of Loch Tay, about a quarter mile from Killin. This fairly modern castle probably was built in 1609, although a castle has occupied this spot much longer. Finlarig Castle has an L-shaped design consisting of a main tower and one wing. While the castle is a dangerous ruin, several features make it fascinating to visit. Even in its ruinous state, substantial portions of the castle remain.

A large sign at the start of the path to the castle warns that the ruin is dangerous and to enter at your own risk. Many parts of the fairly high walls are crumbling and loose.

Remains of a small chapel in far worse shape can be found near the castle. In the 16th century, the Breadalbane family was buried here. Now the chapel consists of four walls filled with rubble. Twentieth century graves of Sir Gavin Campbell, the Marquess of Breadalbane, and his wife are located nearby.

The beheading pit and the hanging tree to the north of the castle fascinated our sons. The pit is a stone-lined square sunk into the ground. Farther north a very old tree stands on top of a hill. Steps leading up the hill to the tree seem to confirm that it was used for hangings. The gentry and important people had the "privilege" of being beheaded while the common folk suffered the indignity of hanging. In the dusk of the winter day, the castle and its overgrown grounds felt eerie.

To get there: *Take the A827 as it heads due north out of Killin. Loch Tay is to the right driving north. Just a quarter of a mile or so out of Killin a road crosses a bridge leading to the right, or east. Take this road straight to the castle. It will pass a cemetery on the right and shortly*

Kinnell Stone Circle, Killin

come to a road leading left. The castle is on a hill to the left at this junction. Park off the road as much as possible and climb the steep path up to the castle.

Kinnell Stone Circle ✱

This lovely circle consists of six stones (and markers where stones once stood) located a half mile east of Killin. At our visit in winter's dusk, sheep wandered between the stones. The sheep keep the grass low, so the stones are easy to see from the fence. The stones appear about waist high and vary in shape.

The Kinnell Farm gates deserve attention. Strange-looking lions crouch on top of each pillar. Our son, who had spent some time in the Loch Tay area, explained that because medieval stonemasons had never actually seen a lion, or even a picture, they carved solely by description.

<u>To get there:</u> *The circle can be found on the south side of the River Dochart, just before the gates of Kinnell Farm, ½ mile east of Killin. We parked just inside the gates of the farm. Alternatively, park in Killin and walk along the farm track. The circle is prominent in a field to the right just before the farm gates.*

<u>Fortingall Yew Tree, Celtic Christian Hand Bell and Stone Circles</u> ★★

Tucked away in the hills above Loch Tay, tranquil and scenic Fortingall seems shielded from the tourists who flock to the loch in summertime. A short detour to this area gives an opportunity to see an ancient tree, a 1,300-year-old Celtic Christian hand bell and stone circles.

The 3,000-year-old yew tree, purported to be the oldest living vegetation in Europe, grows in the Fortingall village churchyard. A low stone wall and iron fence protects this gnarled treasure that began its life during the Neolithic times.

The church houses various relics, the most important being the Celtic Christian hand bell used by the early St. Cedd, a disciple of St. Aidan. It rests in a niche in the wall protected by an iron grate. Dating from 650 AD, it is one of five hand bells surviving in Perthshire. These bells were believed to possess curative powers.

A sign in the church mentions the "Druid stones" located about 250 yards east of the church in a field on the right. Here, several groupings of huge boulders are the only remnants of three stone circles.

<u>To get there:</u> *Fortingall is situated in a hilly area just north of Loch Tay. Take the minor road north from Fearnan from the A827, or a minor road southwest from Keltneyburn off the B846.*

St. Mary's Church, Grandtully

St. Mary's Church is a tiny 16th century parish church with lovely ceiling paintings, not far from Loch Tay. We visited in the last days of June and had the church to ourselves. St. Mary's is in the care of Historic Scotland and in great condition. The long, low, white, nondescript building might be mistaken for a barn belonging to the neighboring farm. Looks are deceiving in this case, because the real treasure is inside.

Once the lights come on, the plain little building is transformed. (Look for the light switch to the left upon entering.) The wood ceiling is covered with symbolic and heraldic scenes in vivid colors. Although the church was built by at least 1533, the elaborate ceiling was not completed until 1636.

To get there: *St. Mary's Church wasn't as easy to find as we'd initially thought, as its road wasn't shown on our 3-miles-to-1-inch map. The typical small sign on the A827 at Grandtully is also easy to miss. St. Mary's Church is located south of the A827 three miles northeast of Aberfeldy (or about seven miles northeast of Kenmore) on an unmarked single-track road. Signs provide directions to the church from its car park.*

Dunfallandy Pictish Stone

The glass and roofed structure protecting this carved Class II stone make it difficult to inspect. Nevertheless, if the light is just right, the cross on one side and the Pictish designs on the other look as though they were carved only recently. The cross side is filled with intricate patterns and interlacing, surround by animals and angels. The reverse side shows scenes and Pictish symbols. We couldn't detect any damage to the stone.

To get there: *From Pitlochry, cross the river Tummel to*

*Ballinluig to the southwest of town following the minor
road to Logierait. Alternatively, from the A9 take the Festival Theatre route and continue toward Logierait. Turn at
Fonals Cemetery sign (also signposted to Festival Theatre) near the BP petrol station, crossing the river. Follow
the minor road for 3½ miles. The stone is signposted at
the church cemetery. Park at the bottom just off main road
and walk up.*

Elcho Castle ★★

Tucked away from the main roads near the city of
Perth and the River Tay, Elcho Castle provides an outstanding example of a nearly intact tower house. Not
many people visit Elcho, so we had the castle nearly to
ourselves and could feel the peace of its secluded setting. While the building dates to more recent times, the
location has associations with William Wallace.

Today Elcho belongs to the earls of Wemyss, as it
has since 1468 when James III gave it to Sir John
Wemyss. In 1929, it was placed in state care by the 11th
earl. The current castle was probably built just after
the 1550s. A 1570 bill to the laird for ironwork possibly

Elcho Castle

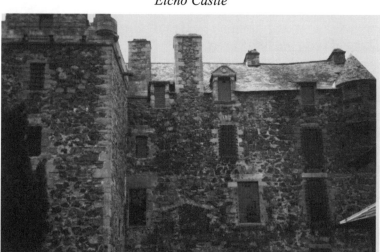

refs to the existing iron window grills and castle door yett (metal gate). Elcho's outstanding state of preservation enables visitors to see how people once lived. Plaster still clings to many walls, and, in one room, possibly the laird's, a plaster cornice remains partially intact. Although floorboards have been replaced, the wooden beams holding them are original. In some rooms, only the beams remain. The castle is famous for its numerous toilets, enough to make any modern home pale by comparison. The custodian sends visiting school children on a hunt to count the toilets or "loos." The correct answer is 17.

Elcho Castle has its share of drama as well. The Historic Scotland caretaker shared a legend in which William Wallace climbed a yew to escape his pursuers, pointing out the yew trees that grow on the grounds. Legend or not, he probably visited the area numerous times during his fight against the English. On one occasion when he reportedly killed one of his own men to escape the English, he felt so guilty he was haunted by the dead man's ghost.

Although it doesn't look it, the castle is actually a tower house. The irregular layout with small towers around the square main tower hides its tower-like structure but adds to its charm. Obviously built for comfort, the strong yett and gun holes in the basement walls demonstrate that defense wasn't neglected either.

To get there: *Elcho Castle is located about three miles to the southeast of Perth on the south side of the River Tay. Take the A912 south from Perth to a minor road to Rhynd. Follow the road to Rhynd for about three miles. Just past Rhynd a road turns left signposted to the castle. It is necessary to drive through a farmyard to reach the castle.*

Medieval painted ceiling, Huntingtower Castle

Huntingtower Castle ★★

Extraordinary events—including romance, treason and villainy—occurred within the walls of Huntingtower. This tower house, witness to so much history, remains amazingly well preserved. A painted ceiling and plaster with its original artwork still decorate the building.

For several hundred years, the castle bore the name House of Ruthven. However, in 1600, after the fall of the Ruthven family, an act of Parliament changed its name to Huntingtower. The Murrays of Tullibardine owned it until 1805.

The Ruthven family left a remarkable history. One of the first Ruthvens vacillated in loyalty between the Scots and the English. He twice pledged allegiance to the English but also fought with William Wallace and Robert the Bruce. The second of the original two towers, only three feet apart, may have been built so that two sons of a later Ruthven could each occupy their own noble residence. A member of the family also died with King James IV at Flodden.

Later, Patrick Ruthven became a strong supporter of

Protestant reform during Queen Mary's time. He entertained Mary twice in 1565, the second on the occasion of her honeymoon with Lord Darnley. He also participated in the murder of David Riccio, the Queen's secretary, afterwards fleeing to England where he died. Ruthven's son, William, helped imprison Mary and later forced her to abdicate. Then, in 1582, William participated in a coup against Mary's son, James VI, an event that became known as the Ruthven Raid. William and other nobles lured the young king to Huntingtower where they held him for 10 months until he escaped in June of 1583. The king initially forgave the raiders, but later, after more mischief, the king abolished the Ruthven name and seized their property.

Subsequent owners of the newly named Huntingtower Castle presided over more peaceful times. Ironically, Lord George Murray was born at Huntingtower and led the Jacobite army in 1745-1746.

In addition to political intrigues, several legends surround Huntingtower. One involved Dorothea, the daughter of an early Ruthven. She developed a fancy for a local fellow of lower rank named John Wemyss. Although her parents didn't approve, they invited him to stay in the older tower. Dorothea, whose room was in the newer, smaller tower somehow managed to get into John's room. When her parents caught wind of her indiscretion, Dorothea ran to the parapet and jumped nine feet four inches to her own tower. At the time, the towers weren't attached and the drop would have been about 60 feet.

In the late 1900s, a single woman who raised chickens lived in the castle. Stories proliferated about her extensive entertainment of men. The local people believed she threw any resulting babies down the well. Some older folk still consider the castle evil.

Huntingtower Castle actually consists of three separate structures. The first two towers were linked together by a middle building, giving the interior an odd mismatched appearance. The numerous wall paintings date to before 1513. Some of these paintings remain vivid, and we were surprised by the contemporary look of some of the designs. In the east tower, the second floor hall retains its painted wood ceiling from about 1540, one of the earliest surviving painted ceilings in Scotland. The dovecot in the garret of the west tower surprised us, and we could only wonder about the clatter created by the resident doves!

To get there: *The castle is very easy to reach, situated about three miles northwest of Perth off the A85 and close to the A9.*

Clava Cairns ★★★

Only a mile and a half from the Culloden battlefield, these cairns provided a very different experience from Culloden. Conscious of its bloody history, we left Culloden in a somber mood. Arriving at the Clava Cairns, we immediately felt the peace and quiet of their leafy park, which evoked a history far earlier than the events at Culloden. Maybe it was just the warm June morning we visited, but the experience was magical. Sunlight filtered through the many tall trees, warming the venerable gray stones of three cairns and speckling the green grass that surrounds them.

A stone circle rings each of the three main cairns. Large kerb stones around the base of each cairn hold the mass of round, smooth rocks that form most of the cairn. Even in its ruined state, the cairn closest to the car park rose much higher than our heads. Imagine the amount of work needed to build such a massive structure.

Four cairns lie within the protected area under Historic Scotland's care. A straight line runs from the northeast to the southwest through two passage grave cairns and a central ring cairn that has no passageway into the tomb. The passage graves on either end are nearly identical in size, an amazing engineering feat 4,000 years ago. Even more remarkable, both were built so that the sun on the winter solstice shines down the passageways, illuminating the backs of the chambers. If one were to stand in the very back of the northeast cairn at the spot the sun would strike and look up the passageway, the view would frame the southwest cairn. In this way, the builders created a dramatic effect. The winter solstice sun would appear to set just above the southwest cairn.

The ring cairn has its own unusual design. If it were possible to view the entire ring cairn from directly above, four rays of rock would be seen extending out from the tomb. From a ground perspective, the rays are a little harder to find. Each ray leads to an individual stone in the cairn's ring of standing stones.

The symbolism expressed in the stones' positioning is not obvious to a casual observer. For example, all three stone circles have taller stones in the southwest and shorter stones in the northeast. This same ordering occurs in the stones around the bases of each burial chamber and again in the kerb stones. Cup and ring marks appear on a number of stones, usually in obscure places like the last passageway stone of the northeast cairn and on several kerb stones and standing stones.

A fourth grave, a tiny kerb cairn, lies almost hidden off to one side. Hardly noticeable, it is just an outline of rocks. This cairn was excavated in the 1950s and a burial was found. Other cairns and standing stones dot the nearby countryside, like the stone in a field northeast of the car park.

To get there: *Take the minor road just west of Culloden Battlefield to the south. This crosses the B851 and the River Nairn at the Clava Bridge. The Clava Lodge is to the left. The next road to the right leads to the cairns.*

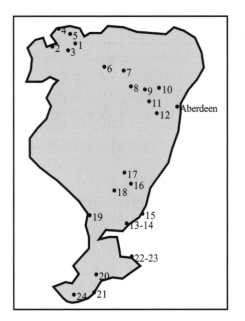

1	Elgin Cathedral	13	Carlungie Earth House
2	Sueno's Stone	14	Ardestie Earth House
3	Pluscarden Abbey	15	Arbroath Abbey
4	Duffus Castle	16	Brechin Round Tower,
5	Spynie Palace		Cathedral, Carved Stones
6	Balvenie Castle	17	Edzell Castle
7	Huntly Castle	18	Aberlemno Pictish Stones
8	Picardy Symbol Stone	19	Meigle Museum
9	Maiden Stone	20	Falkland Palace
10	Loanhead Stone Circle	21	Aberdour Castle
11	Easter Aquhorthies Stone	22	St. Andrews Castle
	Circle	23	St. Andrews Cathedral
12	Crathes Castle	24	Dunfermline Abbey, Palace

Chapter 10
The Northeast and Fife

So many castles exist in the northeast that local tourist authorities have created a castle trail. However, not only castles dot the region. This ancient Pictish kingdom also boasts numerous carved stones, recumbent stone circles, Roman forts, cathedrals and ruins. It is a land of wild mountains, deep glens and rushing rivers, treacherous sea cliffs, fertile farmland and tiny picturesque fishing hamlets.

Elgin Cathedral ★★

Haunting Elgin (pronounced with a hard "g") Cathedral deserves its reputation as one of Scotland's most beautiful ruins. Once called Lanthorn of the North, Elgin's shattered elegance inspired many artists.

Like other Scottish abbeys and cathedrals, Elgin's history is one of building and rebuilding. Construction began in 1224, only to be started again after a serious fire in 1270. By the end of the 13th century, the cathedral attained its current size. Unfortunately, the Wolf of Badenoch, Earl of Buchan, fell out with the bishop and set fire to building. In 1402, Alexander, a son of the Lord of the Isles, attacked the cathedral. Further destruction occurred in 1560, following the Reformation, when local people mined the cathedral for building material.

Elgin's ruins give a sense of its former grandeur. Two imposing stone towers flank the nave entry. When we visited, stone masons were at work repairing the towers. Stone replaced by the masons is light in color, while the original stone has a reddish tinge. Intricate stonework, although severely damaged, graces the entire cathedral, especially the two transepts and the elegant presbytery. The octagonal chapter house with its ribbed roof supported by a single large fluted column is the best-preserved structure. A Class II Pictish stone, erected at the east end of the nave, was found in the center of Elgin. This unusual stone made of granite has clear carvings, particularly on the cross side.

Monks at Elgin did not maintain permanent residence at the cathedral. The Elgin canons or prebendaries were supposed to attend services, but seldom did. Some held jobs or had other priestly duties that kept them away. In order to keep religious services going, the bishop appointed a substitute clergy called the vicar's choral.

We learned a lot from the Historic Scotland custodian, who shared many stories about Elgin. One of these told about a young woman of the town who ran away with a soldier. She returned disgraced and about to deliver a child. Her family disowned her so she sought refuge in the ruined chapter house where she raised her son. The people took pity on her, bringing her food and other necessities. The son later became successful and wealthy and used his fortune to repay the people's kindness. His name adorns a number of Elgin's buildings.

To get there: *We did not find Elgin Cathedral well signposted. We eventually stumbled upon it by driving through town. The cathedral is located on the northeast side of Elgin off the A96. Watch carefully for the Historic Scotland signs.*

Sueno's Stone ★★

We've seen this stone in many photos, but none of them prepared us for its immensity or for the complexity of its carving. This 20-foot-tall cross slab is likely the tallest and most intricately carved stone in Scotland. In order to protect the stone from additional weather damage, a modernistic glass and aluminum protective structure has been built around it. So, we couldn't get really close to the stone, and the sun's reflection on the glass made viewing difficult.

The carvings are exceptional. One side displays a ring-headed cross while the other contains dozens of figures. The stone's name, Sueno, was incorrectly attributed to Viking Swein Forkbeard, who had nothing to do with it. The carvings suggest a 9th or 10th century origin, possibly commemorating the defeat of the Picts by the Scots, the defeat of Orkney Norse by the local Picts of Moray, or the killing of the Scottish king by the men of Moray in 966. No one knows for sure, although it must document a momentous battle. The battle scenes start at the top as two armies meet, progressing until the enemy is defeated, which includes beheading of the captives, possibly the enemy leader.

To get there: *Sueno's Stone stands incongruously at the edge of a housing area next to the A96. We thought we would be able to see it from the highway, but didn't know where to look. Driving east toward Elgin, take the second roundabout into Forres on the B9011. Drive west toward town and watch for a sign to the stone that seems to point toward the subdivision on the right (north). Follow this sign. The stone is about 200 yards from the B9011.*

Pluscarden Abbey ★

To visit Pluscarden is to step back several hundred years. We will never forget sitting in one of the small transept chapels set aside for visitors, smelling the incense, and listening to the monks chant compline. The peacefulness of the small glen, the gentleness of the monks, the hush that came over the hills as the sun sank behind them will forever characterize our happenstance yet memorable visit to Pluscarden.

Alexander II founded Pluscarden Abbey in 1230 as a Valliscaullian priory. One of only three Valliscaullian priories in Scotland (Beauly and Ardchattan were the other two), it became Benedictine in 1454. Even after the Reformation, for about 30 years, monks continued to live at Pluscarden. In 1897, a Catholic antiquarian, John, the 3rd marquis of Bute, bought the monastery ruin and began repairs. In 1943, his son gave the priory to the Benedictines, who started restoring it in 1948. Pluscarden received abbey status in 1974. Today, about 30 monks, priests and novices live there in a fashion similar to their forebear's medieval lifestyle. Restoration work continues.

We arrived at Pluscarden Abbey on a midsummer evening, driving past several of the region's many distilleries and through a peaceful wooded valley to get there. We parked our car at the retreat housing area and walked into the abbey grounds through a gate in the original enclosure wall, one of the best-preserved in Scotland. As we walked up the path, bells pealed down the valley. We discovered that the eight o'clock compline service was about to begin and that guests could attend in one of the transept chapels. With a handful of other people, we watched silent monks file into the choir. Once they sat down, they were out of view and we could only hear their Latin chanting. We imagined the countless times over the centuries these abbey walls had witnessed this same service. In a small way, we participated in an unchanging ritual perpetuating an ancient tradition.

To get there: *We took the B9010 southeast out of Forres. (The B9010 also loops southwest out of Elgin.) Approximately four miles south of Forres and about two miles out of the village of Rafford, a secondary road heads east toward Elgin. Pluscarden Abbey is three to four miles down this road. Visitors are welcome.*

Duffus Castle ★

Visible from the main road, Duffus Castle (pronounced "duffus," not "doofus") rises out of the flat lowland, called the Laich o' Moray, like a man-made mountain. This fine motte and bailey castle served as a fortified house for more than 500 years. Human labor built the huge mound (motte) and ditch surrounding it. The word "bailey" refers to the broad expanse of turf surrounding the motte. Occupied until the early 1700s, Duffus Castle started its life in 1180. First built as an earth-and-timber, Norman-style stronghold, it was converted to stone in the 14th century. At one time, Duffus was one of the strongest fortifications in Scotland. The initial builder was a Flemish soldier of fortune named Freskin who had lands in the Lothian region. King David I, who encouraged him to establish a stronghold in the north, stayed at the early wooden castle in 1151. By 1200, known as the house of Moray, Freskin's descendants had become the most influential family in northern Scotland.

The path to the castle leads over a bridge that crosses a deep ditch. While the tower is the most obvious structure, ruins of a number of other domestic buildings probably built in the 15th century butt up against the motte.

Time has eroded both mound and castle. The northwest corner of the tower has broken off and slipped down the side of the motte where it now rests at a crazy angle. Huge wall cracks show in several places. Historic Scotland is at work to stabilize the castle walls, indicated by scaffolding across the tower.

To get there: *Duffus isn't signposted from Elgin, so we had some trouble finding our road. Take the A941 north out of Elgin toward Lossiemouth, watching closely for the B9012 heading northwest to Burghead. The B9012 takes a left off the A941 on the north side of Elgin about a quarter of a mile from the A96 roundabout. Duffus castle is signposted off the B9012, about five miles from Elgin.*

Spynie Palace ★

Spynie Palace illustrates the luxury high churchmen enjoyed at one time. For 500 years, probably beginning in the late 12th century, bishops of Moray lived in a style grander than many secular lords. Spynie Palace is one of the two largest bishop's palaces in Scotland surviving from medieval times (St. Andrews Castle in Fife is the other). The huge square tower has been restored, and visitors can climb to the top for spectacular views of the countryside.

Although the bishop's seat moved to Elgin, the bishops continued to live at Spynie and regally entertain guests. The bishops provided hospitality here to both James I and James II. King James IV visited on two occasions and Queen Mary once. Later, James VI stayed twice at the palace.

Spynie Palace enjoys a secluded setting. A loch, long since lowered, once lapped at its walls. A water gate in the massive northern wall led from the interior to the loch. Inside, on this wall, one ornamental head that supported a wooden beam remains. A medieval village once partly surrounded the palace, but no trace exists today.

The knowledgeable Historic Scotland custodian told us that the tower, David's Tower, was recently restored from rubble at a cost of three-quarters of a million pounds. A roof covers the tower that has replica medieval windows made half of wood and half of glass. The tower can be rented for weddings, banquets and other events. What an exquisite setting for a banquet!

To get there: *Spynie Palace was one of the easier places to find. Just two miles north of Elgin, it is signposted off the A941 heading toward Lossiemouth. When parking in the car park, many people mistake the little cottage at the entry as the visitor's center, but it is the custodian's home. The visitor center is located down the path past the cottage just under the walls of the palace.*

Balvenie Castle ★

Although a ruin, much of Balvenie Castle is well preserved and documents the development of the castle through its life. If its walls could talk they would tell stories of Scotland's famous families. Balvenie Castle stands prominently on a knoll overlooking the Glen Fiddich distillery and the River Fiddich. It has many nooks and crannies to explore.

Although the castle was associated with great names, not much activity actually occurred at Balvenie. The castle witnessed no sieges or escapes nor did it hold notable prisoners. However, its owners experienced various tragedies. The Comyn earls of Buchan, or the Black Comyns, built the castle in the late 13th century. John Comyn turned against Robert the Bruce and was later defeated and forced into exile. The next family, the Douglasses, experienced similar misfortunes. King James II stabbed a Douglas to death in Stirling Castle. When the ninth earl tried to avenge his death, the Stewart king destroyed the family.

The 13th century walls, still tall and massive, have been extensively damaged. In places, where the outer facing of dressed stone is gone, the inner core of rubble stone reveals the construction of the walls. The castle entrance retains its original rare double-leafed iron gate (yett).

In the early 1500s, John Stewart, the fourth earl of of Atholl added the elegant Atholl Lodging. During his control, Mary Queen of Scots stayed at the castle for two nights. John may have been poisoned later at Stirling Castle.

The Atholl Lodging survives as the most interesting portion of Balvenie Castle. A few spots even retain some plaster, and some of the chambers remain so well preserved we could appreciate how people lived when the castle became more of a home. Information boards show how the rooms may have looked when in use.

Standing back from the front entrance, we could detect various castle construction periods. A line demarcates the old wall at the left from the newer Atholl Lodging.

To get there: *The A941 out of Elgin leads to Dufftown, partly following the lovely River Spey famous for its many whisky distilleries. The castle stands just north of the center of Dufftown. Turn east off the A941 at the Glen Fiddich Distillery, and follow the road past the distillery to the castle.*

Huntly Castle ★★

Situated in a leafy park, Huntly Castle attracts numerous visitors interested in architecture. Many features of this unique castle are noticeable from the south, or front, side. Its ornate oriel windows and inscription

Fireplace carving, Huntly Castle

across the entire south face stand out even from a distance. The word, palace, more aptly describes Huntly Castle.

Huntly Castle actually contains the remains of three castles, the first a late 12th century motte and bailey castle, the second a more permanent castle built in 1376, and the third a palace started in the middle 1400s. Display boards describe the various building periods.

Only the large grassy mound or motte survives from the oldest castle. The other two castles were built on the bailey surrounding the motte. The second castle, built by the Gordons in 1376, replaced the first wooden castle. James VI destroyed this one in 1594, and today only the foundations of the tower house remain. The most noticeable structure is the magnificent palace started in the middle 15th century but extensively remodeled in the 1500s and finally completed in 1600.

Although suffering from age, the palace readily illustrates the splendor enjoyed by its occupants. Many fine stone carvings decorate the walls. Plaster on a basement wall even had graffiti from long ago.

Good access is provided to the various floors for visitors to see many of the castle's features up close. Some of these include striking carvings on the bedchamber fireplaces and the three-story elaborate frontispiece carving over the main doorway inside the grounds. These intricate carvings and opulent living accommodations conveyed the power and importance of the earl.

Much Scottish history features Huntly Castle. Robert the Bruce recovered from an illness in 1307 in the old wooden tower on the motte. James IV, a frequent guest, attended a wedding in the second castle in 1496. Queen Mary of Guise visited the Gordon earl here in 1556. Ironically, years later her daughter, Mary Queen of Scots, defeated Huntly in battle and ransacked the palace.

To get there: *The best way to reach the castle is to drive to*

Huntly and follow the signs to the Nordic Ski Centre at least part of the way. When we visited, the road to the castle was not as well marked as is the route to the Ski Centre. Go through the town center where a few signs point toward the castle located north of town. Drive through a narrow arch, wide enough for cars but not for tour buses and follow the lush, tree-lined road to the small car park at the castle.

Picardy Symbol Stone ★★

This nearly six-foot-tall Class I Pictish stone may be one of the oldest in Scotland, possibly dating from the 7th century. It stands in an iron enclosure at the edge of a field. After all these years, the symbols on this bluish colored stone remain distinct. They include a double disk shape with a Z rod (Pictish symbol shaped like the letter "z") through it at the top, a snake with a "Z" rod through it, and finally a mirror shape on the very bottom.

An early dig in the 1800s discovered a burial underneath a cairn located below the stone. The Iron Age Dunnideer hill fort is visible in the distance and can be climbed, time permitting.

To get there: *Take the B992 to Insch. In Insch, follow the minor road toward Largie. The stone stands about two miles beyond Insch on the south side of the road. When we were there, an electric fence enclosed the field on either side of the stone.*

Maiden Stone ★★

This finely carved Class III Pictish stone may be one of the last of the Pictish carving tradition. The nine-foot-tall stone has a notch on one side and is composed of red-pink granite. It displays a cross on one side and various Pictish symbols confined in panels on the other. Although weathered, the ring-headed cross side remains

Maiden Stone

clearly visible in the right light. The carving on the other face is crisper, allowing the Pictish animals and symbols to stand out.

At the time we visited, a children's author from the area and her husband were photographing the stone. While we admired the stone, they told us a few legends. One tale involved a bet a young woman made that she could finish baking bread before a stranger (the devil) could finish building a road. The devil won and turned her to stone thus explaining the notch where he grabbed her.

Loanhead Stone Circle

To get there: *The site is located off the A96 4½ miles northwest of Inverurie. Take the minor road south from the A96 to Chapel of Garioch. The stone is one mile south of Chapel of Garioch on the west side of the road. A long strip alongside the road allows for parking.*

Loanhead Stone Circle ★★

We saw our first true recumbent stone circle on a gorgeous summer day that also happened to be the summer solstice. Alone at the site, we entered through a small glade that led to the tall gray stones, some more than six feet high. The location, a meadow atop a large hill, afforded us grand vistas of the surrounding countryside with its green hills and rolling farmland. Built approximately 4,500 years ago, this circle experienced ceremonial activity for 1,500 years. Some scholars believe it served as a lunar observatory in Neolithic times.

A recumbent stone circle contains the usual upright stones with the addition of a massive rectangular recumbent stone flanked by two large uprights. Eight other standing stones, purposely graded by height, complete this circle. Cup marks are carved into the stone just east of the eastern flanking stone. A large ring cairn occupies the center of the circle. Where the cairn comes closest to the recumbent stone, a curved arc of kerb stones outlines the cairn stones separating them from the recumbent stone. A Bronze Age cremation cemetery sits next to this Neolithic circle. Low stone walls form two arcs with some small cairns inside the walls.

To get there: *This site makes up part of the Northeast's stone circle trail and is signposted as such. It is located about 4½ miles north of Inverurie, just north of the village of Daviot on an unmarked road. Daviot and the circle are sandwiched between the B9001 and the A920 southeast of the intersection of these two roads.*

Easter Aquhorthies Stone Circle ★★

We visited this recumbent circle on the summer solstice, not particularly meaningful, because like Daviot it also supposedly served as a lunar observatory. On that warm sunny day about eight or nine people shared the site with us, most just relaxing and soaking up the sun. This rather artistic circle was easy to locate off the A96 but required about a half-mile walk to reach it.

Neolithic people selected the stones in this circle for their color. Although all its upright stones are made of granite, eight appear light pink with the ninth a darker red. In addition, the huge recumbent stone appears dark red while its two flankers are gray. As at Daviot, the stones are graded for size.

To get there: *This circle is approached off the A96, just west of Inverurie. The circle is well signposted from both directions.*

Crathes Castle ★★★

An outstanding example of the transition of a defensive tower house to a luxurious home, Crathes Castle is typical of many castles in northeastern Scotland. Best described as an elegant tower house with turrets, this fairy tale castle also boasts an exquisite walled garden.

The castle's excellent condition can be attributed to 14 generations of the Burnett family, who lived in Crathes for 350 years. Crathes was fortunate to escape the ravages of major battles due to the discretion of its owners. Now in the care of the National Trust, Crathes traces its history back to Robert the Bruce who rewarded a follower, Alexander, with an estate in the nearby Banchory. Along with the estate, Alexander also received the post of Royal Forester and a horn as a badge of office. Today, this special treasure, the Horn of Leys, hangs over the fireplace in the High Hall. Other treasures in the house include portions of original painted ceilings and wall

Crathes Castle

friezes, carved panels in the Laird's bedroom and a panelled oak ceiling in the Long Gallery.

Crathes Castle also has its own ghost, a girl in a green dress, first reported in the 1700s. The figure is seen carrying a baby and could be a daughter of the family, murdered as a result of an unfortunate pregnancy.

Although the Trust removed some of the castle's modern fixtures to show how it appeared in earlier days, the castle still radiates warmth and gentility, even coziness. The turret rooms give outstanding views of the lovely grounds and walled garden below. The National Trust limits the number of visitors who tour the castle by assigning time slots. The garden makes a superb "waiting room" if the weather is decent.

<u>To get there:</u> *Crathes Castle is signposted off the A93, three miles east of Banchory, Deeside.*

Carlungie Earth House ✶

Both the Carlungie Earth House and its neighbor, the Ardestie Earth House, provide excellent examples of the size and construction of Pictish souterrains. In fact, Carlungie has been used as a model earth house for comparison purposes. A farmer plowing his field found Carlungie in 1949. To this day, a farm field surrounds the earth house.

Although called earth houses, souterrains were really storage cellars. Similar structures have been discovered in Ireland, Brittany and Cornwall. In Scotland, souterrain construction method varies by location. This one and others nearby were probably built around the 1st and 2nd centuries AD at the same time the Romans occupied parts of Scotland. Indeed, some scholars have speculated that they were used to store grain for the Roman army. Many were specifically backfilled following the Roman departure, as if they were no longer needed.

Because any roofing has disappeared, the entire souterrain layout is easy to see. Its form roughly approximates the shape of an L, running more than 100 feet in length. The paved floor stone sides reach almost six feet high in places. Two entryways exist and a long passage connects the main chamber and a smaller chamber that may have been a workshop. Some paved areas at ground level outside the earth house may have been dwellings.

To get there: *From the parking location for Ardestie on the B962 (see below), continue north toward Drumsturdy. Take the first road to the right. After a short way, a sign on the right points to the souterrain in the drive of a farm. Park in a wide spot along the drive. A gate through the fence leads to a path through the crops to the monument.*

Ardestie Earth House ✷

Ardestie, like Carlungie, displays all the characteristics of a large, well-made souterrain. The roof was removed and the whole thing filled in sometime around the end of the 2nd century. Several large boulders form its walls on the lower courses with smaller flat rocks above and between. A drain in the floor was constructed to remove any water that accumulated in the clay soil.

Ardestie was discovered and excavated in 1949. The excavator described its shape as a banana, with the door the stem and the large chamber the banana.

A number of structures were once located outside the souterrain, but today only part of one remains. A quern and piece of another, some pottery shards, part of a Roman amphora and animal bones were discovered inside. These structures connected with the souterrain through still another structure. No one knows their purpose.

To get there: *A sign on the busy A92 Dundee to Arbroath road at its intersection with the B962 points to the souterrain. Park along the B962 and walk back along the A92 toward Dundee. Go through a gate in the fence and follow a path in field to the souterrain. It can't be seen from the road when the crops are high.*

Arbroath Abbey ★★

Arbroath Abbey set the stage for some of the most important events in Scottish history. Knowing that the Declaration of Arbroath was signed here in 1320 made a visit to this bustling fishing town almost a pilgrimage.

The Declaration of Arbroath was actually a letter to the pope, signed by Scottish nobles pledging support of Robert the Bruce in his efforts to achieve papal recognition as the rightful king of Scotland. Abbot Bernard de Linton, Scotland's chancellor for Bruce, likely drafted this document, celebrated for asserting the independence of the Scots: " . . . For, so long as one hundred remain alive, we will never in any degree be subject to the dominion of the English. Since not for glory, riches or honours do we fight, but for freedom alone, which no man loses but with his life."

King William the Lion founded the abbey in 1178. Construction continued for many years with enough finished by 1214 for the King's body to be buried in front of the altar. The abbey was consecrated in 1233. The gatehouse range was built between the late 13th and early 14th centuries. Part of the existing Abbot's House dates from the time of the church structure with additions made in late medieval times.

Many older buildings in Arbroath owe their stone to the abbey, so little remains of the church or abbey buildings. Parts of the west towers, the south wall and transept, and a little of the presbytery and choir still stand in varying degrees. Only the late medieval sacristy built into the south wall of the choir retains most of its former shape including rooms. Today the gatehouse introduces visitors to the abbey via an audiovisual program and cars drive through the gate that previously accommodated horses and wagons. With the exception of the Abbot's House and foundations, Arbroath's domestic ranges surrounding the two cloisters have disappeared.

A pile of rocks is all that's left of the southeast corner of the chapter house. When the chapter house was excavated in 1938, 10 skeletons of high-ranking Tironensian monks were found buried beneath the floor. Some still wore leather laced boots or buskins on their legs. One was wrapped in the remains of his fine wool habit.

The Abbot's House still exists because it was used for other purposes after the Reformation. Though greatly modified over the centuries, much of it dates from the late 12th to early 13th century. It now serves as an abbey museum. In one room, some remarkable old charters from the 1500s and 1600s are displayed. Curtains cover these precious documents, protecting them from light. Be sure to look behind them.

The story of the abbey's founding is like a legend. Young William the Lion spent time in England where he developed a strong friendship with Thomas Becket. In 1162 Becket became archbishop of Canterbury, and a few years later, William became the Scottish king. After Becket's murder at the instigation of Henry II in 1170, Becket was canonized a saint. He became extremely popular and developed almost a cult following. Eventually, Henry showed contrition for his part in Becket's murder and allowed 80 clerics to scourge him at Becket's tomb. Later, Henry learned that William had been captured by English forces during an unsuccessful invasion of England at the exact hour he left his ceremonial whipping. When William was released in 1178, he founded Arbroath to honor God and his old friend, St. Thomas Becket.

To get there: *We thought Arbroath a difficult town to get around in. Not having a good city map, we drove around and around on its narrow one-way streets, none heading the direction of the abbey. This happenstance tour allowed us to see some of the quaint back streets of Arbroath, especially those near the harbor. Our best advice is to follow High Street to its north end where the abbey stands. We parked on the street.*

Brechin Round Tower, Cathedral and Carved Stones ✱

The town of Brechin is known for its old cathedral and distinctive round tower. One of only two round, Irish-type towers surviving in Scotland, this one soars more than 78 feet high. The old cathedral also shelters several finely carved Pictish stones.

Brechin's round tower, once freestanding, was built about 1100 as part of an early monastery. The tower rose six stories, each containing wooden floors reached by ladders. A tower entrance six feet off the ground also required a ladder. Carved figures of monks and animals as well as a crucifix decorate the stone frame. When used as a bell tower, the bell ringer climbed to the top and rang hand bells out the windows. During times of danger, the tower may have also provided security.

Parts of the cathedral date from the 13th century, although much of it has been restored. Inside, three carved stones are displayed. One Class III stone (carved after Kenneth MacAlpin united the Picts and Scots in 843 AD, showing crosses and figures but no Pictish symbols) contains carvings of David and a lion, a triangular harp, staff, and animals with two seated monks facing each other. A second stone is a fragment of a once magnificent Class III cross slab with Latin inscriptions, unusual for the stone's date. A third stone, resting on a wooden box, is a rare finely carved hogback gravestone from the early 11th century.

To get there: *Drive to the center of Brechin from the A94. An archway off High Street leads to Bishop's Close and the cathedral. We parked on the street.*

Edzell Castle ★★

On our way to Edzell Castle, we drove through the town of Edzell. This unusual town seemed oddly familiar, yet out of place in Scotland. Later, we learned the town was built in Victorian times. Its wide, planned streets reminded us of small communities in the western United States. The castle was another story, however. This early 16th century castle stands a short distance from Edzell, its red stone contrasting beautifully with its surrounding green hills, trees and garden. The focal point of the castle is not the building. Instead, Edzell Castle's graceful ruins adorn a spectacular garden.

The tower house, the earliest structure, is the most prominent feature of the castle structure. It stands in the southwest corner of a courtyard, overlooking the attached walled garden. Although the floors of the tower long ago disappeared, its walls remain intact except for a parapet at the very top. Because Historic Scotland has provided access to an upper platform, the tower house windows provide superb views of the garden below.

Other castle ruins border each side of the courtyard. Buildings that once stood at the south and east ranges of the courtyard were of late 16th century date and have largely disappeared. The west range dates from 1553 and includes the castle entryway, once at the end of a grand boulevard of beech trees that unfortunately had to be cut to pay the owner's debt. This boulevard led to the old village of Edzell and the first castle, a motte and bailey type. The motte is still visible as a high mound.

Today, visitors enter the castle precinct through the summerhouse and garden. The summerhouse is opposite the tower house with the walled garden between.

Sir David Lindsay built the garden in 1604. This magical garden was designed to stimulate the mind as well as the senses. The parterre, or formal planting, fills the center of the garden. Low trimmed yellow and green dwarf box hedge plants shaped into designs form a border around the flower beds. More hedges decorate the corners of the garden, these shaped into the thistle of Scotland, the fleur-de-lys of France, and the rose of England. Lindsay family heraldry and mottoes are etched, or trimmed, into the hedge foliage.

The carved stone panels lining the inside of the garden walls are even more extraordinary. The sculpted panels in special recesses in the walls portray the planetary deities, the liberal arts, and the cardinal virtues. The figures depicted in each panel stand out distinctly, although a few of the panels are reproductions based on the most weathered originals protected in the summerhouse. Small recesses in the walls function as birdhouses, others for plantings.

The delightful summerhouse, built the same time as the garden, displays some of the original wood panels from the castle rooms. The bathhouse, now demolished, stood at the southwest corner of the garden. A Scottish laird with a bathhouse was probably most unusual, because baths didn't become fashionable until Victorian times.

The Lindsays owned Edzell for most of its life. Now, the family is most known for its attractive tartan, copied regularly in current fashions. The Lindsays, often referred to as "lichtsome" or carefree, possessed the estate from 1358 to 1715. They didn't worry much about defense as the castle was built more for comfort than protection. Queen Mary stayed once for a few days, and later her son, James VI, visited twice. Cromwell captured it, and his troops who billeted in the castle for a month harassed the locals. Local people tell of the ghost or "gray lady," one of the Lindsay women, who haunts the place.

To get there: *Follow the B966 north out of Brechin to the Village of Edzell. The castle lies to the west of the village on a minor road, well signposted from the village.*

Aberlemno Pictish Stones ★★

Aberlemno is known for its four carved Pictish stones. These four exceptional stones stand in the open, three along the B9134 and the fourth in the church graveyard. In fact, photographs of these stones frequently appear in books about the Picts. Historic Scotland protects the stones in winter with heavy wooden covers. Someday, the stones may be moved to an indoor shelter.

The oldest stone stands farthest to the east along the road. This shapeless Class I stone displays a snake, a double disc and Z rod, and a comb and mirror, all typical Pictish symbols. Faint cup marks on the back suggest the Pictish carver recycled an old standing stone. This stone and its neighbor were moved here in more recent times. The middle stone was probably once a standing stone as well and contains some very faint markings.

The last or third stone of this group, thought to stand in its original position, is a Class II cross slab. A cross, angels, animals, and an intricate design fill one side. On the reverse, crescent and V rod, double disk and Z rod Pictish symbols compete with depictions of a hunting scene and religious figures.

The final Aberlemno stone, a superb stone located in the church cemetery, best conveys the Pictish stone carvers' skill. Intricate designs fill the cross, and strange twisting animals surround it. On the opposite side, Pictish symbols and a cauldron edge a remarkably clear battle scene, most likely the 685 AD battle of Dunnichen between the victorious Picts and Angles.

To get there: *Aberlemno is located on the B9134, north-*

east of Forfar and southwest of Brechin. Watch for the three stones along the roadside. The churchyard is just off the main road to the south.

<u>Meigle Museum</u> ★★

Meigle Museum houses a fine collection of carved stones. All stones came from the vicinity of Meigle (rhymes with beagle) and were assembled for protection in the museum. Large windows allow natural light to display the carving at its best, especially on sunny mornings. Unfortunately, we visited in the early evening when daylight was waning.

The stone carvings date from the 8th to the 10th centuries. Because so many stones came from the area, Meigle must have been an important Pictish religious center. While no early Class I stones exist in the collection, the carvings depict Pictish society from a warrior perspective. According to art historians, they also exhibit a distinct Meigle carving style.

The Vanora stone, almost eight feet high, dominates the museum. Was this the tombstone of King Arthur's Guinevere? After her capture by Pictish King Mordred and her return to Arthur, she was executed for her infidelity. Legend suggests that the stone's carved lions attacking a figure reenact this event, but in reality it probably depicts Daniel in the lions' den.

The museum also displays recumbent gravestones, created in the late 10th century after the cross-slab tradition died out. Some of the recumbent stones have slots in the top to hold a stone or wooden cross. An unusual hogback stone carved later than the recumbent stones and designed to cover the full grave is shaped as a fish-like creature with its sides resembling roof tiles or scales.

<u>To get there:</u> *The village of Meigle is located on the A94, between Coupar Angus and Forfar, where the A94 bisects*

the B954.   The museum lies a little south of the village center.

Falkland Palace ★★

The history and style of Scotland's royalty, particularly the Stewarts, comes alive at Falkland Palace. Falkland served as a hunting lodge, a retreat and a royal home. At Falkland, dying James V learned of Mary's birth and uttered his famous remark that his dynasty "cam' wi' a lass and will gang wi' a lass." Here, the royals played tennis and archery, danced and enjoyed music, and read novels and poetry. Then, as now, entertaining was a favorite pastime. While portions of Falkland have been restored and other parts lie in ruins, enough still exists to give visitors a strong flavor of royal life.

The name *Falkland* denotes its purpose as a hunting lodge. Falkland means falcon, and falconry was a royal sport. While visiting the palace we learned from a National Trust guide that one of his ancestors, a commoner, had been executed for possessing a falcon.

Although Falkland served as a favorite palace, the Stewarts and their court moved frequently between Edinburgh and Stirling castles, and Linlithgow and Falkland palaces. Traveling was a necessary way of life for the large numbers of people making up the royal court. Traveling allowed them to consume taxes paid in food and other perishables, but they also traveled for sanitary reasons. Primitive toilets emptied onto the ground, and before long, the ensuing royal sewage resulted in unbearable stench and health concerns.

Falkland began as a castle for the Macduffs, earls of Fife, in about the 12th century. The rebuilt base of their tower house rests in the garden on its original location. In 1337, the English destroyed that structure, although some sort of fortification existed during the early 1500s when records documented a garrison at the site.

The Stewarts became linked with Falkland in the mid-

Sinclair and Girnigoe Castles near Wick
Caithness

Old Wick Castle overlooking North Sea, Caithness

Oakbank Crannog reconstruction
Scottish Crannog Centre
Loch Tay, Perthshire

Duffus Castle near Elgin

Carved Pictish cross in church cemetery, Aberlemno

Falkland Palace, Fife

Standing stone, Beorgs of Housetter, Shetland

*Norse settlement
Jarlshof, Shetland
(above)*

*View from
Sumburgh Head
Shetland
(left)*

1300s. James II gave Falkland to his queen, Mary of Guilderland in 1451. In 1455, it was referred to as a palace. James III, James IV, James V, Mary, her son James VI, and both Charles I and II lived at Falkland for periods of time. To this day, Falkland still belongs to the crown and hereditary keepers care for the palace. Unfortunately, when the 3rd Marquess of Bute, a direct descendant of the Stewarts, bought the estate and its hereditary keepership in 1887, he found Falkland neglected and derelict. He completed an accurate restoration on much of the palace, but died in 1900 before he finished.

The gatehouse and south range appear complete, thanks to Lord Bute's restoration work. A large wall dominates the remaining east range, while nothing exists of the north range. The room in the gatehouse of the south range, called the keeper's bedroom, contains a bed that supposedly belonged to James VI. This room, the dressing room and the drawing room have all been restored. After World War II, Michael Crichton Stuart, the grandson of Lord Bute, and his wife lived in the gatehouse. Some of the furniture dates to Stewart times, while others are reproductions. Many original portraits decorate the rooms.

The royal chapel, dating to the time of James V, connects to the gatehouse. An oak screen at the entrance to the chapel was made in the 1500s. Although restored, much of chapel's decoration, such as the painted ceiling, was created in 1633 for Charles I. Other rooms include a tapestry gallery and the old library.

The king and queen's rooms in the east range have been restored to appear as they might have during Falkland's use as a royal residence. However, the royal apartments were not actually located here. The four-posted bed in the king's room, called the Golden Bed of Brahan, dates to the time of James VI.

Falkland's tennis courts, the oldest in Britain, should not be overlooked. Restored in the 1800s, they were originally built in 1539 for James V. Queen Mary dressed as a page and played tennis here, a type of tennis much different from the modern game. The display at the tennis courts describes this complex game in detail.

To get there: The *royal burgh of Falkland lies north of Glenrothes on the A912. Falkland Palace is in the center town.*

Aberdour Castle ★★

This little treasure stands north of Edinburgh just across the Firth of Forth. We took the coastal road to St. Andrews and Aberdour was on our route. Not expecting much from Aberdour, we were pleasantly surprised. The castle exemplifies progression from an old stone building to a luxurious lord's home used until this century. The main intact structure and the adjacent roofless range comprised the lord's home. Next to the roofless range, a wall still stands from one of the oldest stone castles in Scotland, built in the 12th century. Besides this remaining southeast wall, the basement and footings of other early walls can be detected.

The castle began life as a hall house, a two-story affair with a hall built over storage rooms. Later, additional stories were added to make it into a tower house with additional private quarters for the lord.

In the 16th century, the owner Earl Morton, regent of the kingdom during James VI's childhood, built the central range next to the tower house. This section was erected over a much earlier structure that probably once served as the great hall. It housed Morton's private apartments and other rooms such as storerooms and kitchen.

In the 17th century, the sixth earl, William Morton, added the east range, the part still covered by a roof. Its painted ceiling still survives. Other features include a sundial on an outside wall and William's initials, WEM, carved in the stone above the window on the gable end.

The Morton family, a branch of the Douglas family, held Aberdour Castle for most of its active years. The sixth earl guarded Queen Mary during her imprisonment in Lochleven Castle. As a loyalist supporter of Charles I, the seventh earl had to forfeit a lot of property but was allowed to keep Aberdour. The last Mortons moved out in 1725, although other people continued to live in the castle for at least 200 more years. The two gardens give an idea of some of the pleasantries of castle life. Historic Scotland plans to eventually restore the recently discovered terraced garden with its ancient dovecot. The walled garden built in the 1600s enclosed an acre of land.

Easy to overlook, St. Fillan's Church, tucked next to the walled garden, can be reached through a door in the wall. It dates from 1140 when the DeMortimers, then owners of the castle, built it. It contains an unusual Romanesque nave and chancel.

To get there: *Aberdour Castle stands in the center of the town of Aberdour on the A92 between the Forth Bridge and Kirkcaldy.*

St. Andrews Castle

Not only is medieval St. Andrews famous as the home of golf, it also boasts Scotland's oldest university founded in 1411, ruins of an ancient cathedral, numerous Pictish carved stones, and St. Andrews Castle. This ruined castle served as a stage for much Scottish history, including villainy, treachery, intrigues and abuse of power. Most of what now remains was constructed between the 1300s and 1571 as a fortified palace for powerful churchmen. The castle's history is one of building, destruction and rebuilding.

The activity St. Andrews Castle experienced highlights the town's importance as a religious center based around the relics of Scotland's patron saint. Religion also proved its undoing in the years surrounding the Reformation. Cardinal Beaton stands out because he made so many enemies. In 1546, he burned at the stake Protestant preacher George Wishart in front of the walls of the castle. Later, a group of lairds captured the castle by trickery. Murdering Beaton, they hung his body from the walls. The defenders were in turn attacked by government forces, who inflicted a great deal of damage. A final siege occurred in 1546-47 against a Protestant garrison. Before he was hanged, Archbishop John Hamilton completed additional restoration work. After the Reformation, the castle fell into decay, and its stone was used to repair the harbor walls.

During its early history, the English took St. Andrews Castle twice—first, in 1296 only to lose it after Bannockburn in 1314. They took it again in the 1330s, losing it in 1337 following a three-week siege. The Scots destroyed it, but in the late 1300s, Bishop Trail rebuilt it again.

Although little remains of the castle structure, several interesting features attract attention of visitors. The gruesome pit prison, used to hold lower classes, is located in the basement of the sea tower. John Knox accused the church of keeping many Protestants in this ominous place. Another feature not to be missed is the mine-counter-mine. During the 1546-47 siege, the besiegers dug a tunnel through solid rock to gain entry to the castle, while the defenders built a counter-mine that ultimately prevented them. Although a bit damp, the mines can be toured. They are well lighted with good footing.

To get there: *The castle sits in the heart of St. Andrews, right on the water.*

St. Andrews Cathedral ★★

This ancient monument stood at the epicenter of medieval Christian Scotland, hard to believe when gazing at its gaunt and shattered shell. Begun in 1160, St. Andrews Cathedral was once Scotland's largest, built in a location sacred even to the Picts. Legend tells us that St. Rule, guardian of St. Andrew's relics (bones), fled Greece to save them. When his ship foundered off the coast of Fife, he brought the bones to St. Andrews.

Today, this once renowned and magnificent cathedral consists only of the west doorway and south wall of the nave, the south transept, and the beautiful tall east gable. The windows in the nave's south wall give an idea of its previous beauty and architectural grace. Some are round and some are pointed with Y tracery, demonstrating transition from Romanesque to Gothic style. The east gable displays round-headed Romanesque windows.

The big square tower and its chancel belonged to St. Rule's Church, built in 1120, before the cathedral. A vigorous climb to the top of this tower affords superb views of the city. Entrance to the tower requires tokens purchased from the Historic Scotland visitor center. A word of warning: the circular stair is very narrow and the turnstile at the bottom very tight!

Other priceless treasures reside in Historic Scotland's museum in the visitor center located in the abbey's rebuilt cloister or living area. These include a superb collection of Pictish gravestones and cross slabs. The one-of-a-kind Pictish sarcophagus from 800 AD is the major treasure of the collection. This elaborately carved sarcophagus may have held St. Andrew's bones or those of another important person.

To get there: *The cathedral ruins stand next to the castle on the edge of the sea right in St. Andrews.*

Dunfermline Abbey and Palace ★

Dunfermline Abbey, although not a major tourist attraction, deserves a prominent place in Scottish history. This abbey founded in 1070 by Queen Margaret became one of the richest in Scotland and served as the burial place for many Scottish monarchs including Robert the Bruce.

We first learned about saintly Queen Margaret and her connection with Dunfermline ("Dun fairm lin") Abbey after a visit to Edinburgh Castle's tiny St. Margaret's Chapel. Queen Margaret loved Dunfermline so much she established its first small priory with a few monks from Canterbury. This exceedingly pious queen was rowed across the Forth from a place that became known as Queensferry. A Saxon princess, Margaret received refuge in Scotland following the Norman Conquest. She married Scotland's King Malcolm III (Canmore) at Dunfermline around 1069. After her death, Margaret was canonized and her tomb at Dunfermline became a shrine.

In addition to Margaret and Malcolm, other Scottish royalty received burial at Dunfermline after Iona came under Viking influence. In 1329, the body of Robert the Bruce was interred at Dunfermline while his friend Douglas took his heart on a crusade to the Holy Land. Today, an elaborate gold tomb beneath the pulpit of the parish church marks Bruce's grave. The Museum of Scotland in Edinburgh displays a piece of gold cloth that covered his body.

Margaret's son, King David I, built the church between 1128 and 1250. Through his efforts and those of other Scottish monarchs, the priory founded by Margaret gradually developed into the third richest abbey in Scotland.

Following the Reformation in 1560, the abbey declined under the care of commendators. However, in 1587, James VI repossessed the abbey and gave it to his queen, Anne of Denmark, who completed some restoration work on the guesthouse to make it into a palace. Their son, future King Charles I, was born at Dunfermline in 1600.

Over the years, the cathedral fabric weakened, becoming noticeable as early as 1563. After 1620, sections had to be rebuilt and heavy buttresses placed to support the nave. Today, these buttresses form a striking feature of the nave's exterior. In 1672, parts of the choir blew down, and the crossing fell in 1716. Other than the nave, the remainder of the current church is the result of restoration in the 1800s.

Cathedral features of note include the original Norman nave with its massive decorated pillars, the carved doorways, the west front towers and the demolished Chapel of St. Margaret. Architecturally, the nave resembles that of Durham Cathedral, not surprising because the masons came from Durham. At one time, St. Margaret's shrine drew crowds of pilgrims who brought offerings, an important source of income for the monks. Today only fragments of this eastern extension built in the mid-1200s survive. A plaque marks the chapel location, now open to the elements.

Most of the rest of the abbey has vanished. Of monastic buildings, only the refectory (monks dining hall) and the undercroft beneath it still exist. Other remaining structures include the gatehouse and parts of the royal guesthouse/palace once used by the abbey's royal benefactors.

The abbot's house next to the abbey is worth a peek. This medieval building contains a restaurant, gift shop and a small Dunfermline museum.

To get there: *We parked in the car park on Chalmers Street near the tourist information center and walked to the abbey by way of High Street and Kirkgate. The town of Dunfermline sits at the north end of the Forth Bridge and west of the M90.*

Shetland

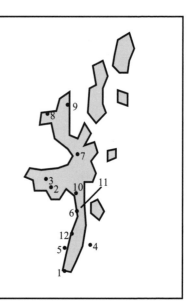

1 Jarlshof
2 Staneydale Temple
3 Scord of Brouster
4 Mousa Broch
5 St. Ninian's Isle
6 Scalloway Castle
7 Busta Standing Stone
8 Giant's Stones
9 Beorgs of Housetter
   Cairn, Standing Stones
10 Tingwell Stone
11 Clickhimin Broch
12 Catpund Steatite Quarries

Orkney

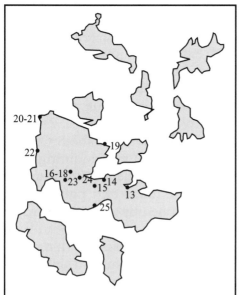

13 Earl's Palace, Bishop's Palace, St. Magnus Cathedral	19 Broch of Gurness
14 Rennibister Earth House	20 Brough of Birsay
15 Cuween Hill Chambered Cairn	21 Earl's Palace, Birsay
16 Stones of Stenness	22 Skara Brae
17 Barnhouse Settlement	23 Unstan Chambered Cairn
18 Ring of Brodgar	24 Maes Howe
	25 Orphir Church, Earl's Bu

Chapter 11

Shetland and Orkney

Shetland

These islands cluster far away from mainland Scotland, in fact, so far that visitors must either spend hours on a ferry to get there or go by air. For hundreds of years, the Shetland Islands belonged to Norway. Closer to Norway than to the north coast of Britain, their Viking and Scandinavian heritage endures. More than 100 islands comprise the Shetlands, so it's no small wonder the sea strongly influences the life of their residents. The islands bear stark testimony to the force of the North Atlantic with rugged sea cliffs rising to meet desolate, treeless slopes. The only trees we saw on Shetland were enclosed behind tall stone walls or sheltered by buildings in Lerwick. Even so, their gnarled and wind-ravaged branches gave ample evidence of the force of the North Atlantic gales. The islands sustain little agriculture, likely due to weather as well as the inhospitable peat-covered rock that makes up most of the soil. The Shetland Islands are known throughout the world for their diminutive ponies, sheep and sheepdogs, understandable in a land with limited sustenance for animals.

The remote Shetlands weren't always so hostile to humans and animals. Abundant evidence of habitation as early as 4500 BC can be found throughout the islands. In fact, the very isolation of Shetland has preserved its prehistory in a way not possible farther south. Because visitors to these islands must make a special effort to get there, their natural charm has not been corrupted by mass tourism.

We chose to fly from tiny airport in Wick on Scotland's northeast end to Sumburgh Airport at the southern tip of Shetland's main island. While we had no preconceptions about Shetland's appearance, we were thrilled when our small plane landed, its wings nearly brushing the sides of the enormous cliffs of Sumburgh Head. These high sea cliffs rise out of the ocean like a giant ship's prow. Later, we visited Sumburgh Head to gaze down its sheer steep sides to the ocean and watch the myriad sea birds wheel amidst the waves and rocks. Expecting to find an airport smaller than Wick's, instead we encountered a busy, modern terminal with numerous helicopters. We soon learned that Shetland serves as a staging point for the North Atlantic oil rigs.

Jarlshof ★★★

Jarlshof practically sits at the end of the runway at Sumburgh Head. Buzzing helicopters visible from the ancient ruins form an incongruous backdrop. Jarlshof, one of the most important archaeological sites in Britain, was far more than we expected. This one spot contains homes of Bronze Age and Iron Age people, the Viking era, and finally the medieval period. It's possible to cover nearly 5,000 years of history within a few minutes walk. Best of all, visitors can actually wander freely among the houses, touch the walls, duck under low doorways. We saw little cubbyholes for storage, passageways, grinding querns for grain, stone beds and cupboards, and all sorts of little rooms. Shetland's limited number of tourists means that Jarlshof is still accessible, unlike the ruins of Skara Brae in Orkney that must be protected from further crowd damage.

People lived almost continuously at Jarlshof for more than 4,000 years. The earliest Neolithic homes are located near the visitor center. The oldest house, about 4,500 years old, consists of a small oval structure. The walls don't appear very substantial, but little is left of them. Two pits in the floor contained fragments of human bone, stone axes, a stone knife, and a cow's four hooves. A nearby midden heap (garbage dump) contained 4,500-year-old pottery.

Wheelhouse, Jarlshof

Four later houses dating from the Bronze Age remain in better shape. About 800 BC, one of them served as a workshop for an itinerant Irish bronzesmith indicating that this Bronze Age community must have been wealthy. One of the two other middens contained hundreds of stone tools and broken pottery. The house with the bronzesmith's workshop featured two attached souterrains.

The large number of excavated Pictish artifacts, including two male profile portraits, indicates that Picts lived here. Did the Picts build the wheelhouses and broch? Although no definite answer is possible, souterrains usually suggest Pictish origin. Regardless, the Iron Age wheelhouses remain in superb condition, as does the broch built later. The wheelhouse name refers to their construction. Wheelhouses have round outer walls and piers that radiate inward, like a wheel with spokes. The spokes presumably partitioned rooms and held up the roof. Researchers found spindle whorls for spinning yarn and a weaving comb inside the houses and broch. They also discovered finer pottery, and more advanced querns, bone pins, awls and even slate axes, indicating use of Stone Age tools even during the Iron Age.

The Norse inhabited the site next and built the widest settlement. Earliest recorded Viking raids occurred just before 800 AD, so Norse settlement here probably started around that time and could have lasted for as long as 16 generations. Viking homes were shaped as long rectangles that housed humans on one end and animals on the other. Interestingly, this design coincides with the Lewis "black houses" used well into this century. Over the long years of Norse occupation, many changes and modifications occurred to the original structures, so it's hard to identify other buildings. They could have been barns, smithies, a temple or bathhouse. Artifacts found in the Viking settlement include a dazzling array of fine domestic and work items including iron objects that haven't rotted. Unlike objects from earlier periods, these objects give a clear picture of Norse life.

The medieval Norse farmhouse stands at the east end of the early Norse settlement. Not much remains because part of it was removed to reveal the Bronze Age houses. Built sometime in the early 1300s, this house provided shelter for about 200 years.

In 1469, James III of Scotland gained control of Shetland. Scots immigrated to the new territory, and in the 1500s Robert Stewart was granted lordship of Shetland. New Hall, the building closest to the Norse settlement, came into existence around that time. It became a kitchen in 1604 when the Old House of Sumburgh was built. This building dominates the site because of its height. In fact, the top of the stairs in the laird's house provides a good viewpoint for the entire site. The laird's house was originally called Sumburgh House. Sir Walter Scott named it Jarlshof in his novel, *The Pirate*.

To get there: *Twenty-two miles south of Lerwick, Jarlshof*

stands right next to Sumburgh Hotel and very near Sumburgh airport. In fact, visitors share the car park with the hotel.

Staneydale Temple ★

Staneydale Temple and surroundings contain scattered remains of a Neolithic farming community. Nothing like Jarlshof in ruins, it drew us further afield and into Shetland's landscape. The half-mile walk to the site gave us an opportunity to experience Shetland's remote moorland firsthand. The sun, the wind, the solitude, the closeness to nature as well as the jumbled Neolithic structures, made the short hike memorable.

Black and white poles mark the route to Staneydale Temple. On the way, beside the third pole, we passed the remains of a Neolithic house. This house consists only of a rock oval with an entrance facing south and downhill. We had some difficulty determining its features, although the house contains rooms and a porch.

We also could see stone fence boundaries and a burial cairn on top of a hill. Here and there, we saw clearance cairns or piles of rock Neolithic farmers cleared from the fields. Other stones looked like they might have been standing stones, but we couldn't tell for sure.

Staneydale Temple, a huge grass-topped rock structure restored to about four feet high, dominates the hillside. Built by superb craftsmen, its exterior design resembles a shoe heel or a horseshoe, similar to local chambered tombs. The large interior hall is oval in shape. The end farthest from the doorway contains six alcoves. The room's center once supported two poles probably used to hold the roof. Scientists have reported that one of the poles came from a type of pine found in North America, likely driftwood that ended up on a local beach.

The effort to build Staneydale Temple must have been monumental, thus demonstrating its importance. No one really knows its purpose. Rather than a central hearth as in the homes around it, it had hearths around the edge. Also, unlike nearby homes strewn with rubbish, it was clean. Staneydale Temple may actually have served as a temple or perhaps a meeting hall. Interestingly, the sea is not visible from it, one of the few places in Shetland where the sea can't be seen.

To get there: *Take the A971 from Lerwick toward Walls. About two miles the other side of Bixter, a minor road heads south to Gruting. Drive down this road for approximately 1½ miles. Staneydale site is marked with a sign that points up the hill to the west. We parked off the road and looked for the black and white route marker posts that lead across the moor.*

Scord of Brouster, a Neolithic Settlement ★

The Scord of Brouster is considered one of the most complete Neolithic farming communities in Shetland. Although the settlement can be viewed from the road, a climb to the ridge top affords a view of the entire complex of houses, stone field fences and enclosures as well as a ring cairn of a later date. An interpretive sign located at the top describes the settlement.

The top of the ridge also provides spectacular vistas of this barren and rocky landscape. Looking at the farms of these ancient people, it's hard believe this place was once covered by scrub laurel, hazel and birch and that these farmers grew crops and raised livestock. The climate was milder in those days and the wind not so fierce.

To get there: *The Scord of Brouster is located not far from Staneydale Temple. We drove to the site via the A971 heading toward Walls and Sandness. We turned off on the Sandness fork at Bridge of Walls. The settlement is north of the road about a quarter mile past the bridge.*

Mousa Broch ★★★

We went to Shetland to see Mousa Broch. For years we'd read about the most complete broch in the world, dreaming that someday we'd see it for ourselves. Mousa Broch was all we hoped for, even if we had seen nothing else in Shetland. Mousa Broch stands on its own little uninhabited island aptly named Mousa. The only way to visit the broch is by boat.

We were not sure we would actually get to go until about an hour before we boarded our boat, because small ferryboats cannot operate in rough seas. Although the June day of our planned crossing dawned bright and sunny, a brisk wind made the trip "iffy." We waited at the ferry dock on the Wick of Sandsayre with three other couples. Fortunately, the seas remained calm enough, and the *Solon* ferried us to Mousa in about 15 minutes. On the way, we saw a puffin skim the water and huge seals looking a bit like giant slugs lounging on Mousa's shoreline. Most of the way to the island, we could see Mousa Broch, looming larger and larger in the distance. Mousa has no pier, only some rusty handrails bored

Mousa Broch

into the rock. The *Solon* let us off to explore the island for two hours. Our captain gave us firm instructions to be back on time so he could get on to his regular job that afternoon.

Once on the island, we all headed for the broch. A path leads from the ferry landing to the broch around the east edge of the island. Soaring more than 40 feet tall, this circular tower looks as though a giant potter's wheel shaped it. The curved drystone walls are crafted with such precision that the outside surface is completely smooth.

Inside, Historic Scotland thoughtfully provided flashlights (torches). A heat-cracked rock hearth and well occupy the center of the broch. We explored the various guard and storage compartments and climbed the narrow stairs inside the broch walls to the top. At the top of the stairs, a wire mesh door keeps birds out. We walked out onto the circular ramparts to be rewarded with glorious views of the surrounding sea, mainland Shetland and Mousa Island. We also could look down through a protective wire mesh screen into the center of the broch. When inhabited, the circular tower would have been open to the elements with reed roofs placed around interior walls to shelter occupants.

After leaving the broch, we walked to a ruined two-story stone house on the hill behind the broch. The wood floors and roof had rotted away, and the carcass of a dead sheep lay in one of the rooms. One of the front windows framed the broch. Imagine having a 2,000-year-old broch as a yard feature!

We used the rest of our time to hike around the island. On the south end of the island, we passed one of the ancient burnt mounds, thought to be cooking rocks, and two lovely bays filled with frolicking seals and bordered by white sandy beaches. Wildflowers and birds filled the island with variety and color. Once we got too close to a nest and a pair of birds flew at us. Another time, we almost stepped on a duck sitting on its nest.

To get there: *The only way to reach Mousa Island is by boat. Make reservations by calling a number available from tourist information. We suggest allowing enough time on Shetland so you'll have several opportunities to go if the weather turns bad. We also recommend taking drinking water, as Mousa has no facilities.*

St. Ninian's Isle

Visitors to St. Ninian's Isle are rewarded with grand scenery as well as the ruins of an old church where a spectacular Pictish silver hoard was discovered in 1958. Weather permitting, the walk across the unique sand causeway to the island not only provides good exercise but also great views of ocean and nearby green islands with steep cliffs that fall away to the sea. Sheep populate the islands, and we wondered if some of them ever fall off the precipitous cliffs.

The church foundations can be seen from the mainland for those who know where to look. At the end of the causeway, St. Ninian's Isle rises up abruptly. The long hourglass-shaped strip of sand connecting the island to the mainland causeway is called a tombolo. The remains of the church rest high on a bench to the right of tombolo.

Once we reached the island, we followed an indistinct and steep sandy path to the site. A fence guards what's left, and an interpretive sign describes the site. The church was rediscovered only in 1955 after lying hidden in the sand for several hundred years. Maps from 1608 and 1654 showed its location. Burials in the cemetery ranged from Iron Age cist graves to mid-18th century Christian, indicating that generations of people considered the island sacred.

Excavations of the church revealed Iron Age occupation but most of the remains date to the 12th and 13th centuries. In 1958, a local schoolboy helping with the dig made an extraordinary discovery. Under the nave of the medieval church but inside a much earlier church, he found a Pictish treasure of silver brooches, sword pieces, a spoon, and bowls. A rotted wooden chest of larch contained 28 pieces of silver and part of a porpoise jawbone. The treasure was buried in about 800 AD—possibly because of raiders. The Lerwick museum exhibits replicas of the hoard.

To get there: *Take the A970 south from Lerwick to the B9122 heading southwest. Take a minor road west to Bigton. Leave your car at a car park just beyond Bigton and walk across the tombolo to St. Ninian's Isle.*

Scalloway Castle ★

The infamous Earl Patrick Stewart built his castle in Scalloway in 1600. The main structure, the tower house, remains fairly complete to this day. The castle dominates the town of Scalloway almost as much as in Earl Patrick's time. Decorative corbelling and corner turrets, including a long stairway complete with fake gun holes, make Scalloway appear very much a castle.

Scalloway, once the ancient capital of Shetland, had been an important center since Norse times. So, Earl Patrick Stewart wisely chose it as his main Shetland residence to match his elegant castle in Kirkwall, Orkney. Earl Patrick had many enemies, possibly for good reason. He forced the local people to build his castle and demanded huge amounts of peat for his castle fireplaces. After his downfall in 1609, his castle continued in use as an administrative center for the king's representatives.

Originally, water surrounded a larger castle on three sides. Today, only the rectangular, four-story tower house is left. A small square tower or "jamb" protrudes from the southwest corner of the main structure. Visitors enter the castle through a door in the jamb. An inscription for Earl Patrick above this door once sported royal arms.

Inside, only the first two floors remain including the great hall. Historic Scotland has erected an informative display about Earl Patrick Stewart in one of the ground floor rooms.

To get there: Drive *through Scalloway to find the castle. Obtain the key from the knitwear shop next door.*

Busta Standing Stone

This huge granite boulder situated high above Busta Voe (a voe is an inlet) stands in a pasture near a minor road. Local legend relates that the angry devil threw the stone here. However, early Shetlanders probably exerted a lot of effort to move this 20-ton piece of rock into place.

To get there: *Take the A970 north. Just past the town of Brae after the A970 bends around Busta Voe, take the minor road that heads south following the west side of the voe. Watch for the stone in a field between the road and the voe.*

Giant's Stones

These stones overlook the tiny hamlet of Hamnavoe in the northwest mainland of Shetland. The two stones stand about 60 feet apart, one about six feet tall, the other a little shorter. The smaller stone is somewhat triangular in shape while the other resembles a large thumb. Both stones have a predominant dark red coloration. White lichen covers some of the surfaces. We noted that the road past the stones appeared red in color as did the beach.

No particular reason justifies the stones' placement in this location. They don't seem to be aligned toward a specific landmark, and the sea, while nearby, is not easily seen here. A third stone once may have existed here as well.

To get there: *These stones are situated in the northwest part of the mainland. Take the west branch of the A970 toward Hillswick. Before getting to Hillswick, turn on the B9078 that heads west to the region of Shetland called Esha Ness. Follow the B9078 two to three miles until reaching a minor road that goes north to the little hamlet of Hamnavoe. About a mile after this turn, the stones stand on the right, just off the road. Talk about being off the beaten track!*

The Beorgs of Housetter Cairn and Standing Stones ★

This superb monument is located in the far north mainland. A bonus in our search for Shetland's archaeological sites was the opportunity to explore some of its more remote areas. We found these stones particularly enchanting. The ancient people who created this composition showed they had a sense of style and artistry.

Locals call this 4,000-to-5,000-year-old site the Giant's Grave. The builders erected a grayish white rock cairn between two beautiful red standing stones in front of the Beorgs of Housetter, a high steep ridge facing east toward the Loch of Housetter. The standing stones guarding the tomb are both about six feet high. We noticed that some of the rock cascading down the Beorgs was red, some gray and some white, which afforded a striking backdrop for the monoliths and graves. A ruined chambered tomb of red rock, called Trowie Knowe, stands a little north of the giant's grave. Unfortunately, these cairns are in sad shape. Antiquarians broke into both, and the rock once covering them has been used extensively for road fill.

To get there: *This site is almost as far north on Shetland's mainland as you can drive. Only seven miles farther north, the A970 ends at a farmhouse at Isbister. Driving north, watch for the Beorgs (a steep ridge) on the west and Housetter Loch on east. The cairns and stones stand on flat ground on the west side of the road below the ridge. We parked just north of the stones.*

Tingwell Stone

We could almost touch this 4,000-year-old standing stone from our car. Located as it is at the edge of the road and the edge of a golf course, access is not a problem. This six-foot, square-shaped stone stands near a narrow strip of land that separates two lochs.

To get there: *Look for the golf course on the B9074 about a 1½ miles north of Scalloway. The stone is on the east side of the road. We parked briefly in a driveway at a gate next to the stone.*

Clickhimin Broch ★★

Clickhimin Broch is probably the only broch in the world in the suburbs of a modern town, surrounded by a modern housing complex. From a block or two away it even looks like a modern structure. Today the setting resembles a city park and the structures would form a superb playground if the high walls didn't pose a danger. Because of its take-it-for-granted location, Clickhimin Broch might appear a less important monument, when in reality it is a very complex structure.

Clickhimin Broch stands on the southwestern edge of Lerwick, its small peninsula jutting out into Clickhimin Loch. The broch occupied an island reached by a causeway at one time, but the water level was dropped in the late 1800s. A major problem in visiting Clickhimin is its location on the major highway (A970) entering Lerwick from the south and lack of parking nearby. We parked down the street and walked to the broch. But we had trouble crossing the A970 as morning workers poured into Lerwick. Who would have believed rush hour on Shetland?

Clickhimin has about a 2,000- to-3,000-year history of occupation. Excavation revealed a sequence that began with a Bronze Age farmhouse located behind the broch to the northwest. This house remains almost intact. Next came a strong defensive ring wall and an impressive blockhouse at the entrance facing the causeway. The blockhouse stands by itself just inside the wall's gateway, so visitors walk through the wall and then straight through the blockhouse gate. Guard cells stand on either side of this second gate, one of which may have served as a prison.

The Iron Age broch was probably built shortly after the construction of the blockhouse and ring wall. The broch still reaches two stories high all the way around and may have once towered higher. A house built later inside the broch obscures its interior features. Unlike others we have seen, this broch had two smaller entrances in addition to its main entrance.

A highlight of Clickhimin is easy to miss. Just outside the defensive wall in front of the entire complex, a small stone structure has been erected to cover a rock with a pair of footprints carved on it. Although difficult to distinguish due to weathering, these footprints resemble some found in Argyll, where the early Scots used them for royal inauguration ceremonies.

To get there: *Clickhimin Broch is located on the southwest side of Lerwick off the A970.*

Catpund Steatite Quarries

The Catpund Steatite (soapstone) Quarries served as an ancient industrial site. For thousands of years, from Bronze Age through Viking times, steatite was used for making bowls, lamps, spindle whorls, beads and other items. Some items found at Jarlshof even match blanks and discarded pieces discovered at the quarries.

Soapstone cuts easily, so early people favored it for

raw material. The stone contains a high talc content and feels soapy, hence its common name.

Catpund Burn flows through the quarries, with outcrops of steatite all along its length. In some places, blanks are visible. Blanks were sections made ready for removal, but never taken. The fenced area along the burn on the west side of the road shows the clearest evidence of mining, places where blanks were removed, as well as tool marks, cuts and other indications of quarrying.

To get there: *The quarries are found just off the A970 between Lerwick and Sumburgh. They are not marked, so we had some difficulty finding them. Drive south past the little town of Mail. Just over a half mile from Mail, beyond some cliffs on the right side, a right hand slip road runs parallel to the main road. The burn is accessible from this side road. Take the stile over the fence. A sign warned us to beware of rams. If you see sheep, especially a ram, don't turn your back!*

Orkney

After Shetland's windswept rawness, Orkney seemed mellow and pastoral. Clearly, the soil in Orkney is far richer. Where Shetland was barren and rocky, Orkney appeared lush and green. Cows grazed in the pastures, farm machinery worked the fields. We were amazed at the amount of agriculture in Orkney in contrast to Shetland. Small hills covered with peat and heather intermingle with grassy slopes. We could even see some mountains in the distance on Orkney's main island.

As in Shetland, Orkney identifies heavily with its Norse tradition, although the residents view themselves as uniquely Orcadian. When we told a Historic Scotland worker at Maes Howe we were writing a book about ancient Scotland, he looked at us quizzically and asked in all seriousness, "Why then are you including Orkney?" We responded by asking if he considered Orkney to have

Norse affiliation rather than Scottish. "Neither," he said. "We are Orcadian."

Orkney consists of about 40 islands, all rich in prehistory. Almost daily farmers accidentally uncover new sites; they may not tell the authorities because they don't want visitors trampling their fields. On this first visit to Orkney, we stayed entirely on the main island.

Earl's Palace, Bishop' Palace, and St. Magnus Cathedral ★★

Right in the heart of Kirkwell, the Earl's Palace, the Bishop's Palace, and grandest of all, St. Magnus Cathedral, stand just across the street from one another. Today, only the cathedral remains functional while the ruined Bishop's Palace and Earl's Palace commemorate grander and more turbulent times. Historic Scotland manages the Bishop's and the Earl's Palaces with the tiny visitor center located on the grounds of the Earl's Palace.

Earl Patrick Stewart, the fellow with a bad reputation for oppressing his subjects both in Orkney and Shetland, built his Orkney palace in 1606. The palace occupies park-like grounds and provides a fine example of Renaissance architecture, supposedly the best in all of Scotland. How magnificent it must have looked when first built, especially the striking turret-like oriel windows just five feet above the ground. The intricately carved entry doorway remains beautiful although weathered. Inside, a grand staircase leads up to a great hall dominated by a massive and elegant fireplace. The triple tall windows at the south end of the hall give a feeling of spaciousness and light. The palace remains complete enough for visitors to wander around and inspect several rooms.

The Bishop's Palace located across the street provides a tangible reminder of the power of the bishops. Other than its five-story tower and very high walls, not

Earl's Palace, Kirkwall

much is left of the roofless palace. The rectangle that used to be the hall-house is visible inside the walls, but the upper floors no longer exist. Here, King Haakon of Norway died after his defeat by the Scots at the Battle of Largs in 1263. In the late 1500s, Bishop Reid built most of the current structure. We enjoyed climbing to the top of the tower in the Bishop's Palace where we got some great views and pictures of Kirkwall and St. Magnus Cathedral. The tower is the best-preserved portion of the palace. A statue of St. Olaf still survives, recessed in an arched niche in an outer wall.

St. Magnus Cathedral stands proudly just across the street from both palaces. Grand and venerable in its reddish stone, its oldest sections date to 1137, although it took 300 years to completely finish. It was dedicated to Earl Magnus who was murdered on Egilsay in 1116. His bones and those of St. Rognvald were discovered hidden in its piers in the late 19th and early 20th centuries. Its Romanesque architectural style is often compared favorably with Durham and Dunfermline.

To get there: *Look for the spire of St. Magnus in the center of Kirkwall.*

Rennibister Earth House ★

Rennibister Earth House is located in a farmyard right next to a farmhouse. In some ways, its location is most appropriate, because 2,000 years ago earth houses formed the centers of farmsteads. The Rennibister Earth House is a fine example of such a souterrain.

The main chamber is entered through a hatch inside a wrought iron fence smack in the middle of the farmyard. We opened the hatch and climbed down a ladder. At the bottom, the main chamber forms an oval with five recesses in the walls. Four stone pillars support a corbelled roof. Originally, the earth house was entered through a tunnel extending out from the main chamber. Today, lintel stones cover this long passage. The tunnel entrance is still visible in the middle of the modern farm drive.

Rennibister was discovered in 1926 when the wheel of a farm implement crashed through the roof of the chamber. Inside, searchers found the floor of the main chamber covered with scattered bones of six adults and twelve children. No one knows why it contained bones when souterrains were primarily used for storage.

To get there: *Take the A965 west out of Kirkwall for about four miles. The farm is on the right heading west. A sign guides you into the farm drive. Do not actually drive into the farmyard; instead, park in the grassy car park provided, and walk to the farm. At the farm, another sign points to the site. Go past the farmhouse where you'll see the wrought iron fence.*

Cuween Hill Chambered Cairn ★

We were glad we took our flashlight to explore this

tomb. Although Historic Scotland provides a torch at the entrance, it was helpful to have a second source of light. We duckwalked to the main chamber along the 16-foot-long passage just as the Neolithic people might have. This remarkable tomb exhibits exceptionally fine craftsmanship. The stone courses lining its interior were laid with precision and accuracy similar to a modern brick building.

Cuween contains four cells leading off the main chamber, one a double chamber. The ancient builders constructed the front walls and roof with stone blocks, but the backs of the main chamber and side chambers were cut into solid bedrock. When the tomb was entered in the 19th century, antiquarians found skulls of 24 dogs in the main chamber and remains of eight humans in both the main chamber and cells.

To get there: *Take the A965 to Finstown where a secondary road leads south. Follow the secondary road for about a mile until a Historic Scotland sign gives directions to a rough farm track that ends in a car park large enough for four or five cars. The cairn sits at the top of a long path up a hill, perhaps as far as a quarter of a mile. Once you reach the top, use the stile to cross the fence.*

Stones of Stenness Circle and Henge ★★★

Although only a few stones remain, the Stones of Stenness reminded us of the grandeur of Callanish. After seeing so many pictures, we were surprised to find that these stones seemed even more gigantic in real life. No picture can accurately communicate their magic. Like modern sculptures pointing to the sky, these ancient monoliths conveyed both a dramatic and awesome feeling.

Visible from a distance, the stones stand between two lochs, Harray and Stenness. Two outlying stones associated with Stenness, the Barnhouse stone southeast next to the A965 and the Watch Stone northwest on the narrow sliver of land between the two lochs, add to the mystique of the place. No one understands the connection between the outlying stones and the Stenness grouping. Today only four stones survive in the circle and henge that once contained twelve. Three incredibly tall, angular, pointed stones reach to about 15 feet. The fourth stone is smaller, about six to seven feet, with a pronounced bend. We think it fortunate that these four survive at all because the circle was deliberately destroyed in the 18th century. Restoration in the 19th century saved these.

A henge originally encircled the stones, but little remains. The ancient people laboriously cut the ditch for the henge out of bedrock and oriented the henge entryway toward the Barnhouse Settlement. At the bottom of the ditch, archaeologists found pottery and human and animal bones dating to about 3000 BC. The center of the circle contained a square made up of four flat stones laid on the ground. Nearby, traces of postholes have been discovered.

To get there: *Take the B9055 north from the A965. You can't miss them.*

Barnhouse Settlement

Barnhouse Settlement may have been the village of the people who erected the Stones of Stenness, because both sites date to about the same time. Discovered in the early 1980s, only the foundations remain of several 5,000-year-old Neolithic structures. Despite centuries of destruction from plowing and perhaps deliberate demolition by the people who abandoned the site, the settlement resembles Skara Brae.

The settlement consisted of six houses with stacked turf walls and turf roofs and drains leading to the nearby loch. People inhabited Barnhouse Settlement for about 300 years. Toward the end of this time, they constructed a large ceremonial building with a platform surrounded by a stone wall. Possibly used to control access, the entryway design was elaborate and complicated. The building's interior would have been the largest in Orkney. Did the ceremonies here involve the Stones of Stenness?

To get there: *From the Stones of Stenness, follow the path along the north side of the henge toward the Loch of Harray. A sign points toward the settlement.*

Ring of Brodgar ★★★

Along with Callanish and Stonehenge, the Ring of Brodgar ranks as one of the most impressive stone circles in Britain. This giant 312-foot circle, contains 36 of its original 60 stones, some as high as 15 feet. Most of the stones remain whole, while others consist of broken stubs protruding from the ground. The Ring of Brodgar, in its pristine setting between two bodies of water, would be an ideal spot to reflect on the meaning of life or ponder the nature of the universe. Good times to visit are early morning or evening when the sun casts long shadows and the colors of the sky and clouds produce dramatic effects.

This perfect circle occupies a slight plateau, surrounded by an enormous ditch cut out of solid rock. Once about 6 feet deep and 27 feet across, this ditch is still striking even covered with peat. Unlike many henges, this one has no outer bank. Two entryways at opposite ends of the circle lead across the ditch and face the lochs.

The solitary Comet Stone stands on a little mound east of the circle. Two other stone stumps show at the edge of its platform. Although no one knows for sure its purpose, it does provide a good place to view the entire ring.

Age estimates for the ring range from 5,000 to 4,500

Ring of Brodgar and henge

years. Its center has not yet been excavated so nothing is known about what may be inside. A Viking carved his name, Bjorn, on one of the stones at the northernmost point of the arc.

Burial mounds surround the circle. Two large ones stand southeast of the henge. A rare disk barrow, usually found in southern England, is situated northwest of the ring.

To get there: *Take the B9044 northwest from the A965 between the two lochs. It's impossible to miss.*

Broch of Gurness ★★

Touring the Broch of Gurness seemed a little like visiting a real home in an inhabited Iron Age village. The houses, their rooms and furniture remain in such excellent condition we could easily visualize people bustling around intent on daily chores. At one time, about 30 to 40 families lived in this sizeable community. This well–preserved complex may represent the most extensive broch-settlement monument in Scotland.

The intriguing site consists of a broch almost completely surrounded by Iron Age homes. Three sets of

ditches and ramparts encircle the village. The broch
might have soared to over 36 feet at one time. The broch's
original purpose was likely defensive, but, in later years,
it was transformed into a comfortable home for a family
of means. The grave of a well-to-do Viking woman buried in fine woolen cloth with a number of possessions
was excavated on one of the ramparts.

The broch is clearly the centerpiece of the village. Its
entrance through thick walls supported a large lintel
stone still showing adz marks left from working the stone.
All other stones consisted of shale, probably taken from
the sea cliffs near the site. Workers carefully fitted all
the stones with appreciable skill. The broch's interior
contains various rooms, a hearth near a well and a well-
used quern for grinding grain. The broch displays classic broch features—double walls, a stairway to the top
within the walls, and guard cells at the entrance. We
walked around on top of the walls for a good view of the
village houses and the broch's internal layout.

To get there: *Take the A966 between Birsay and Finstown.
About halfway and across from the island of Rousay, look
for a minor road heading northeast with directions to the
Broch of Gurness.*

Brough of Birsay ★★

This site provides an outstanding example of Pictish
and Norse settlements that spanned centuries. However,
we weren't sure we'd get to see it. A visit to the Brough
of Birsay entirely depends on the tide. Located on an
island reached by a causeway, the Brough of Birsay can
be accessed only at low tide. We were fortunate, because
the morning of our visit the tide was out and would not
return for two hours. If we didn't get back, we'd have
been stranded for six hours. We took our chances. Until
we got to the island we didn't know the tide schedule.

The walk over to the island on the rocky causeway

was a bit of an adventure. On both sides huge waves lashed at the cliffs. Fierce storms had probably hollowed out this causeway between the island and the mainland. We later learned that storms have unfortunately destroyed portions of the Brough of Birsay settlement. Concrete walls now protect remaining structures. (Note: "Brough" is pronounced the same as "broch," or "rock.")

About all that remains of the Pictish community is located to the east of the 12th century Norse church. Traces of a simpler earlier church, likely Pictish, have been discovered under the current church. Excavators found remnants of 7th and 8th century oval houses under some of the later houses. The famous carved stone depicting three bearded warriors holding spears and square shields was found shattered into fragments on this site. A replica stands in the churchyard with the original in the Museum of Scotland. Other evidence of Pictish life includes scraps from a bronze workshop that produced fine jewelry.

Vikings lived on the site for about 300 years and their houses fill the hillside just north of the church. These Norse hall houses are typical of the 9th and 10th centuries. Later Norse homes of the 10th and 11th centuries were built close to the cliff edge nearest the causeway. Rooms and stone ducting for underfloor heating can be detected in the remaining rock of these homes. An 11th century sauna here also provided a familiar measure of comfort in the harsh environment.

The monastery and its Romanesque church from the 12th century are the site's greatest Norse legacy. Although small, the church dedicated to St. Peter hints at its once fine structure. The church consists of only three parts, the rectangular nave at the west end, the chancel that looks like a small square room east of the nave, and the semicircular apse at the far east end. Some flagstones in the floor of the nave mark the site of a grave. The cloister buildings were located north of the church for either Benedictine or Augustinian monks. The Museum of Scotland in Edinburgh contains most of artifacts found here. Interestingly, some Pictish items were found in Norse houses, so the Picts and Norse possibly co-existed for some time.

To get there: *The island is located about 20 miles northwest of Kirkwall. Follow the A966 or the A986 to the village of Birsay. Follow the signs to the Point of Buckquay and a large car park. Ask the local people about the tide schedule before you go.*

Earl's Palace, Birsay

Only stacks of stone and a few ruined walls suggest the previous splendor of this palace. Built around 1574 by Robert, Earl of Orkney, it was designed as a fortified house. Therefore, the outside walls with their gun ports appear plain in contrast to the Earl's palace in Kirkwall.

This palace played an important part in the rebellion of Patrick Stewart, Robert's son, who seized it from the government in 1614 and defended it against the sheriff of Kirkwall's men. Because of this rebellion, Patrick and his son were executed a year later.

To get there: *Follow the A966 to the village of Birsay.*

Skara Brae ★★★

In 1850, a furious Atlantic storm blew across Orkney, ripping sand from its shoreline. Near the Bay of Skaill, the storm exposed several structures that would become one of the most extraordinary prehistoric finds in Europe. This 5,000-year-old Neolithic village attracts thousands of visitors every year. Photographs of its near-perfect homes have become almost as familiar as photographs of Stonehenge. No trip to Orkney would be complete without a visit to Skara Brae.

House, Skara Brae

Skara Brae still exists today because of the foresight of one man. William Watt, Laird of Skaill, had enough scientific interest to protect and explore the structures exposed by the storm. His support helped preserve the site, so that a large-scale excavation conducted in the late 1920s revealed an entire village occupied for 600 years and created before both the Pyramids of Egypt and Stonehenge.

Skara Brae is unique for many reasons. The undamaged village houses look as though the occupants have just left. In some places the walls still stand to about six feet. Central hearths, stone furniture, non-perishable household and personal goods remain untouched in the houses.

The best houses visible today represent the last reincarnation of even earlier houses built on the site. Some parts of these earlier dwellings also have been excavated. The village consisted of about 50 people who lived in six subterranean houses connected by narrow covered passages. A seventh structure just outside the village probably served as a workshop. The entire village was constructed inside a huge midden heap, made from decomposed animal and vegetable waste from the earlier village.

Most visitors find the furniture and personal items especially fascinating, a tangible connection with our present lifestyle. Stone furniture consists of box beds, stone storage boxes for bait, display dressers, benches and seats, and more permanent cupboards in the walls. Some of the nooks had drains in the floors and thus may have served as the earliest toilets. Carved designs decorate some of the wall stones. Personal artifacts include game pieces, awls, axes, small pots, and bead jewelry, pendants, and stickpins. Other strange objects found on the site may represent religious items.

Because of the priceless and fragile nature of the village, visitors must walk on designated paths above the homes, and plastic barriers protect some of the homes. Interpretive signs explain various parts of the village at specified viewpoints.

In 1998, a new state-of-the-art visitor center/museum opened at Skara Brae. An excellent video describes the site and reflects on its mystery. Artifacts found at Skara Brae are displayed in an interactive and computerized exhibit. A reproduction of one of the houses stands outside the visitor center. The path leading from the visitor center to the site incorporates a timeline beginning with the present day and moving through major world events back to the time Skara Brae was built. This timeline helps visitors measure Skara Brae's antiquity against other familiar events.

To get there: *Skara Brae is located on the west coast of the Orkney mainland near the Bay of Skaill. Take the A967 and connect with the B9056 that runs right by Skara Brae. Watch for signs, and expect to tour with a lot of visitors. The car park is huge.*

Unstan Chambered Cairn *

After duckwalking through Unstan's long entry passage to its large interior chamber, we were startled by a deep voice behind us. Straightening up, we realized it belonged to a man in blue coveralls holding a shovel. Instead of some ancient ghost, he was actually a Historic Scotland worker with the cleaning crew we'd seen outside. Talking with him, we learned that he and his crew not only cared for the monuments, but were skilled stonemasons as well. As always, we found the insights provided by the friendly Historic Scotland worker to be as interesting as the actual monument.

Unstan Chambered Cairn, with easy access from the main road, is a good example of a 4,500-year-old Orkney tomb. A modern skylight lights the tomb, so flashlights aren't necessary. The long main chamber contained large upright flat slabs that divided it into burial compartments. The recent dead may have been placed in the small cell in the wall until decomposed, when the bones were moved to the compartments. Over 30 pots were discovered in this tomb. Similar pots found on Orkney have been named Unstan Ware. Human bones, arrowheads and other implements also have been excavated.

To get there: *This tomb is located about three miles northeast of Stromness off the A965. A small gravel road leads to a farmhouse. Park at the car park near the farm garage and walk to the tomb along a fenced path.*

Maes Howe ***

The scale and type of construction of 5,000-year-old Maes Howe reminded us of later Egyptian tombs. Maes Howe, one of the finest tombs in Europe, also displays the best collection of Viking runes outside of Scandinavia. All visitors to Maes Howe receive a guided tour and thorough explanation of its many features by Historic Scotland staff.

Maes Howe rises up out of a farm field like a huge green mound. This 22-foot-high earth-covered rock cairn actually rests on platform surrounded by a shallow ditch. The long entry passage requires visitors to squat or stoop very low in order to prevent scraping heads and backs on the stone ceiling. A huge rock used to close the passage occupies a recess on the left side of the entry passage. When pushed the stone rocks slightly, verifying how easily it can be moved. Further along the entry passage large flat slabs, one about 17 feet long, form the walls.

Once inside the main chamber, electric lights controlled by the guide permit maximum visibility. The chamber was constructed as a 14-foot square with three side chambers that have waist-high entrance openings. Four huge upright stones, one in each corner, act as buttresses. The walls consist of thick stone slabs stacked atop one another.

The engineering ability of these primitive people once again amazed us. On the winter solstice, the sun shines down the passageway and lights up the rear wall of the main chamber. The entryway aligns with the Barnhouse Standing Stone.

When excavated, Maes Howe yielded nothing except small pieces of human skull that were lost before they could be analyzed. Vikings broke into the tomb more than once seeking treasure. Perhaps they cleared it out.

One treasure, however, survived intact on the walls. The Vikings decorated the main chamber with numerous runes. When translated, this fascinating form of Norse writing tells a lot about the people who made them, even their humor. The rune carvings actually represent an early form of graffiti doodled by bored Vikings passing time in the cairn. A fine sketch of a dragon complements the runes.

<u>To get there:</u> *Take the A965 between Kirkwall and*

Stromness. The tomb stands on the north side of the road, the visitor center in an old mill on the south side. Tickets purchased at the visitor center allow entry to Maes Howe in groups led by Historic Scotland guides.

Orphir Church and Earl's Bu

The remains of Orphir or St. Nicholas' Church represent the only medieval circular church left in Scotland. Sadly, part of it was mined for stone to build a parish church that was eventually torn down. The apse and part of the round wall survive from the original church. Some low foundation walls near the church may have been the Earl's Bu or drinking hall.

Norse Earl Haakon Paulsson, who died in 1122, possibly built the church in the 12th century, after a pilgrimage to Jerusalem. The church design is based on the Church of the Holy Sepulchre in Jerusalem. The *Orkneyinga Saga*, an important document of the Norse period written about 1200 AD, describes Orphir as a magnificent church. It also describes the Earl's drinking hall.

To get there: *Take the A964 toward Scapa Flow. At Cairnton in the Orphir region of Orkney's mainland, take the secondary road to the hamlet of Gyre. We parked at the Orkneyinga Saga Center, closed at the time. The building is unmistakable with half a Viking boat in front.*

Appendix

Timeline

Age	Years	Characteristics
PALEOLITHIC (Old Stone Age)	10,000 BC - 7000 BC	Only a few nomadic hunters and gatherers live in parts of Scotland where the glaciers retreated.
MESOLITHIC (Middle Stone Age)	7000 BC - 4000 BC	Largely nomadic hunters and gatherers range all over Scotland, living in seasonal camps. People occupy the near islands and mainland coastal or river areas. Many lithic (stone tool) scatter sites exist near rivers. Shellfish, fish, and seabirds seem more important for food than game animals.
NEOLITHIC (New Stone Age)	4000 BC - 2500 BC	Farmers, short in stature with long skulls, live in permanent settlements, cultivate barley and raise sheep and cattle. People develop manufacturing centers for tools and gain time for leisure.

Examples	Region	Representative Sites
Hand axes and tanged single stone points are used for spears.		Very few sites exist in Scotland
Midden heaps are common. Microliths (small stone blades for use in arrows or spears) are characteristic as well as stone blades and flakes for scraping and use as knives. Other stone tools include hammer stones and anvils as well as limpet hammers used to gather shellfish. People use harpoons, limpet scoops (for shellfish), fishhooks, and other tools made of bone.		We visited no Mesolithic sites, although some exist
Collective chambered tombs (both passage and long cairns) begin to be built. Fine stone axe heads are very important. People erect standing stones (both alignments and circles) and henges.	Close to Central Cities	Cairnpapple
	Toward the English Border	Cairnholy I and II, Torhouse Stone Circle, Machrie Moor
	Argyll and the Islands	Linear Cemetery (Kilmartin), Temple Wood, Kintraw Cairn and Standing Stone
	Western Isles	Barpa Langass, Cleitreabhal, Steinacleit
	Skye and the Northwest Highlands	Vatten Cairns
	Central Highlands and Perthshire	Croft Moraig Stone Circle, Machuinn Stone Circle, Kinnell Stone Circle
	The Northeast	Loanhead of Daviot, Easter Aquhorthies
	Shetland and Orkney	Staneydale Temple, Scord of Brouster, Ring of Brodgar, Stones of Stenness, Skara Brae

Age	Years	Characteristics
BRONZE AGE early	2500 BC - 1400 BC	People's heads are rounder, and they stand taller than Neolithic predecessors. They bury their dead singly in cists. Burials often include metal objects. These people are characterized by their pottery and thus called Beaker people. There is no evidence of conflict with the earlier inhabitants. The people have knowledge of metallurgy and make bronze weapons and tools. They also use gold.
middle	1400 BC – 900 BC	Two-piece closed molds allow casting to be done. People use a wider range and quality of weapons, functional as well as decorative. Evidence shows changes in society, including signs of society in some sort of crisis. Population dramatically decreases. The Hekla volcano eruption in Iceland in 1159 BC may have contributed.
late	900 BC - 700 BC	Evidence for regular contact with the continent exists. Economy is pastoral, with sheep and cattle-raising the main activity, supplemented by fishing. Some grains are still farmed. Highly skilled metalworking is evident, and gold decorates weapons. Society appears more warlike with some Celtic characteristics. Metalwork that may have been used for horses appears.
IRON AGE early	700 BC - 70 AD	Celtic speakers are now likely. Evidence shows migrations of people. A new type of metallurgy, iron working, appears. Horses are used. A warlike and tribal society is stratified into classes. Written and archaeological evidence indicates presence of headhunting and sacrifice. Large-scale fortifications exist, often showing concentrations of many people, probably in capitals of various tribes. Smaller district and sub-district forts can be identified as well as farmsteads. Ancient written sources show about 17 tribes live in what is now Scotland. People grow crops and raise horses, cattle and other livestock.

Examples	Region	Representative Sites
Bronze tools and weapons are used mainly for ceremonies as well as for status.	Close to Central Cities	Cairnpapple
Short daggers are common. Some single standing stones and alignments are erected. Agricultural evidence survives in plow marks and remnants of field boundaries.	Toward the English Border	Machrie Moor, Rispain Fort
	Argyll and the Islands	Linear Cemetery (Kilmartin), Dunadd
Standing stones as monuments persist. Dirks (replacing daggers), rapiers and spearheads are used. Fine earthenware beakers are characteristic of the era.	Western Isles	Macleod's Stone, Steinacleit, Clach an Trushal, Callanish
	Skye and the Northwest Highlands	Uig Stones, Hill O' Many Stanes, Cairn O' Get
	Central Highlands and Perthshire	Fortingall Stone Circles
Hillforts. Bronze tools and weapons take on functional uses.	The Northeast	Cremation cemetery at Loanhead of Daviot
	Orkney and Shetland	Jarlshof (houses), Clickhimin Broch (house), Catpund Steatite Quarries
Hillforts are present, many of them vitrified. Iron tools and weapons are used.	Close to Central Cities	Rough Castle, Bearsden
	Toward the English Border	Mote of Mark
	Argyll and the Islands	Kildonan Dun, Dunadd
	Western Isles	Cleitreabhal, Dun Bayble, Dun Carloway, Dun Bharabhat
	Skye and the Northwest Highlands	Dun Beag, Ullinish Souterrain, Dun Fiadhairt, Dun Hallin, Dun Grugaig, Dun Ringill, Dun Telve

Age	Years	Characteristics
IRON AGE **late**	70 AD - 500 AD	Romans arrive in Scotland affecting everything. Christianity also arrives. Written records now help describe people living in Scotland. The Scotti of Ireland invade southwest Scotland and create the kingdom of Dalriada. Displaced bands of possible nobles and their warriors come to Scotland from the south. These bands are made up of Iceni and Brigantes who bring distinctive types of fine metalwork. The Romans may have constructed a number of hillforts and then abandoned them before completion.
THE DARK AGES	500 AD - 1100 AD	Romans leave Britain. Saxons invade England. Large movement of people occurs. Scotland consists of four main groups: Picts in the north, Britons in the south (Strathclyde), Anglo-Saxons in the southeast, and Scots in the southwest (Dalriada). By the late 800s, the Vikings invade and soon become a fifth group. Sometime between 830 and 860, Kenneth MacAlpin, a Scot, unites the Scots and Picts. This is the beginning of Scotland as a nation and the age of the Celtic Saints. Churches and monasteries are built throughout Scotland, usually of wood, wattle and daub.

Examples	Region	Representative Sites
High quality metalwork uses bronze, iron, and gold. Brochs and duns, crannogs, souterrains, hut circles, and wheelhouses are built. Romans construct baths, forts, Antonine Wall, signal towers, roads.	Central Highlands and Perthshire	Oakbank Crannog
	The North-east	Carlungie Earth House
	Shetland and Orkney	Mousa Broch, Clickhimin Broch, Broch of Gurness
Early Pictish cross slabs with symbols and a cross are carved. Later, cross slabs are made without the Pictish symbols.	Close to Central Cities	Dumbarton Castle
	Toward the English Border	Mote of Mark, Whithorn Priory
	Argyll and the Islands	Columba's Footprints (Southend), Dunadd, Iona's Reilig Oran
	Western Isles	Howmore
	Skye and the Northwest Highlands	St. Columba's Island
	Central Highlands and Perthshire	Fortingall Celtic Christian Handbell, Dunfallandy Pictish Stone
	The North-east	Sueno's Stone, Picardy Symbol Stone, Maiden Stone
	Shetland and Orkney	St. Ninian's Island, Jarlshof, Broch of Birsay, Rennibister Earth House

Age	Years	Characteristics
MEDIEVAL and RENAISSANCE	1100 AD - 1699 AD	The Normans strongly influence Scotland. In 1124, King David of Scotland invites his Norman friends and gives them lands. He initiates a feudal system of land ownership in the south. Large, grand monasteries and cathedrals are built. The Celtic church succumbs to the Roman church, which gains wealth and power. In 1314, Robert the Bruce defeats Edward II at Bannockburn to win independence from the English. The Declaration of Arbroath is signed in 1320. In 1560, the Scottish Reformation occurs. Life is hard and short, but population grows as well as the settlements in which most people live. Frequent warfare, pestilence, and sometimes famine occur. England's Queen Elizabeth I beheads Mary, Queen of Scots in 1587. James VI of Scotland becomes James I of England after Elizabeth's death in 1603.

Examples	Region	Representative Sites
Towns and villages prosper. Magnificent cathedrals, abbeys, priories, and churches are constructed. This is the time of great castles and palaces.	Close to Central Cities	Craigmiller Castle, Culross, Linlithgow Palace, St. Michael's Church, Bannockburn, Dumbarton Castle, Glasgow Cathedral, Tantallon Castle
	Toward the English Border	Border abbeys, Hawick Motte, Smailholm, Greenknowe, Traquair, Caerlaverock Castle, Dundrennen Abbey, Sweetheart Abbey, Whithorn Priory
	Argyll and the Islands	Castle Sween, Campbeltown Cross, Dunaverty Castle, St. Columba's Church, Carnasserie Castle
	Western Isles	Trinity Temple, St. Clement's Church, St. Moluag's Church
	Skye and the Northwest Highlands	Dunstaffnage Castle, Ardchattan Priory, Aros Castle, Moy Castle, Iona Nunnery, MacLean's Cross, St. Oran's Chapel, Iona Abbey
	Central Highlands and Perthshire	Finlarig Castle, St. Mary's Church, Elcho Castle, Huntingtower Castle
	The Northeast	Spynie Palace, Huntly Castle, Balvenie Castle, Elgin Cathedral, Pluscarden Abbey, St. Andrews Castle & Cathedral, Arbroath Abbey, Edzell Castle, Crathes Castle
	Shetland and Orkney	Scalloway Castle, Earl's Palace, Bishop's Palace, St. Magnus Cathedral

Glossary

abbey a monastery with a group of monks or canons headed by an abbot; larger than a priory.

annexe addition to a Roman fort after construction of the fort and its walls.

antechamber an outer room or waiting room that leads to a main room.

aumbry a small cupboard or recess in a wall to store religious items.

bailey space enclosed by the outer wall of a castle, below the mound of the motte, as in a motte and bailey castle.

beaker a particular kind of reddish pottery made by a group of people, called Beaker, who ushered in the Bronze Age.

broch circular tower, varying in height, built of drystone walls, usually with just one entrance, hollow galleries and chambers or cells in the walls.

burn small stream.

cairn a manmade pile of stones, usually covering a tomb.

canon priests, not monks, who lived in a community following church rules.

capstone massive flat stone used to roof a tomb or other chamber.

car park parking lot.

caravan British word for trailer, camper or motor home.

castle large fortified structure built for defense and protection.

causeway trail, path or road built above the natural level of usually wet or marshy ground or water.

Celts Iron Age people who once ranged over much of western Europe, including Britain until pushed into pockets like Ireland, Cornwall, Wales, Brittany, and Scotland.

chambered tomb tomb characterized by a burial chamber or room covered over with rock or earth.

chancel part of a church east of the nave and crossing; includes choir and presbytery.

chapter house usually a splendid room, south of the church, where the monks met to discuss business.

choir area of church located east of the nave and the crossing; part of the chancel where monks sat to sing services.

cist grave made of flat stones to form a box or coffin; sometimes cut from solid rock; may be used for storage.

claustral monastery domestic buildings grouped around the cloister.

cloister an open square with covered gallery usually on the south side of a church where the monks walked and read.

commendators lay people given the title and income of an abbot; often absentee and appointed by the royalty.

corbel a stone or wood beam projecting out of a wall to support another structure.

corbelling layers of stone overlapping inward to form roof after walls reach a particular height; used instead of arches.

croft small farm, often worked by renters.

Covenanter someone loyal to the doctrines of the Scottish Reformed Presbyterian Church.

crannog an artificial, manmade island usually found in lochs.

crenellations tooth-like notch in castle battlements.

crossing usually refers to the part of a church where the transepts, nave and choir meet; often, a tower rises above the crossing.

Culdee member of the early Celtic Christian clergy.

cup mark cup-like carving in stone created by pecking out the shape with a hammer stone; often have rings around them and date from the early Bronze Age.

curtain wall stone wall that encloses a castle.

donjon a strong keep or tower inside a castle.

dovecot a pigeon house.

drum tower round or drum shaped tower.

drystone building of stone without the aid of mortar or cement.

dun a small drystone Iron Age fort without the characteristics of a broch.

earth house subterranean storage chamber made of rock, reached by a rock-lined tunnel; also called a souterrain.

equinox when the sun crosses the equator so that day and night are of equal length.

flagon a container with a narrow neck, spout and handle.

flying buttresses a buttress that supports a wall, connected by an arch that keeps the wall from bulging outward.

forecourt a space in front of a building or other structure like a tomb; usually partly enclosed but open to the sky.

galleried walls the hollow walls of a broch, sometimes used for stairs or rooms.

gatehouse fortified building, usually a tower, at the entrance to a castle.

glaisrig female sprite or fairy.

gled old Scots word for hawk.

Gothic pointed arch style of building that evolved after Romanesque.

great hall large room for entertaining and feasting in a castle or palace.

green men carved stone faces originating from Celtic pre-Christian mythology; remind people of the close connection between nature and humans.

guard cells small rooms built into the wall of a broch, usually just off the entryway; may have been used for defense.

henge a large ditch dug in a circle for ceremonial reasons; usually the dirt or rock from the ditch formed a bank; from the Neolithic or Bronze Age.

Jacobite a person who supported the Stewart dynasty as rulers of Britain.

kerb stones large stones surrounding a pile of rocks that form a cairn.

kirk Scottish word for church.

land an Edinburgh house situated in Old Town on a narrow piece of land.

lilia Latin for lily; pits the Romans dug in front of forts with sharp stakes at the bottom.

lintel stone a stone laid horizontally over the top of a door.

loo a British word for toilet.

machicolations open place in a projecting castle parapet or fighting platform through which defenders could throw boiling water, rocks, spears and other items down on attackers.

manse house where a minister lives.

mercat cross cross set up in a village or town where the market was held.

midden a mound of garbage made from household waste.

minster name for early churches having monks; usually important places.

minstrel gallery a balcony or walkway at the upper level of a great hall for musicians.

monks men who follow the rule of monastic life and have made a vow of chastity and poverty.

mortar and pestle tools used to grind grain.

motte manmade earthen mound for a wooden Norman castle.

nave westernmost part of the church set aside for use by the congregation; only part the public could enter.

Northumbria a region of northeast England inhabited in early times by Saxon people.

ogham an early form of Irish writing brought to Scotland in the 400s AD. It appears as a series of short diagonal and horizontal lines running through a long vertical line.

palace home of a king or noble; unlike a castle, not heavily fortified.

palisade a defensive wall or fence made of wood posts or stakes, often sharpened at the top.

pantile a roof tile with an S curve in it laid so that the large curve of the S overlaps the small curve of the next tile.

peat partly decayed vegetation found in ancient marshes and bogs; used as fuel when dry.

pele a fortified home, usually a tower, with no battlements.

Pictish stones stones carved by the ancient Picts; Class I stones—early plain rough unshaped stones with Celtic symbols; Class II—stones with symbols in relief, include a cross, Pictish and other symbols; Class III stones—most recent with a cross and other figures but no Pictish symbols.

piscina basin usually set in the south wall near the altar of church; used for washing religious vessels.

portal stones huge standing stones at the entrance of a tomb chamber.

portcullis heavy iron or wood door raised or lowered by a hoisting mechanism that slides up and down in grooves on either side of a castle entrance.

prebendaries honorary priests.

presbytery easternmost part of church for exclusive use of clergy; east of the choir, included in chancel.

priory subordinate branch of an abbey, smaller in size, headed by a prior.

quern flat stone used to grind grain.

rampart a defensive bank of earth usually holding a parapet or a palisade.

recumbent a massive stone laid flat with a standing stone called a flanker on either end; usually in the southeastern part of the stone circle.

refectory monks' dining hall.

Reformation movement started by Martin Luther to reform the Catholic Church and resulted in Protestantism; occurred by 1560 in Scotland.

reredorter the toilet building of a monastery.

Romanesque round headed arch style of building brought to Scotland by Normans; based on Roman architecture.

rubble walls walls built with stones of all different shapes with outside faces made flat.

runes early written script developed in Scandinavia.

sacristy room in a church for religious items and clothes.

scarcement stone ledge used to support beam that held an upper floor.

sheela-na-gig of late Irish origin and late medieval date intended to ward off evil; a female or male figure displaying its genitalia.

solstice when the sun is at its farthest point from the equator; occurs once in summer and once in winter.

souterrain underground chamber sometimes called an earth house probably used for storage; usually with a stone roof and drystone sides, sometimes a paved floor; entered by a tunnel.

spindle whorl a round stone weight with a hole in the center through which a wooden stick was run; used for spinning fibers into yarn.

squint an opening in a wall for people excluded from the congregation to watch the service.

steatite soft stone, easy to work; soapstone.

string courses a horizontal layer of stone laid in a wall to provide decoration.

tenement　parcels of land in Edinburgh for multistoried "lands."

torch　British term for a flashlight.

tower house　tall multi-storied stone fortified home; usually a square tower.

transept　parts of a church that usually project out to the north and south; form short arms of a cross.

turnpike stair　a spiral stairway.

turret　little tower that projects from a castle or palace.

undercroft　vaulted cellar.

V rod　Pictish symbol that looks like a double headed arrow in the shape of a V carved above other Pictish symbols.

vitrified fort　fort that had timbers between the inner and outer faces of the walls set on fire causing the stone to fuse together; not known if intentional or the result of an attack.

voussoir　wedge-shaped stone that makes up part of an arch.

wheelhouse　circular stone house with inside partitions arranged so they appear like spokes of a wheel.

yett　a strong iron gate at the entrance of many castles and fortified homes.

Z rod　Pictish symbol that looks like a double headed arrow in the shape of a Z carved over other Pictish symbols.

Useful Resources

General/Tourism

•British Tourist Authority—www.visitbritain.com; 800-462-2748
•Scottish Tourist Board—www.holiday.scotland.net
•Historic Scotland—www.historic-scotland.gov.uk
•National Museums of Scotland—www.nms.ac.uk
•Edinburgh festivals—www.go-edinburgh.co.uk

Many regional authorities support or maintain websites, such as: Orkney (Orknet)—www.orknet.co.uk; Argyll, the Isles, Loch Lomond, Stirling and Trossachs—www.scottish.heartlands.org

Accommodation (also see regional tourist authority websites or write to the regional tourist boards)

•Automobile Association—www.theaa.co.uk/Hotels
•Scottish Tourist Board—www.holiday.scotland.net

The Scottish Tourist Board publishes four excellent guides, available in local bookstores, from the British Tourist Authority or the Scottish Tourist Board—*Scotland: Hotels & Guest Houses; Scotland: Bed & Breakfast; Scotland: Caravan & Camping; Scotland: Self Catering*

Driving

The Highway Code, HMSO. (This useful manual can be purchased in British bookstores. We suggest you contact James Thin Ltd, 53-59 South Bridge, Edinburgh EH1 1YS; www.jthin.co.uk.)

Packing and Travel Clothing

Cardone, Laurel. *Fodor's How to Pack.* New York: Fodor's Travel Publications, Inc., 1997.

Gilford, Judith. *The Packing Book.* Berkeley: Ten Speed Press, 1996.

McAlpin, Anne B. *Pack it Up!* Seattle: Flying Cloud Publishing, 1990.

References

A Guide to Forest Walks and Trails: Forests of Knapdale, Kintyre & Kilmichael.
N. p.: Forestry Commission, n. d.

A List of Ancient Monuments in Scotland. N.p.: Historic Scotland, n. d.

Aikman, Christian. *Castle Tioram in Moidart.* N. p.: n. p., 1995.

Apted, Michael. *Aberdour Castle.* Ed. Chris Tabraham. 1961. Edinburgh:
Historic Scotland, 1996.

Armit, Ian. *The Archaeology of Skye and the Western Isles.* Edinburgh:
Edinburgh UP, 1996.

Ashmore, Patrick. *Calanais: The Standing Stones.* Stornoway: Urras nan
Tursachan Ltd, 1995.

—. *Jarlshof: A Walk Through the Past.* Ed. Chris Tabraham. Edinburgh:
Historic Scotland, 1993.

—. *Maes Howe.* Ed. Christopher Tabraham. 1989. Edinburgh: Historic
Scotland, 1995.

Ashmore, P. J. *Neolithic and Bronze Age Scotland.* Historic Scotland. London:
B. T. Batsford Ltd., 1996.

Baldwin, John. *Edinburgh, Lothians and Borders.* Ed. Anna Ritchie. Exploring
Scotland's Heritage. Edinburgh: HMSO, 1997.

Bannockburn. Edinburgh: The National Trust for Scotland, 1991.

Barclay, Gordan, and Doreen Grove. *Cairnpapple Hill.* Ed. Chris Tabraham.
Edinburgh: Historic Scotland, 1998.

Blundel, Nigel. *Ancient Scotland.* London: Promotional Reprint Company Ltd.,
1996.

Bord, Janet, and Colin Bord. Atlas of Magical Britain. *1990. London:
Bracken Books, 1993.*

Bradley, Richard. "Excavations at Clava." *Current Archaeology* 148 (1996):
136-142.

Bramman, John, et al. *Visits to Ancient Caithness.* 3rd ed. Thurso: Caithness
Field Club, 1982.

Breeze, David J. *Ardoch Roman Fort: Braco, near
Dunblane: A Guide.* Dunblane: Rotary Club of Bridge of Allan and Dunblane,
1987.

Bridgland, Nick. *Hermitage Castle.* Ed. Chris Tabraham. Edinburgh: Historic
Scotland, 1996.

Brooks, J. A. *Welcome to Iona.* Norwich: Jarrold Publishing, 1987.

Burl, Aubrey. *A Guide to the Stone Circles of Britain, Ireland and Brittany.*
New Haven and London: Yale UP, 1995.

Chapter House Museum: Dunkeld Cathedral. Dunkeld: The Friends of Dunkeld
Cathedral, 1996.

Clarke, David, and Patrick Maguire. *Skara Brae.* Ed. Christopher Tabraham.
Edinburgh: Historic Scotland, 1995.

Clarke, Simon. *Trimontium: A Roman Frontier Post and its Phases.* N. p.: The
Trimontium Trust, n. d.

Close-Brooks, Joanna. *The Highlands.* Ed. Anna Ritchie. Exploring Scotland's
Heritage. Edinburgh: HMSO, 1995.

Cruden, Stewart. *Castle Campbell.* Ed. Chris Tabraham. 1952. Edinburgh: Historic Scotland, 1994.

—. *The Brochs of Mousa and Clickhimin: Shetland.* Edinburgh: HMSO, 1951.

Donaldson-Blyth, Ian. *In Search of Prehistoric Skye.* Insch: ThistlePress, 1995.

Dun Bharabhat, Great Bernera NB15583355. N. p.: n. p., n. d.

Dudley, Marjorie, and Wilber Dudley. *Look Over Your Right Shoulder.* Verona: Park Printing House, Ltd., 1984.

Elliot, Walter. *The Trimontium Story.* N. p.: The Trimontium Trust, n. d.

Fawcett, Richard. *The Architectural History of Scotland: From the Accession of the Stewarts to the Reformation 1371-1560.* Eds. Charles Mckean and Deborah Howard. Edinburgh: Edinburgh UP, 1994.

—. *Dunkeld Cathedral: A Short History and Guide.* Dunkeld: The Society of Friends of Dunkeld Cathedral, 1990.

—. *Argyll's Lodging.* Ed. Chris Tabraham. Edinburgh: Historic Scotland, 1996.

—. *Beauly Priory and Fortrose Cathedral.* Ed. David J. Breeze. Historic Buildings and Monuments. Edinburgh: HMSO, 1987.

—. *Stirling Castle.* Edinburgh: HMSO, 1990.

—. *Elgin Cathedral.* 1991. Edinburgh: Historic Scotland, 1995.

—. *St Andrews Castle.* Ed. Chris Tabraham. Edinburgh: Historic Scotland, 1992.

—. *St Andrews Cathedral.* Ed. Chris Tabraham. Edinburgh: Historic Scotland, 1993.

—. *Elcho Castle.* Edinburgh: Historic Scotland, 1997.

—. *The Abbey and Palace of Dunfermline.* Ed. Chris Tabraham. Edinburgh: Historic Scotland, 1990.

Fisher, Andrew. *A Traveller's History of Scotland.* 3rd ed. New York: Interlink Books, 1997.

Fojut, Noel, Denys Pringle, and Bruce Walker. *The Ancient Monuments of the Western Isles.* Ed. Denys Pringle. Historic Scotland. Edinburgh: HMSO, 1994.

Fojut, Noel, and Denys Pringle. *The Ancient Monuments of Shetland.* Ed. Chris Tabraham. Historic Scotland. Edinburgh: HMSO, 1993.

Fojut, Noel. *The Brochs of Gurness and Midhowe.* Ed. Chris Tabraham. Edinburgh: Historic Scotland, 1993.

Fraprie, Frank Roy. *Castles and Keeps of Scotland.* New York: Barnes & Noble Books, Inc., 1993.

Grove, Doreen. *Caerlaverock Castle.* Ed. Chris Tabraham. Edinburgh: Historic Scotland, 1994.

—. *Glenluce Abbey.* Ed. Chris Tabraham. Edinburgh: Historic Scotland, 1996.

—. *Dirleton Castle.* Ed. Chris Tabraham. Edinburgh: Historic Scotland, 1995.

Hamilton, Ronald. *The Pluscarden Story.* Elgin: Moravian Press, Ltd., 1997.

Hannah, Ian C. *The Story of Scotland in Stone.* Stevenage: The Strong Oak Press Ltd., 1988.

Hartley, Christopher. *Gladstone's Land.* Edinburgh: The National Trust for Scotland, 1992.

Heggie, Douglas C. *Megalithic Science: Ancient Mathematics and Astronomy in*

Northwest Europe. London: Thames and Hudson Ltd., 1981.

Hill, Peter, and Dave Pollock. *The Whithorn Dig.* N. p.: Whithorn Board of Management, 1992.

Historic Scotland: The Sites to See: A Guide to Over 300 Historic Sites Spanning 5,000 Years. Edinburgh: Historic Scotland, n. d.

In the Footsteps of Early Man: An Introduction to the Archaeology of Skye & Lochalsh. Portree: Skye and Lochalsh Museums Service, n. d.

James, David, and Bostock, Simant. *Celtic Connections.* London: Blandford, 1996.

Jackson, Anthony. *The Pictish Trail: A Travellers Guide to the Old Pictish Kingdoms.* Kirkwall: The Orkney Press Ltd., 1989.

Johnstone, Anne. *The Wild Frontier: Exploring the Antonnie Wall.* Ed. Sheila Mackay. Edinburgh: Moubray House Press, 1986.

Keppie, Lawrence. *Scotland's Roman Remains.* Edinburgh: John Donald Publishers Ltd., 1990.

Kilmartin Glen. Lochgilphead: Kilmartin Glen Project, n. d.

Laing, Lloyd, and Jenny Laing. *The Picts and the Scots.* Phoenix Mill: Alan Sutton Publishing Limited, 1994.

Lawson, Bill. *St. Clement's Church at Rodel Isle of Harris.* Northton: n. p., n. d.

Leslie, Andrew. *Passport's Guide to the Best of Scotland.* Chicago: Passport Books, 1997.

Levison, David, ed. *St Marys Collegiate Church Haddington.* N. p.: n. p., n. d.

Lockhart, Ann. *Celtic Saints.* N. p.: Pitkin Pictorials, 1995.

Macdonald, C. J., and Neil Urquhart. *The Eagle Stone: A Mysterious Legacy from the Picts.* N. p.: n. p., 1996.

MacIvar, Iain. *Blackness Castle.* Ed. Chris Tabraham. 1982. Edinburgh: Historic Scotland, 1993.

—. *Dumbarton Castle.* Ed. Chris Tabraham. 1958. Edinburgh: Historic Scotland, 1993.

—. *Balvenie Castle.* Ed. Chris Tabraham. 1986. Edinburgh: Historic Scotland, 1995.

MacKie, Euan W. *Scotland: An Archaeological Guide.* London: Faber and Faber, Ltd., 1975.

Mackie, R. L., and Stewart Cruden. *Arbroath Abbey.* Ed. Chris Tabraham. 1954. Edinburgh: Historic Scotland, 1996.

Magnusson, Magnus, ed. *Echoes in Stone.* Edinburgh: Ancient Monuments Division, Scottish Development Department, 1983.

Meldrum, Edward. *The Cairns of Clava.* N. p.: n. p., 1983.

Menzies, Lucy, et al. *St. Margaret Queen of Scotland.* Ed. Charles Robertson. N. p.: The St. Margaret Chapel Guild, 1994.

Miers, Richenda. *Scotland's Highlands & Islands.* N. p.: Cadogan Books, n. d.

Morris, William J. *A Walk Through Glasgow Cathedral.* 2nd ed. Glasgow: University of Glasgow, 1995.

Muir, Richard. *Traveller's History of Britain and Ireland.* 1983. London: Bloomsbury Books, 1992.

Nigg Old Trust. Fearn: Cromarty Courthouse, 1996.

Oram, Richard. *Scottish Prehistory.* Edinburgh: Birlinn, 1997.

"Orkney." *Current Archaeology.* 154 (1997): 372-380.

Pastime Publications Ltd. *Scotland for the Motorist 1996.* Edinburgh: Pastime Publications Ltd. In Association with the Scottish Tourist Board, 1996.

Pearson, John. *Around Stirling.* Perth: John Macmillan Pearson, 1995.

Ponting, Gerald, and Margaret Pointing. *The Stones Around Callanish.* Stornoway: Stornoway Gazette, 1984.

Ponting, Margaret R., and G Ronald Curtis. *Mini-Guide to Prehistoric Harris (2).* Callanish: Margaret R Ponting and G Ronald Curtis, 1988.

—. *Mini-Guide to Prehistoric Harris (1).* Callanish: Margaret R Ponting and G Ronald Curtis, 1988.

Ponting, Gerald. *A Mini-Guide to Eoropie Teampull: Isle of Lewis.* Callanish: G & M Ponting, 1982.

Prebble, John. *The Lion in the North.* London: Penguin Group, 1981.

Pringle, Denys R. *Doune Castle.* 1987. Edinburgh: Historic Scotland, 1995.

Pringle, Denys. *Craigmillar Castle.* Historic Scotland. Edinburgh: HMSO, 1990.

—. *Spynie Palace.* Ed. Chris Tabraham. Edinburgh: Historic Scotland, 1996.

—. *Huntingtower.* Ed. Chris Tabraham. 1989. Edinburgh: Historic Scotland, 1996.

—. *Linlithgow Palace.* Edinburgh: HMSO, 1989.

Puttfarken, Thomas, et al. *Falkland Palace and Royal Burgh.* Ed. Hilary Horrocks. Edinburgh: The National Trust for Scotland, 1995.

Reclaiming the Romans: The Newstead Project. N. p.: National Museums of Scotland, n. d.

Renfew, Colin, ed. *The Prehistory of Orkney: BC 4000-1000 AD.* Edinburgh: Edinburgh UP, 1985.

Richardson, James, and Marguerite Wood. *Dryburgh Abbey.* Ed. Chris Tabraham. 1937. Edinburgh: Historic Scotland, 1996.

Richardson, J. S. *Dundrennan Abbey.* Ed. Chris Tabraham. 1981. Edinburgh: Historic Scotland, 1994.

—. *Sweetheart Abbey.* Ed. Chris Tabraham. 1958. Edinburgh: Historic Scotland, 1995.

Richardson, J. S., and Margureite Wood. *Melrose Abbey.* Ed. C. J. Tabraham. Edinburgh: HMSO, 1989.

Ritchie, Anna and Graham Ritchie. *Scotland: An Oxford Archaeological Guide.* Ed. Barry Cunliffe. Oxford: Oxford UP, 1998.

—. *The Ancient Monuments of Orkney.* Ed. Patrick Ashmore. Historic Scotland. Edinburgh: HMSO, 1995.

Ritchie, Anna, and David J. Breeze. *Invaders of Scotland.* Historic Buildings and Monuments. Ediniburgh: HMSO, 1991.

Ritchie, Anna. *Meigle Museum: Pictish Carved Stones.* Ed. Chris Tabraham. Edinburgh: Historic Scotland, 1997.

—. *Orkney.* Ed. Anna Ritchie. Exploring Scotland's Heritage. Edinburgh: HMSO, 1996.

—. *Picts.* Historic Scotland. Ed. Christopher Tabraham. Edinburgh: HMSO,

1989.

——. *Prehistoric Orkney*. Historic Scotland. London: B.T. Batsford Ltd., 1995.

——. *Scotland B C*. Edinburgh: HMSO, 1988.

——. *Shetland*. Ed. Anna Ritchie. Exploring Scotland's Heritage. Edinburgh: HMSO, 1997.

——. *The Brough of Birsay*. Ed. Chris Tabraham. 1986. Edinburgh: Historic Scotland, 1998.

Ritchie, Graham, and Anna Ritchie. *Scotland: Archaeology and Early History*. Edinburgh: Edinburgh UP, 1991.

Ritchie, Graham, and Mary Harman. *Argyll and the Western Isles*. Ed. Anna Ritchie. Exploring Scotland's Heritage. Edinburgh: HMSO, 1996.

Ritchie, Graham, ed. *The Archaeology of Argyll*. Edinburgh: Edinburgh UP, 1997.

Ritchie, J. N. G. *Brochs of Scotland*. Aylesbury: Shire Publications Ltd., 1988.

Robertson, Anne S. *The Antonine Wall*. Ed. Lawrence Keppie. Glasgow: Glasgow Archaeological Society, 1990.

Ross, Stewart. *Ancient Scotland*. Moffat: Lochar Publishing, 1991.

——. *Scottish Castles*. Moffat: Lochar Publishing, 1990.

Salter, Mike. *The Castles of Lothian and the Borders*. Malvern: Folly Publications, 1994.

Shepherd, Ian. *Aberdeen and North-East Scotland*. Ed. Anna Ritchie. Exploring Scotland's Heritage. Edinburgh: HMSO, 1996.

Simpson, W Douglas. *Bishop's Palace and Earl's Palace: Kirkwall Orkney*. Ed. Denys Pringle. Edinburgh: HMSO, 1991.

——. *Edzell Castle*. Ed. Chris Tabraham. 1952. Edinburgh: Historic Scotland, 1993.

Sked, Paul. *Culross*. Edinburgh: The National Trust for Scotland, 1994.

Skinner, Basil. *Pluscarden Abbey*. N. p.: The Pilgrim Press Ltd., 1997.

Stell, Geoffrey. *Dumfries and Galloway*. Ed. Anna Ritchie. Exploring Scotland's Heritage. Edinburgh: HMSO, 1996.

——. *Dunstaffnage and the Castles of Argyll*. Ed. Chris Tabraham. Edinburgh: Historic Scotland, 1994.

Stevenson, Jack. *Glasgow, Clydeside and Stirling*. Ed. Anna Ritchie. Exploring Scotland's Heritage. Edinburgh: HMSO, 1995.

Summers, Gilbert. *Exploring Rural Scotland*. Ed. Andrew Sanger. Lincolnwood: Passport Books, 1990.

Sutherland, Ian. *Sinclair & Girnigoe Castles*. Wick: Signal Enterprises, n.d.

Tabraham, Christopher. *Scottish Castles and Fortifications*. Ed. David J Breeze. Historic Buildings and Monuments. Edinburgh: HMSO, 1986.

Tabraham, Chris, and Fiona Stewart. *Urquhart Castle*. Ed. Chris Tabraham. Edinburgh: Historic Scotland, 1991.

Tabraham, Chris, and Doreen Grove. *Tantallon Castle*. Ed. Chris Tabraham. Edinburgh: Historic Scotland, 1994.

Tabraham, Chris. *Bothwell Castle*. Ed. Chris Tabraham. Edinburgh: Historic Scotland, 1994.

—. *Edinburgh Castle*. Ed. Chris Tabraham. Edinburgh: Historic Scotland, 1994.

—. *Huntly Castle*. Ed. Chris Tabraham. 1985. Edinburgh: Historic Scotland, 1995.

—. *Smailholm Tower*. Ed. Chris Tabraham. 1985. Edinburgh: Historic Scotland, 1993.

The Automobile Association and the Ordnance Survey. *Ordnance Survey Leisure Guide: Scottish Highlands*. Basingstoke: Publishing Division of The Automobile Association and the Ordnance Survey, 1994.

The Bernera Iron Age Village at Bostadh. N. p.: n. p., n. d.

The Highway Code. N.p.: HMSO, 1993.

The Site of Whithorn Priory. N. p.: n. p., n. d.

Tranter, Nigel. *Tales and Traditions of Scottish Castles*. 1993. New York: Barnes & Noble Books, 1997.

Traquair House. N. p.: Traquair House and Jarrold Publishing, 1992.

Turner, Val. *Ancient Shetland*. Historic Scotland. London: B. T. Batsford Ltd., 1998.

—. *Archaeology of Shetland*. Lerwick: Shetland Islands Tourism, n. d.

Walker, Bruce, and Graham Ritchie. *Fife, Perthshire and Angus*. Ed. Anna Ritchie. Exploring Scotland's Heritage. Edinburgh: HMSO, 1996.

Whittaker, Jean. *Mull: Monuments and History*. N.p.: Brown & Whittaker, 1995.

Wickham – Jones, C.R. *Scotland's First Settlers*. London: B.T. Batsford Ltd/ Historic Scotland, 1994.

Williams, David. *Scotland's Best-Loved Driving Tours*. 3rd ed. New York: Macmillan Travel, 1998.

Yeoman, Peter. *Medieval Scotland*. Historic Scotland. London: B. T. Batsford Ltd., 1995.

Yoxon, Paul, and Grace M. Yoxon. *Guide No. 4 to Prehistoric Skye*. Broadford: Skye Environmental Centre, 1987.

Index of Sites

Order Information

In Search of Ancient Scotland, A Guide for the Independent Traveler, $17.95 each.

To order, send check or money order in U.S. funds to:

> Aspen Grove Publishing
> P. O. Box 1493
> Mead, WA 99021-1493

On direct orders to U.S. addresses, we pay shipping (book rate) and handling.

Sales tax: please add 8.2% sales tax for books shipped to Washington State addresses.

Please help us keep this book current!

If you visit sites in this book and find changes or have comments and suggestions, we would be very interested in hearing from you. Please write Aspen Grove Publishing at the above address.